THE CAMBRIDGE GUIDE TO READING POETRY

At the heart of this book is a belief that poetry matters and that it enables us to enjoy and understand life. In this accessible guide, Andrew Hodgson equips the reader for the challenging and rewarding experience of unlocking poetry, considering the key questions about language, technique, feeling, and subject matter which illuminate what a poem has to say. In a lucid and sympathetic manner, he considers a diverse range of poets writing in English to demonstrate how their work enlarges our perception of ourselves and of our world. The process of independent research is modelled step-by-step, as the guide shows where to start, how to develop ideas, and how to draw conclusions. Providing guidance on how to plan, organise, and write essays, close readings, and commentaries, from initial annotation to final editing, this book will supply you with the confidence to discover and express a personal response to poetry.

ANDREW HODGSON is Senior Lecturer in the Department of English Literature at the University of Birmingham. He is the author of *The Poetry of Clare, Hopkins, Thomas, and Gurney: Lyric Individualism* (2020), has edited and introduced an edition of *The Selected Poems of John Keats* (2019) for the Macmillan Collector's Library, and has written essays on numerous English poets.

THE CAMBRIDGE GUIDE TO READING POETRY

ANDREW HODGSON
University of Birmingham

CAMBRIDGE
UNIVERSITY PRESS

University Printing House, Cambridge CB2 8BS, United Kingdom

One Liberty Plaza, 20th Floor, New York, NY 10006, USA

477 Williamstown Road, Port Melbourne, VIC 3207, Australia

314–321, 3rd Floor, Plot 3, Splendor Forum, Jasola District Centre, New Delhi – 110025, India

103 Penang Road, #05–06/07, Visioncrest Commercial, Singapore 238467

Cambridge University Press is part of the University of Cambridge.

It furthers the University's mission by disseminating knowledge in the pursuit of education, learning, and research at the highest international levels of excellence.

www.cambridge.org
Information on this title: www.cambridge.org/9781108843249
DOI: 10.1017/9781108915212

First published 2021

Printed in the United Kingdom by TJ Books Ltd. Padstow, Cornwall

A catalogue record for this publication is available from the British Library.

Library of Congress Cataloging-in-Publication Data
NAMES: Hodgson, Andrew, author.
TITLE: The Cambridge guide to reading poetry / Andrew Hodgson.
DESCRIPTION: New York : Cambridge University Press, 2022. | Includes index.
IDENTIFIERS: LCCN 2021023819 (print) | LCCN 2021023820 (ebook) | ISBN 9781108843249 (hardback) | ISBN 9781108824125 (paperback) | ISBN 9781108915212 (ebook)
SUBJECTS: LCSH: Poetics. | Poetry – Appreciation.
CLASSIFICATION: LCC PN1042 .H56 2022 (print) | LCC PN1042 (ebook) | DDC 808.1–dc23
LC record available at https://lccn.loc.gov/2021023819
LC ebook record available at https://lccn.loc.gov/2021023820

ISBN 978-1-108-84324-9 Hardback
ISBN 978-1-108-82412-5 Paperback

for L. G. G.

. . . it nourisheth, and instructeth our youth; delights our age; adorns our prosperity; comforts our adversity; entertains us at home; keeps us company abroad, travels with us; watches; divides the times of our earnest, and sports; shares in our country recesses, and recreations [. . . it is] a dulcet, and gentle philosophy, which leads on, and guides us by the hand to action, with a ravishing delight, and incredible sweetness.

– *Ben Jonson,* Timber, or Discoveries *(1641)*

Poetry turns all things to loveliness; it exalts the beauty of that which is most beautiful, and it adds beauty to that which is most deformed; it marries exultation and horror, grief and pleasure, eternity and change; it subdues to union under its light yoke all irreconcilable things. It transmutes all that it touches, and every form moving within the radiance of its presence is changed by wondrous sympathy to an incarnation of the spirit which it breathes: its secret alchemy turns to potable gold the poisonous waters which flow from death through life; it strips the veil of familiarity from the world, and lays bare the naked and sleeping beauty, which is the spirit of its forms.

– *Percy Bysshe Shelley,* A Defence of Poetry *(1821)*

'To be a poet is to have a soul so quick to discern that no shade of quality escapes it, and so quick to feel, that discernment is but a hand playing with finely ordered variety on the chords of emotion – a soul in which knowledge passes instantaneously into feeling, and feeling flashes back as a new organ of knowledge. One may have that condition by fits only.'

'But you leave out the poems,' said Dorothea. 'I think they are wanted to complete the poet.'

– *George Eliot,* Middlemarch *(1871–2)*

Contents

Introduction: Reading Poetry

Using This Book

This is a guide to reading and enjoying poetry, intended for students from high school upward and for the general reader. It covers three broad topics: Reading a Poem, Studying a Poet, and Writing about Poetry. The material on the first of these topics, which takes up the main body of the book, is composed of short interlocking sections, each introducing a perspective from which to approach a poem, illustrated with examples taken from a range of poets writing in English. The book is designed to be read cumulatively, to show how consideration of one element of a poem will invariably glide into another, but each section can be taken as a stand-alone unit, and the contents pages should help you locate the discussions on any particular issue.

The best way to develop as a reader of poetry is through practice. The more poems we read, the more we become familiar with the things poems do and the ways they work. The book is a companion to that process. Its emphasis is on asking questions as you read. It aims to supply the knowledge and assurance to enter into dialogue with poems, to spend time with them, and to enjoy what they have to show us. It hopes to give you the confidence to discuss the poems that you have read. Perhaps the words most commonly uttered by students in a classroom or university seminar are 'I'm probably wrong, but . . . ' And while the world would no doubt be a pleasanter place if everyone were to handle their opinions with such caution, it's good, too, to feel secure in our judgements. The book shows how to develop that security by reading actively and accepting that our comprehension of a poem will always be gradual and capable of evolution. Above all, the book encourages you to practise reading slowly. It doesn't claim that reading poetry is easy, but it does say that its challenge is what makes it so rewarding. In a world of immediate gratification, poems invite us to take our time. When we have the tools to grapple with it, poetry's supposed difficulty becomes part of its pleasure.

The second section of the book deals with the task of studying the life and work of an individual poet. How do we build up an impression of their career? How do we find out about their life and times? How can we benefit from what other people have said about them? Finally, since most students are required not just to read but also to write about poems, and since writing itself is a way of working out what we think and feel about a poem, the book closes with some reflections on that process.

When quoting from poems, I have supplied the date of first publication (where known) in parentheses; on occasions when a poem was published after an author's death, I have given a rough date of composition instead. The aim has been to give some sense of chronology rather than to document the minutiae of any given poem's textual history. I have quoted wherever possible from standard critical editions.

I would like to thank the anonymous reviewers of the initial manuscript of the book for their promptings and suggestions. Emily Hockley and Sarah Starkey at Cambridge University Press have offered wonderful support. Kilmeny MacBride has been a sensitive and sharp-eyed copy-editor. I am grateful, too, to the following people, without whom the book would be far poorer: Will Bowers, Oliver Clarkson, Steve Ellis, Jessica Fay, Tom Lockwood, and, most of all, Stefanie John.

Why Read Poetry?

Why read poetry? Surely there are more profitable things to study? Surely there are more gratifying ways to spend your time? When you wake up in the morning, you might have all sorts of things to read – many of them with more urgent claims on your attention than the book of poems lying by the bed. There are messages from friends, newspaper reports, opinions pouring onto social media, bills and bank statements to deal with; perhaps, if you are at school, poetry is competing with subjects that apparently have a more practical application: biology, economics, computer sciences. So why reach down to find, say, the following poem by Christina Rossetti (1862)?

Song

She sat and sang alway
    By the green margin of a stream,
Watching the fishes leap and play
    Beneath the glad sunbeam.

I sat and wept alway
    Beneath the moon's most shadowy beam,
Watching the blossoms of the May
    Weep leaves into the stream.

I wept for memory;
    She sang for hope that is so fair:
My tears were swallowed by the sea;
    Her songs died on the air.

The answer at the heart of this book is that poetry affords pleasure and wisdom. Reading poetry enriches our experience of life. To be able to read Rossetti's lines and appreciate their verbal distinctiveness, their formal patterns, their emotional insight, their vision of what life is, is to make the world a different, perhaps more fulfilling place.

Many things give pleasure, of course: playing sport, bird watching, eating chips, knitting, contemplating a beautiful landscape, even dancing – and a lot of these activities offer more immediate joys or require less work than reading a poem. But pleasure takes different forms. The very fact that the fullest satisfactions of a poem are neither easily nor immediately accessible is a sign that the pleasure offered by poetry has particular depth and quality. The rewards of patiently devoting one's resources to a complex subject are richer than the sugar rush that comes from wolfing down a bar of chocolate.

Rossetti's poem does afford immediate pleasures. On a first reading we might simply enjoy the sounds of the words, the patterns of the rhymes, the attractiveness of the images. The more closely we look and listen to these qualities, the more intricate they reveal themselves to be. Reading becomes its own reward as we linger over the poem's repetitions and variations; its innovations on a sequence of four- and three-beat rhythms, familiar from nursery rhyme and folk song; the similarities and contrasts between the three parts of the poem's structure. The words are arranged with a care and subtlety that makes them worthy of attention for their own sake. Wake up and spend ten minutes following the unfolding of Rossetti's poem, and our time is not frittered away, as it might be in reading a webpage or a text message. Instead, the poem allows us to escape temporarily from the randomness of day-to-day experience into a meaningful verbal pattern.

Returning to the poem another morning, our attention might pass from the poem's sensuous qualities to its emotional impact. Here is a memorable expression of the centrality of hope and sadness to human life and of the transience of that life. And we might find that the poem calls on us to exercise our intellect, as we consider the persuasiveness of the different perspectives it presents. We might start to see that while the poem offers a pleasurable experience in itself, it also informs and illuminates other experiences. The care with which it is constructed promises a corresponding care over what it has to communicate. Through their richness and complexity, the words draw attention to the richness and complexity of life. Rossetti presents two contrasting outlooks, one joyful, one mournful, and brings us to the view, finally, that neither attitude will change our fate. The poem sharpens our sense of the pathos of the human predicament, and, in its brevity, shows how to accept that pathos without wallowing in it.

Poems enrich the moments we spend reading them. In doing so, they deepen our understanding and appreciation of life beyond those moments. They offer representations of life that help to refine and enlarge our conception of experience. Every poem says, implicitly: 'Look at the world in this way: isn't life like this?' Or, sometimes: 'isn't this the way life could be?' We don't have to endorse that view of the world; we are merely invited to share in it, temporarily. Crucially, poems work by inviting us to view the world through the prism of the experience they offer. Rossetti does not tell us, flatly, that 'whether we are hopeful or regretful, we all end in the same way', as though the job of a poem were to deliver information. Instead, her poem allows us to entertain two opposed perspectives, each with its own validity; it conducts us to its final revelation through representations of hopefulness and mournfulness in a way that does not force its vision of experience upon us. The poem's significance is inseparable from the story that it tells and the way in which it tells it.

One way of putting it might be to say that poems combine two valuable things: beauty and truth. They show us that beauty is not merely decorative but enables us to comprehend experience; it is a way of communicating and preserving an understanding of life. In 'Satire III' (1633), John Donne animates a truth about truth itself:

> On a huge hill,
> Cragged, and steep, Truth stands, and he that will
> Reach her, about must, and about must go;
> And what the hill's suddenness resists, win so.

That is a tricky thought, but the trickiness is part of the point. Donne shows us that arriving at 'Truth' – knowledge, understanding – requires effort. It is often difficult, like following the winding path to the top of a steep hill. And Donne's lines, in their convoluted, halting progress, allow us to feel that difficulty. They seem, magically, to bring truth to life. Just as we don't always go for a walk merely to reach a destination, so there is something innately pleasing as well as instructive about the way Donne's lines tell us the truth. Their repetitive patterns (the couplets of rhyme, the labouring phrase 'about must and about must go') take us through something like the looping progress round the hill that they describe. And the arrangement and positioning of words also recreate something of the difficulty of the journey: 'Cragged' has a craggy prominence at the start of its line; to reach the full sense of 'he that will / Reach her' we have to reach our eye from the end of one line to the beginning of another; it is satisfying that it is only as we arrive at the final two words of the sentence that we 'win' a full understanding of its sense – a sense that would have been easier, but less rewarding, to untangle had the line been written, perhaps more naturally, 'and so win what the hill's suddenness [i.e. its steepness] resists'.

What sorts of thing can poems show us? The answers are almost limitless: we will encounter numerous examples throughout the book. In a wide sense, however, we might say that poems reveal something about human beings and our relation to each other and our world. Poems embody a knowledge of how we belong in the world; they show us the way things are, the way things might be, and the way things should be. Let's take a pair of seemingly contrasting illustrations. A nursery rhyme such as 'Rock-a-bye Baby' (c. 1765) –

> Rock-a-bye baby on the tree top.
> When the wind blows the cradle will rock.
> When the bough breaks, the cradle will fall.
> And down will come Baby, cradle and all.

– is evidently different in gravity and outlook to this stanza from the *Rubáiyát* of the medieval Persian polymath Omar Khayyam, translated by Edward Fitzgerald (1859):

> But leave the Wise to wrangle, and with me
> The Quarrel of the Universe let be:
> And, in some corner of the Hubbub coucht,
> Make Game of that which makes as much of Thee.

Khayyam's lines are more obviously freighted with wisdom (even if, riddlingly, the thrust of that wisdom is to leave the 'Wise' behind). But what finds expression in both poems is a vision of human experience, and a sense of how we might come to terms with it. Those visions are to some degree contradictory – Khayyam sees life as a game, the nursery rhyme as a struggle – but there is truth in both of them. The poems don't deal in matters that are subject to proof, as in the sciences, but rather of different ways of seeing and responding to the world. And even if we don't share their vision, we find it expressed in words which are true to the experience they convey. The neatly patterned feel of Khayyam's poem suggests how we might treat as a 'Game' the workings of a 'Universe' which 'makes as much' of us; the unrelenting momentum of the nursery rhyme, in which things get worse one line at a time, smuggles into a lullaby a frightening sense of nature's destructive power.

The poems we have looked at so far suggest that life involves a measure of unhappiness. How can we square this with the thought that poetry offers pleasure? One answer is that there is a deeper pleasure in knowing and understanding life than in being deceived. Another is that poems show how we can reconcile ourselves with life's inevitable difficulties. Beauty often reminds us that good things can coexist with – even emerge from – the bad. In the face of painful awareness a poem's words and patterns can rescue significance; they can offer consolation and redeem the situation they address. Even as 'Rock-a-bye Baby' warns of nature's violence, it is a pleasure to sing: art can soothe suffering. The speaker of Rossetti's poem says that she 'wept', but the poem itself is a 'Song', something that brings consolation and joy. In poems dealing with happier circumstances – say a tribute to a landscape or a loved one – the beauty of a poem's words might be a way of consecrating as well as comprehending what they describe, as though in tribute to its value. Poems help us to understand life, but they also affirm life's significance. They give life meaning.

Poems are ways of preserving experience. Rossetti's song describes both its voices vanishing; Rossetti herself is now long vanished (she lived from 1830 to 1894). Yet Rossetti's words are lasting. They give enduring form to Rossetti's distinctive vision and sensibility and allow later readers to share in them and be shaped by their influence. As we read, we are lifted beyond our everyday concerns, and put in touch with something of permanence. That is not to say that a poem will always mean the same thing – for us, or for other readers. A poem endures, in part, because it acquires new significances in the changing circumstances in which it is read. Return the next morning to yesterday's paper, an answered text message, a bill that has been paid, and its significance will likely have dwindled; return to Rossetti's poem, and its significance will have endured, perhaps evolved. Come back years later, carrying new understandings of hope and disappointment, and we might find still different significances. The truth and pathos of its apprehension of human transience will last; our pleasure in the sounds and patterns will remain; we might even find it moves us, or illuminates experience, in a new and unexpected way.

A work of art, wrote John Keats, is 'a friend to man' ('Ode on a Grecian Urn' (1820)). It consoles and cheers us with the company of minds from distant times and places. To read poetry is also to find the company of other readers, living and dead. Every reader will have their own response to a poem. We will all have our own sense of the depth and significance of the truths a poem embodies; we are all drawn to share with others our sense of what is beautiful. This is why the act of reading poetry passes naturally into the act of contemplating and discussing poetry – the practice of literary criticism. Literary criticism might be something that we undertake in formal ways, say as a student at school or university, but even outside of any academic context, it is natural to reflect upon what we have read. And, done well, literary criticism becomes another of poetry's joys and values. Perhaps the saddest and most frustrating things one hears as a teacher is students saying that, while instinctively they like reading books, and even poems, that pleasure is spoiled by being made to criticise them in an academic context. One of the hopes of this book is to persuade you that, when it has love of and gratitude for literature at its heart, thinking about, discussing, and even writing about poetry is part of the pleasure of reading it. Criticism should, as James Reeves says, be 'a development of one's pleasure rather than an eradication'; it is 'an act of love'.[1] The process of reflection helps us to work out what we think and feel about a poem, and why we like or dislike it – it is a way of organising our response. As that process passes into debate with other readers, it offers the pleasure of winning people round to our view and, equally, the pleasure of changing our minds and being persuaded to see the truth or beauty of something we had not recognised.

Someone sceptical about the value of studying poetry might leap in at this point and complain that such matters are all subjective: what society needs is people capable of dealing in facts, not squabbling over things that are 'just a matter of opinion'. To an extent, they would be right: whether a poem is good or bad, true or beautiful, *is* subjective; it is a matter of persuasion rather than proof – just as poems themselves deal in a realm of knowledge not limited to fact. But then how many times in life do we face dilemmas for which there is no factually correct resolution? There is no way of *proving* that choosing to marry a certain person or deciding to pick one particular career path or electing a particular government is definitively the right course of action. But such choices are no mere matter of whim, either. We have to weigh the evidence and decide which option we dislike least. You can't say for certain that it is a better idea to marry the generous and attractive suitor over the mean-spirited alternative, but you can stack up the evidence pretty convincingly in favour. And this is exactly the kind of thinking literary criticism involves. The eighteenth-century critic and lexicographer Samuel Johnson put it best when he said that in practising literary criticism we 'improve opinion into knowledge'.[2] Everyone has the right to an opinion, of course, but that is not to say that everyone's opinion is of equal merit or that we should be satisfied with the opinions that come instinctively into our head. Some opinions will be better-informed, better-substantiated, and better-made than others (people who proudly 'say what they think' often haven't done a great deal of thinking). The distinction Johnson makes between 'opinion' and 'knowledge' asserts that to have an opinion is not enough, and that in holding an opinion we have the obligation to alter, refine, and improve it as best we can. That process requires looking closely and skilfully at the evidence and orchestrating our observations into a coherent case. It enables us to enter a community, balancing our individual preferences against a common standard of taste. And that, again, is what this book offers help with.

Literary study in schools and universities frequently comes under attack. Governments back subjects such as science, technology, and mathematics, which boast more obvious practical benefits. And who doesn't want to feel that they are studying something valuable, for themselves and others? 'What is the use of poetry?' comes the question. One answer, which it is always fun to offer, is that poetry's lack of utility is exactly the point. What, if it comes to that, is the use of love, or music, or wine? Poetry reminds us that there are more virtues in life than being merely useful. Studying it is an education in things that have a value beyond the everyday: truth, beauty, feeling, imagination, tradition. And as a result, poetry will always trouble those who go through life valuing things according to their practicality, fashionableness, or financial worth. A broader response, though, is to draw attention, as we have been doing in the paragraphs above, to the thought that poetry matters for its ability to shape our values, perceptions, sympathies, and sense of community, our powers of debate, argument, and comprehension. Reading poetry involves expanding our knowledge, understanding, and appreciation of life; it sharpens our ability to perceive and apprehend complexity; it trains us to evaluate and persuade others of the substance of our views and trains our receptiveness to the views of others – and where is the society which doesn't need more of that?

What Is a Poem?

Many of the things I have just said about why we should read poetry could apply to literature, or indeed art, of any kind. What makes something a poem? The question is harder to answer than it might first appear, and can be an unfruitful one. Samuel Johnson, when posed the question by his friend and biographer James Boswell, pointed out that definition is sometimes redundant: 'Why, Sir, it is much easier to say what it is not. We all *know* what light is; but it is not easy to *tell* what it is.'[3] Being able to say what a poem is is not as useful as being able instinctively to recognise one. And, as Johnson said elsewhere, 'To circumscribe poetry by a definition will only shew the narrowness of the definer': good poems reshape our sense of what a poem can be.[4] Still, it is helpful, before we start reading, to have in mind some expectations about what we might encounter. And if, as with light, we know a poem when we see one, then it should be possible to sketch out what the features are in a poem that allow us to recognise it, even if working backwards in this manner doesn't yield a categorical definition. Everyone would agree to call Rossetti's 'Song' a poem, for instance – but why? Without trying to be exhaustive or definitive, I'd like to suggest three qualities which will characterise any poem we encounter.

First, let's give some thought to terminology. If the question were 'what is poetry?' one answer would be that poetry is the opposite of prose. That answer would suggest something about the quality of experience we anticipate: a 'poetic' (elevated and intensified) and not a 'prosaic' (ordinary) one. It would also suggest something about the writing's form: poetry is organised differently on the page. We should not hold too fast to those expectations, however: poems can be prosaic, and prose can be poetic; and if form is the defining quality, then the more accurate opposite to prose might be *verse*, as we shall see. And while 'poetry' can oppose itself to 'prose', there is no such thing as 'a prose' for a poem to define itself against.[5] A poem would seem to be not so much the opposite of a novel or a play as a family relation: a different way of accomplishing a similar task. Another answer to the question 'what is poetry?' might be that it is a label for all imaginative literature, and that poems, novels, and plays all fall under its umbrella. And that, in fact, is a good starting point from which to narrow things down: a poem is a work of imagination. It is an act of creativity in response to the problems or pleasures of human life. As an act of imagination, its nature is fictional. That is not to say that the arguments, feelings, situations, or stories that it embodies are entirely invented, but that they always involve some degree of selection and representation; they operate on a separate plane from the events of life itself. The women in Rossetti's poem may well have been real individuals who sat and sang or wept, but the poem presents their actions less as a record of real occurrences than as possible contrasting responses to life. Even poems which respond to historical people or events – Tennyson's 'The Charge of the Light Brigade' (1855), to take a well-known example – do so by imagining a voice that carries that response. Before every poem, we might imagine reading the words 'What if somebody said . . . ' And yet for a work of imagination to compel our attention, its representation of life must have the intensity of something real. A poem invites us to contemplate feelings, circumstances, and actions that we know not to be real as though they were so. Works of imagination, that is, appeal to our imagination. They allow us to transcend our present circumstances; they can project us into other times and places by investing them with their own reality and allow us to reflect back on life from them. They can encourage us to think about how the world might exist differently. Yet imagination is not fantasy. A poem is not a daydream. A poem does not attempt to replace reality, but to exist within it. Rossetti's lines do not say, 'life is sorrowful, but art can allow us to escape it', they say, 'step out of your day-to-day existence, contemplate these opposed responses to life and the thought of how little either affects things, and return to life with your understanding clarified'. Even when a poem presents us with an ideal world, it lets us know we must return from it. In the deepest and most lasting art, the imagination confronts and accommodates itself to reality, rather than fleeing it; it is shaped by, and gives shape to, an understanding of the conditions of this world.

A next step might be to say that a poem is an act of imagination which takes place through language. A poem imagines a voice using words for any number of familiar purposes – to express feeling, shape argument, describe the world, tell stories, dramatise character, and so on. It does so with special flair and control: it takes care over what it says and how it says it, and so encourages us to read with the care and patience we have started to describe. We expect a poem to be resourceful and imaginative in its handling of the expressive possibilities of language; we want it to find out new and surprising ways of speaking about and defining experience, rather than falling back on cliché and imprecision. There is a world of difference, for instance, between Rossetti writing 'She always sat and sang' and 'She sat and sang alway', where the odd spelling has an appropriately archaic, biblical ring to it, and the disturbance to the ordinary order of the phrasing shifts attention onto the word at the end of the line. Along these lines, the poet W. H. Auden once said that the best definition of poetry was 'memorable speech'. What we can expect to encounter in a poem, Auden suggests, are words which stimulate us emotionally and intellectually (for that is what will make them memorable), and which do so not just through their individual surface meanings, but through their sensuous qualities and arrangement into patterns, which create the impression of an intimate speaking voice.[6] Still, even that definition is not absolute: all poetry might be 'memorable speech', but not all 'memorable speech' is poetry. We might add that poems do not just use language imaginatively, they use language in the service of imagination: they use words to create, as well as to communicate. The voices Rossetti's poem imagines are not real, but the poem itself is. It is a verbal artefact, consisting of words arranged into patterns which give them lasting form and an existence in the world. The expressive possibilities of these patterns – the system of organisation which we call *verse*, the medium in which almost all poems are composed, is what gives a poem's utterance force and substance, and will be one of the main considerations of this book.

Finally, we know Rossetti's poem is a poem because it presents itself as one. It does so both explicitly and implicitly. It was included in a book called *Goblin Market and Other Poems* in 1862; its title announces it to be a 'Song'; and it is arranged on the page in a manner that suggests it wishes us to contemplate how it is expressed as well as what it expresses. This last criterion might seem troublesome, since it appears to grant free rein for any piece of writing to declare itself as poetry. I can write the following words more or less at random and announce them to be a poem:

How-
ling anguish tears
my(?) soul
(Un-)
bear-
ably?

There are two possible responses to the claim. The first is to accept that anything that calls itself a poem is a poem, but to say that the status of being a poem is in itself no sign of any value, and to argue that if the writing above, for instance, is a poem then it is a very bad one, full of cheap feeling, clichéd, gimmicky language, and void of meaningful formal design. Alternatively, we could object that the writing's claim to be a poem is shallow and unpersuasive. It is not enough merely for something to advertise itself as a poem – the real identification is done in deeper, more nuanced ways, through technique, imagination, and engagement with tradition. An analogy might be with a pile of bricks which cons itself and its audience that it is a work of art merely because it is stuck in an art gallery and has a label next to it bearing the name of the person who has assembled it. Such a work asks, or even demands, that we think of it as a work of art, but it does nothing to *invite* us to do so, by animating a response to life or situating itself in relation to past works of art which have shaped and defined an evolving consensus of what a work of art is. It is a lifeless idea; it seems concerned only to gain the status of a work of art, not to realise the possibilities of art. We agree that Rossetti's 'Song' is a poem, in part, because it shares features that qualify other pieces of writing as poems, and has sought to emulate them, even as it extends them in new and distinctive ways.

In the end, there is no ideal embodiment of what a poem is. There are only individual pieces of writing which we call poems, each of which is, amongst other things, an answer to the question 'What Is a Poem?' Words mean what we collectively agree them to mean: definitions can change, and a good poem will always try to expand our understanding of what a poem is; but it must engage, too, with our existing notion of a poem: something that devotes imagination to language, and devotes language to the service of the imagination.

Understanding Poetry

Among the disorientating things Lewis Carroll's Alice finds when she goes *Through the Looking-Glass* (1871) is a book containing the following puzzling writing:

sevot yhtils eht dna ,gillirb sawT'
;ebaw eht ni elbmig dna eryg diD
,sevogorob eht erew ysmim llA
.ebargtuo shtar emom eht dnA

'It's all in some language I don't know', says Alice, before realising that if she holds the page up to a mirror 'the words will all go the right way again':

'Twas brillig, and the slithy toves
Did gyre and gimble in the wabe:
All mimsy were the borogoves,
And the mome raths outgrabe.

Still Alice is bewildered. 'It seems very pretty, but it's rather hard to understand! . . . Somehow it seems to fill my head with ideas – only I don't exactly know what they are!'

Every reader of poetry feels like Alice at some point. Poems can be strange. They unsettle our familiar sense of things. They can look perplexing on the page and can be difficult to process once they have started filling your head. It is tempting to think of poetry as a sort of code which needs a special trick to decipher. And it is natural, to begin with, to find something 'rather hard to understand' off-putting. We are supposed to like things that are 'accessible'. But isn't the strangeness of the lines Alice encounters rather appealing, too? We might not know what it means to 'gyre and gimble in the wabe', but it is surely a pleasingly unusual thing to speak about. We don't always recoil from words we don't understand. I am not sure what David Bowie means when he sings about sailors fighting in dancehalls in 'Life on Mars?' (1971), if he means anything at all, but that doesn't stop me, or millions of others, enjoying his weird words; our perplexity might even be part of the reason why we enjoy them – they may not obviously mean anything, but they have meaning. In any case, telling ourselves too quickly that we don't 'understand' the words of a poem can obscure the ways in which they take effect – through their rhythms, their sounds, their printed shape – for which 'understanding' is hardly the right verb. Alice would realise that her response was actually quite sensitive if only she looked at it the right way: the language she encounters *is* 'very pretty' (look at it, read it aloud to yourself), and its tantalising ability to 'fill your head with ideas', even if you are not sure what those ideas are, is part of its magic. It is not that the meaning doesn't matter, rather that Carroll is using the language to create meaning in unusual ways. Perhaps part of the point of the poem is to allow us to experience what it feels like to be on the very borders of understanding something.

Of course, not all poems are so flamboyantly riddling. Some of the most memorable moments in poetry are the most direct: from John Milton's staccato account of Eve picking the fruit from the Tree of Knowledge, and consequently bringing about the Fall of the human race, in *Paradise Lost* (1667) ('she pluck't, she ate'), to the two words that the nineteenth-century poet George MacDonald arranged under the title 'The Shortest and Sweetest of Songs' (1893):

Come
Home.

These words are as easy to understand as those that Alice encounters are obscure. They are 'simple, sensuous and passionate', as Milton once said poetry should be.[7] But it doesn't follow that just by deciphering their sense we have responded to all that MacDonald is doing with them. The way MacDonald separates and arranges the words 'come home' encourages us to wonder about their aural and visual similarities (is this really a 'sweet' song? is it a 'song' at all?) so that they come home to us in a new light. If we imagine the words being spoken, they might ring in our ears with the harmony of forgiveness, the discord of chastisement, or the desperation of a plea. The poem invites attention to the words in all their aspects.

T. S. Eliot said that 'genuine poetry can communicate before it is understood';[8] the inverse is also true: poetry communicates above and beyond immediate 'understanding'. A poem is not a coded message from which a more straightforward meaning is waiting to be extracted. It is an artefact made out of language which invites us to attend to more than just the words' semantic content (their dictionary definitions). Reading is not a matter of looking for 'hidden meanings' that a poet has smuggled away, but of perceiving and interpreting the significance of the experience a poem affords in all its richness. What would it mean to have 'understood' Rossetti's 'Song', for example? One answer might be that it would involve being able to give a paraphrase: 'She sat and sang by a stream. I sat and wept under the moon. I wept for memory. She sang for hope. Both our voices faded into nothingness.' But this raises further questions. What are the effects of Rossetti writing the poem in the precise way she has? How sensitively does it apprehend its occasion? How imaginatively does it respond to it? We want to describe and appreciate how the poem conducts itself. And in succession a host of further questions blossom: how does the poem relate to other poems by Rossetti and by her contemporaries? How is it connected to Rossetti's life and to the society in which she lived? How have other people responded to the poem? Why does it matter? Poetry is so fascinating because 'understanding' it is a gradual and continually evolving process.

The most important thing, to begin with, is to rid ourselves of the suspicion that we *don't* understand poetry and to welcome the awareness that understanding is gradual, may well take place slowly, and may evolve endlessly. When reading a poem, be patient. Make friends with unfamiliarity and uncertainty. If the writing is difficult to 'understand', ask how it affects your senses, rather than your intellect. If 'understanding' seems to come easily, remember that a poem is not a message, but an aesthetic experience, and think about how the way in which the words are presented might complicate or enrich their surface meaning. Trust yourself to take your time.

Connecting with Poetry

Poems can help us to understand ourselves. In a scene from Alan Bennett's *The History Boys* (2004), the teacher Hector describes his pleasure in a poem by Thomas Hardy. The 'best moments' in reading, he suggests, occur when we encounter a perception or emotion which we had thought unique to us and find it set down memorably by someone else completely unfamiliar, perhaps long dead; it is as though a hand has reached across time and space to hold our hand. It is a beautifully imagined scene, and it is undoubtedly true. The idea comes near to a remark that Hardy himself was fond of quoting, that 'the ultimate aim of the poet should be to touch our hearts by showing his own'.[9] Many poets have felt the same. Philip Larkin, for instance, described a poem as 'a verbal device' that preserves a particular experience and 'will set off the same experience in other people, so that they too will feel *How beautiful, how significant, how sad*, and the experience will be preserved'; he concluded: 'I suppose the kind of response I am seeking from the reader is, Yes, I know what you mean, life *is* like that'.[10] According to this line of thinking, the most satisfying poems bring about a glow of recognition. They speak to our own experiences, perhaps representing those experiences more precisely and poignantly than we are able to ourselves. Samuel Johnson once gave some lines spoken by a terrified character in William Congreve's play *The Mourning Bride* (1697) as an example:

> It strikes an awe
> And terror on my aching sight; the tombs
> And monumental caves of death look cold,
> And shoot a chilness to my trembling heart.
> Give me thy hand, and let me hear thy voice;
> Nay, quickly speak to me, and let me hear
> Thy voice – my own affrights me with its echoes.

'He who reads those lines enjoys for a moment the powers of a poet', says Johnson: 'he feels what he remembers to have felt before, but he feels it with great increase of sensibility; he recognises a familiar image, but meets it again amplified and expanded, embellished with beauty, and enlarged with majesty.'[11] Everybody has been frightened before. But Congreve's lines – thanks particularly, perhaps, to the way their repetition 'let me hear thy voice' realises what it is to have one's pleas rebound back upon oneself – take that experience and define it for us more precisely and forcefully. The pleasure we take in them involves having a familiar experience presented to us afresh.

That poetry should offer strangeness amid familiarity – 'amplification' and 'expansion' upon our known experiences, as Johnson puts it – is crucial. For there are problems with making the degree to which a poem speaks from a perspective which we recognise the be-all and end-all. For starters, assuming that we can only enjoy poems which describe a familiar experience excludes us helplessly from the vast majority of poems that have been written: waiting for the experience described in a poem to happen to us is hardly a practical approach to getting to grips with it (though poetry may prepare us for experiences we will have in later life). More importantly, it would be a narrow and shallow mind that turned to poetry with the thought that only those poems which chime with its vision of the world or those which are written in a voice close to its own have any value. Poetry expands as well as affirms our sense of ourselves and of the world. It can extend our sympathies and lead us to adopt unfamiliar perspectives. It 'increases' our 'sensibility', as Johnson puts it. It shows us that there are things of value beyond our own narrow concerns. From time to time, you hear grumbles that poetry should make itself more 'relevant' (usually by using more accessible language or addressing contemporary concerns); students and even reviewers cherish work which is 'relatable'. But those who long for poems they can 'relate to' should question their own powers of relation. Nobody would disagree that poetry should concern itself with matters of human significance – that it should present 'human sentiments in human language', as Johnson said Shakespeare did.[12] But humans are very various, and one of the pleasures of poetry is that it shows us this – Shakespeare's more than anyone's. Poetry pleases through surprise as much as recognition. It allows us to expand and deepen our self, to invite new voices into our consciousness. When Henry Vaughan begins his poem 'The World' (1650) with the remark

> I saw Eternity the other night,
> Like a great Ring of pure and endless light,
> All calm, as it was bright . . .

he is not describing any experience I can recognise or can imagine happening to me over an average evening. But his lines' blend of casual observation with transcendent vision (replace 'Eternity' with, say, 'that film' and you get a feel for how natural the idiom is), the mix of 'calm' and intensity conveyed through the perseverance with the same rhyme sound, opens up a sense of what such an experience must be like. Reading Rossetti's poem, to return to our initial example, we are allowed to entertain a rather forlorn and fatalistic outlook on human experience; we do not have to share it or even be persuaded by it to register its force. 'The main purpose of imaginative literature is to grasp a wide variety of experience, imagining people with codes and customs very unlike our own', the poet and critic William Empson said.[13] Vaughan's and Rossetti's lines give two small examples of how poetry can capture and communicate those 'codes and customs' (the different moral, artistic, emotional, and intellectual ideas that exist in different societies) in a precise and memorable form. Poetry 'speaks to us', often in direct accents, but it does not always tell us what we already know. The onus is on us to meet the poem on its own terms; as we do so, we allow it to refine our sense of existence, and of our selves. C. S. Lewis, author of the Narnia books, described the most important quality in a reader as a willingness to 'surrender': 'Look. Listen. Receive. Get yourself out of the way'. 'Reading great literature', Lewis says, 'I transcend myself; and I am never more myself than when I do'.[14]

Notes

1. James Reeves, *The Critical Sense: Practical Criticism of Prose and Poetry* (London: Heinemann, 1956), 15–16.
2. Samuel Johnson, *The Rambler*, No. 92 (1751), *The Yale Edition of the Works of Samuel Johnson: The Rambler*, ed. W. J. Bate and A. B. Strauss (New Haven, CT: Yale University Press, 1969), 122.
3. James Boswell, *Life of Johnson*, ed. R. W. Chapman (Oxford: Oxford University Press, 1970), 744.
4. Samuel Johnson, 'Pope' (1779), *The Lives of the Poets: A Selection*, ed. Roger Lonsdale, sel. John Mullan (Oxford: Oxford University Press, 2009), 437.
5. See Christopher Ricks, 'The Best Words in the Best Order', *Along Heroic Lines* (Oxford: Oxford University Press, 2021), 1–18.
6. W. H. Auden, introduction to *The Poet's Tongue*, ed. Auden and John Garrett (London: G. Bell and Sons, 1935), v.
7. John Milton, *Of Education* (1644), in *The Complete Prose Works of John Milton: Volume II, 1643–1648*, ed. Ernest Sirluck (New Haven, CT: Yale University Press, 1959), 403.
8. T. S. Eliot, *Dante* (London: Faber and Faber, 1965), 8.
9. Thomas Hardy, *The Life and Work of Thomas Hardy*, ed. Michael Millgate (London: Macmillan, 1984), 131.
10. Philip Larkin, 'How or Why I Write Poetry', *Further Requirements: Interviews, Broadcasts, Statements and Book Reviews, 1952–1985*, ed. Anthony Thwaite (London: Faber and Faber, 2002), 78.
11. Samuel Johnson, 'Congreve', *Lives of the Poets*, 226.

12. Samuel Johnson, 'Preface to *The Plays of William Shakespeare*' (1765), *Selected Writings*, ed. Peter Martin (Cambridge: Harvard-Belknap, 2009), 357.
13. William Empson, *Arguifying: Essays on Literature and Culture*, ed. John Haffenden (London: Chatto and Windus, 1987), 218.
14. C. S. Lewis, *An Experiment in Criticism* (Cambridge: Cambridge University Press, 1961), 141.

CHAPTER 1

Reading a Poem

What Does the Poem Say?

In an episode of the British sitcom *Peep Show* (2003–15), the hapless layabout Jez sits with a copy of Emily Brontë's *Wuthering Heights* (1847), which he has acquired in a bid to impress a woman. Struggling over the novel's opening pages, he turns to his flatmate Mark and asks in a puzzled and fragile voice, 'How do you read?' It is a comically simple question for a man in his thirties to ask, but it is also a good one. I think the answer has two parts. The first is to allow a poem to absorb our attention – to cut out distraction and concentrate on the aesthetic, emotional, and conceptual experience that the words afford. Jez struggles with this because he has the television on in the background ('everything bad begins with "turn the telly off" . . . '), and we will struggle, too, the more distractions we have to hand. Find a quiet, comfortable space, exercise patience, and we will soon find ourselves grateful to immerse ourselves in contemplation of the words on the page. The second part, which a book such as this can do more to help with, involves reflecting on the experience of reading in ways that refine and deepen our appreciation of it. And that process of reflection might itself be divided up. First, it involves establishing accurately and in detail what is there on the page in front of us; it is an act of description. Second, it involves analysing not only what the writing says – or shows us – but *how* it says or shows us it (keeping in mind that the how and the what in literary works are often closely entangled). Third, it involves interpreting and evaluating what we have encountered: what and how much does it mean? In our eagerness to arrive at the third question, it is easy to neglect the previous two, and yet because a poem's vision of experience is inseparable from the experience that it in itself offers, those questions are essential to ensuring that our judgement of a poem has precision and depth. Of course, poems are not just objects for passionless scrutiny. We care about them because they move us, teach us, animate our sense of the world. We want to contemplate their value and significance: why does the poem matter – for the poet, for its audiences, and for us? But we can only begin to answer these questions once we know in detail what we are talking about. Patient attentiveness to the shape and substance of a poem's words is the foundation and fountain of all further understanding. Consequently, our focus in the coming pages will primarily be on attuning ourselves to the experiences poems offer. But as we tour the resources through which poets create meaning and give shape to a voice, we'll keep in mind the wisdom and humanity that flow through those voices and see how technical questions lead invariably to a poem's vision of life.

One way to start is to forget that we are reading a poem at all. A poem imagines a voice, and we should respond to it as we would to any other – by attending to what it has to say. The voice could be talking about anything, though we will usually find that it speaks with strange flair, precision, and insight. Here is the nineteenth-century Indian poet Toru Dutt's translation of Charles Baudelaire's 'La Cloche Fêlée' (1857; tr. 1876):

The Broken Bell

'Tis bitter-sweet on winter nights to note,
Beside the palpitating fire reclined,
The chimes, across the fogs, upon the wind,
Now loud, now low, now near and now remote.
What recollections on that music float!
Blessed the bell that through the darkness blind
Sends honest greetings, consolations kind,
And solemn warnings from its lusty throat.
'Tis like a wakeful soldier,—mine, alas!
The soul-bell in me, can but give one cry,
Like that a wounded soldier—o'er whom pass
Riders and horses, and around whom lie
The dead and dying in a tangled mass—
Utters, unable or to move or die.

'It's a mixed blessing to hear the bells chiming across a winter night. What memories they provoke! Some bells send consolation, as though standing guard over us; the bell within me, my soul, rings out in helpless pain, like a wounded soldier.' In paraphrasing the content of a poem like this, we are describing its *argument*. If we read with a pen and paper to hand, we can always make a sketch of a poem's argument our starting point. It might take time, there might be moments of difficulty or confusion which we need to come back to, but the result will be the basis of a far richer enjoyment. We bring out the shape of a poem's thought: in the lines above we hear meditation pass into gratitude and then sorrow; the ending is gruesome, yet we are left with an expression of anguish that doesn't feel self-pitying, since the pity is directed toward the soldier who provides the image for the poet's grief. At the same time as it seems to take us to the heart of a poem, describing the argument gives us something to measure the poem against: why has the poet put it like that and not like this? It is a springboard for many of the questions which we will go on to pursue about a poem's form, choice of language, and arrangement of ideas.

Paraphrase can be an equally effective way of bringing into focus passages from longer works. Here is the prince Sarpedon persuading his friend Glaucus not to be afraid of dying in battle in George Chapman's translation of Homer's *Iliad* (1598–1616), an epic poem which tells the story of the Trojan war:

O friende, if keeping backe
Would keepe backe age from us, and death, and that we might not wracke
In this life's humane sea at all, but that deferring now
We shund death ever – nor would I half this vaine valour show,
Nor glorifie a folly so, to wish thee to advance:
But, since we must go though not here, and that, besides the chance
Proposd now, there are infinite fates of other sort in death
Which (neither to be fled nor scap't) a man must sinke beneath –
Come, trie we if this sort be ours and either render thus
Glorie to others or make them resigne the like to us.

'If holding back from battle would allow us to escape death entirely, I wouldn't be encouraging you to rush in; but since we all must die eventually in some way or other let's see if we're fated to die in battle – and either give glory to others or achieve it for ourselves.' Or, more briefly: 'We've all got to go sometime, why not now?' Comparing these bland summaries with Chapman's sentence illustrates the value of following an argument in all its twists and turns. How a poem says something matters as much as what it says, but, as the precision and care with which Chapman depicts Sarpedon's argument shows, the two are hard to separate. The opening address that signals Sarpedon's awareness that the truth he is outlining is a painful one, the swiftly curtailed dalliance with the idea that avoiding death now might be to 'shun' it forever, the magnanimous expansion out from the first-person voice to acknowledge that the two soldiers' circumstances, though painful, are not special, and that death is something which every human 'must sinke beneath': all are crucial to the force of the lines, and all can be observed and enjoyed by just describing, slowly and carefully, the course of their argument. It is the stage of reading that is most commonly skipped, yet it is the foundation of all further responses. But establishing a poem's argument, though it may show us that it says strange and valuable things, remains only the starting point for the questions which will take us deeper into its workings, the first of which might be: 'How does it begin?'

How Does the Poem Begin?

The Old English epic *Beowulf* (c. 700–1000), one of English poetry's points of origin, begins with the word 'Hwæt', which modern editions usually translate as a sharp outcry aimed at settling the chatter of an assembled crowd. Poems nowadays tend to be read silently in private and not in a noisy mead hall, but an opening still faces the fundamental task of drawing our mind away from the world around and into that of the poem. What we encounter first is generally a title – a signal of the poem's subject, or a description of what it is: *An Essay on Criticism* (1711), 'Ode to Evening' (1746), or even, as in the case of the Rossetti poem we started with, simply 'Song'. This last instance doesn't tell us much, you might think – but titles can work as much by withholding as revealing information, and Rossetti's compacts different functions, too: her poem *is* a song, but the title also signals that 'Song' is one of its subjects. At the other extreme are those titles which almost overburden us with information: the subheading of Henry Vaughan's 'A Rhapsody. Occasionally written upon a meeting with some of his friends at the Globe Tavern in a chamber painted overhead with a cloudy sky and some few dispersed stars, and on the sides with landscapes, hills, shepherds, and sheep' (1646) develops into something like a stage direction, specifying the precise 'occasion' that prompted the poem. Titles establish expectations we can test against what we encounter in the poem, and it is always worth returning to a title upon finishing a poem, to ask how its promises have been fulfilled.

Some poems have no title at all, thrusting attention onto the voice which breaks the silence in the opening line. The first line of a poem is a threshold; it is the point at which the near infinite possibilities of what a poem might be and the uncountable potential angles of approach to a topic crystallise into the utterance of a unique voice and vision. Here are some examples:

> 'The wind doth blow today, my love,
> And a few small drops of rain . . . '
>
> (Anon., 'The Unquiet Grave')

There is a garden in her face . . .

(Thomas Campion, 'There Is a Garden in Her Face' (1617))

A thousand martyrs have I made,
All sacrificed to my desire . . .

(Aphra Behn, 'A Thousand Martyrs' (1688))

What has this bugbear death to frighten man,
If souls can die as well as bodies can?

(John Dryden, 'Lucretius: Against the Fear of Death' (1685))

Suddenly I saw the cold and rook-delighting Heaven . . .

(W. B. Yeats, 'The Cold Heaven' (1914))

When beauty breaks and falls asunder
I feel no grief for it, but wonder.

(Louise Bogan, 'Juan's Song' (1923))[1]

A description of the weather, a riddling image, a boast, a question, a vision, a statement about loss. Each voice grabs our attention – letting us in on an intimate conversation between lovers, flashing an image before our eyes, adopting a surprising attitude. Each gives us clues to the situation that the poem imagines – the circumstances and purpose to which its voice speaks. Each mimics the way in which someone might begin to talk, but each is refined and elevated too, by patterns of rhythm and rhyme which draw us from the chaos of experience into the ordered world of art. And the voices don't just grab our attention, they hold it, too, by leaving something unresolved: how can someone have a 'garden' in their face? What is the knowledge that will help us overcome our fear of death? Why is heaven 'cold'?

A couple of lines are enough to spark all sorts of questions: who is speaking and in what situation? What are they saying? How are they saying it? Who, if anyone, are they saying it to? Once we have gathered an initial sense of the poem's situation, we might ask further questions: why has the poet started here? Where might this starting point lead? In beginning to sketch answers, we can get quickly to the heart of a poem. Let's go back to the opening lines of Dutt's version of Baudelaire:

'Tis bitter-sweet on winter nights to note,
Beside the palpitating fire reclined,
The chimes, across the fogs, upon the wind,
Now loud, now low, now near and now remote.

The lines express the thoughts and feelings of an individual while also implying that those thoughts and feelings have a general truth. We are invited to contemplate a time and a place – a winter night beside a fireside whose 'palpitations' mirror the poet's own – which might be the poem's setting or might just be the scene that is occupying the speaker's mind. In either case, the poem's starting point is a state of domestic cosiness whose 'bitter-sweet' nature we are assumed to recognise. As the fourth line sets going a series of reverberations on its opening word 'now', its sounds seem to recreate the echoing of the bells in the poet's mind. And as we imagine ourselves into that state of mind and the situation it occupies, we might start to wonder what is 'bitter-sweet' about these chiming bells, and whether the apparent warmth of the opening will be sustained. Asking how the poem begins leads us into the question of how it will develop.

The opening of Robert Browning's *Mr Sludge, 'The Medium'* (1864) presents a less composed voice, emerging from a less certain situation:

> Now, don't, sir! Don't expose me! Just this once!
> This was the first and only time, I'll swear,—
> Look at me,—see, I kneel,—the only time,
> I swear, I ever cheated . . .

Unlike Baudelaire, Browning doesn't begin at the beginning, with a statement that the poem is going to unpack or meditate upon. Instead, the lines give the feeling that we have just happened upon the middle of a conversation. Baudelaire's voice, as translated by Dutt, is measured, premeditated; Browning's is spontaneous, chaotic. Browning's fellow Victorian Gerard Manley Hopkins caught this sort of impact nicely when he described Browning as having 'a way of talking (and of making people talk) with the air and spirit of a man bouncing up from table with his mouth full of bread and cheese and saying that he meant to stand no blasted nonsense':[2] like someone breaking into speech out of nowhere, the poem takes us by surprise. We get a barrage of jumbled information. Whoever is speaking (given the panic, it doesn't seem to be the poet himself, who one would assume might compose himself before beginning) is on the defensive, having been caught 'cheating' in some way or another. We might assume, then, that what the poem is going to offer is an exploration of deception and self-justification. The voice seems flustered and nervous: perhaps the poem is going to be a study in these states of mind. There is also the possibility, given the words seem to be spoken to someone who wields authority over their speaker, that the poem is going to explore the dynamics of a particular power relationship. While it is the urgency of the voice that grabs our attention, it is the uncertainty that surrounds it that makes us want to read on.

One final example, from John Keats's *Hyperion* (1820):

> Deep in the shady sadness of a vale
> Far sunken from the healthy breath of morn,
> Far from the fiery noon, and eve's one star,
> Sat gray-hair'd Saturn, quiet as a stone,
> Still as the silence round about his lair . . .

Keats draws us in to a linguistic world far stiller than Browning's. He gives us a setting – a 'vale' or valley – and a character – 'gray-hair'd Saturn' – but little sense of action or emotional crisis. The writing seems paralysed: the sounds of 'morn' and 'stone', 'star' and 'lair' drag against one another, apparently unsure whether to rhyme or not. The movement matches the stillness and silence and sadness of the main figure on the scene, Saturn, who we may know is one of the Titans of Greek mythology; but even if we know nothing about Saturn, we can deduce that the poem is going to tell us a story which involves him, and we might start to wonder why a poem would want to reach for its material so far back in time. The first thing we learn about Saturn is that he is 'gray-hair'd' – which might strike us as a peculiarly human quality for a supposedly super-human figure: in his 'sunken' and 'quiet' state he seems troubled. Still, it is less easy to identify a central theme or problem in these lines than in the two previous examples. Indeed, we might think that the writing doesn't so much address a concern as embody one: how is the poem going to wake itself from its mood of listlessness and defeat?

What Kind of Poem Is It?

The opening lines of a poem establish expectations; they give us a sense of what a poem is trying to achieve. Take the opening lines of Dryden's translation from Lucretius, which we encountered above:

> What has this bugbear death to frighten man,
> If souls can die as well as bodies can?

It would be odd, in the wake of these lines, to expect the rest of the poem to go on to present a frivolous love story or a description of a beautiful landscape, and it is no use if we go on reading to complain that the poem doesn't offer these things up. The lines establish that the poem will be a discussion of death and immortality. Likewise, Campion's opening makes clear that we are dealing with a love poem and suggests that the poem is going to express its love by comparing the joy afforded by a woman's expression to the pleasure one might take in a garden:

There is a garden in her face
Where roses and white lilies grow;
A heav'nly paradise is that place
Wherein all pleasant fruits do flow.

Our response to a poem depends upon the way it fulfils, or surprises, or disappoints the expectations it establishes. As William Empson says: 'you must rely on each particular poem to show you the way in which it is trying to be good'.[3] Each poem will 'try to be good' in its own way. It will pick its own aspect of life to deal with and develop its own manner of dealing with it. This is why there can be no general set of rules for reading a poem: each poem makes its own. Reading involves opening ourselves to a poem's distinctive apprehension of experience (and so, the assumption we sometimes encounter in academic study that a poem needs to be approached through some or other 'theory' is liable to render us deaf to its eloquence). Some poems will try to be good in ways that are unlike any other poem we have encountered, and this can be disorientating. Consider the opening line of Charles Olson's 'Merce of Egypt' (1953):

I sing the tree is a heron
I praise the long grass.
I wear the lion skin
over the long skirt
to the ankle. The ankle
Is a heron

I look straightly backward. Or I bend to the side straightly
to raise the sheaf
up the stick of the leg
as the bittern's leg, raised
as slow as
his neck grows
as the wheat.

Encountering these lines cold, they are likely to be baffling. Even the title begs questions. The best way to cure our bafflement is to pursue the question of what the poem might be up to. A good edition of Olson's work will tell us that the title refers to Merce Cunningham, a dancer who worked with Olson. That offers a hint about the lines' subject and perhaps suggests the perspective from which they are spoken: they seem to be describing the movements of a dancer or a dance. And with that idea in mind, they suddenly make more sense. The strange statements made by the poem are evidently made to perplex us. But if we start to think of them as an effort to translate into language the ways in which a dancer speaks to us through his postures and movements (which seemingly mimic various wading birds), they edge towards a kind of sense – even if the final result might be to make us feel the distance as well as the similarities between poetry and dance. Going on to consult Olson's poetic principles as outlined in his essay on 'Projective Verse' (1950), where he defines a poem as 'energy transferred from where the poet got it . . . by way of the poem itself to . . . the reader',[4] we can affirm and develop this understanding. Olson's conception of a poem as a means of transmitting 'energy' enables us to see the words as a way of conducting the movements of a dancer into language and on into the movements of our voice as we read. When a poem offers an initially disorientating experience, we can often come to terms with it by asking what the poem is trying to do.

The more we read, the more we will become adept at judging which poems are 'trying to be good' in an idiosyncratic way, like Olson's, and which ones return to topics and situations which other poems have treated before them. To notice these recurrent trends is to think about a poem's *genre* – the particular kind of poem that we are reading. A poem's genre establishes the terms on which it is to be taken; it situates a poem among a family of poems which attempt similar things. To say that a poem belongs to a particular genre is not to say that it is the same as all the other poems in that genre, but it is to indicate a broad set of shared characteristics or concerns. It is to outline in general terms the way in which a poem is 'trying to be good'. As we have seen, we can get clues about a poem's genre from the way it begins. A title may describe the poem as an elegy, or an ode, or a ballad, etc. (see the Glossary on page 236). Then there are indications from the quality and situation of the voice. Simply from the brief openings to the poems by Dutt, Browning, and Keats quoted above, for instance, we can allocate them to three longstanding genres of *lyric*, *dramatic*, and *narrative* poetry. A lyric poem, such as Dutt's, promises the expression of an individual's feelings or sensibility; a dramatic poem, such as Browning's, projects itself into the voice of someone other than the poet: we deal with a character from the outside; a narrative poem, such as Keats's, tells a story.

Those categories are broad. Lyric in particular is a capacious and flexible grouping, capable of diffracting into numerous sub-genres, related both to the forms a poem takes and to the situations it deals with. Even Olson's poem fits within it: it is as though the 'I' that we expect to find in a lyric poem speaks here on behalf of the words of the poem themselves. The 'I' is also the dancer Merce Cunningham, however, and it also makes sense in that light to see the poem as a piece of dramatic writing. Genres can overlap: there are dramatic lyrics, pastoral elegies, and satiric ballads – a poem might try to do more than one thing at once. There are also narrower thematic categories: traditions of poems about country houses, about waking up with one's lover ('aubades'), about the loss of creative powers, and so on through countless situations. And genres evolve over time. Each new poem in a particular genre will grow out of its conventions but take them in a new direction: as a result, it will reshape our understanding of what any given genre is. What readers expected from a lyric poem in 1600 was different from what readers expected in 1900.

The more we read, the more we will become familiar with the conventions, associations, and histories of particular genres. But how can knowledge of a poem's genre prove helpful? Consider the following 'Hokku' (1919) by Yone Noguchi:

> Bits of song – what else?
> I, a rider of the stream,
> Lone between the clouds.

Hokku (or 'haiku') originated in Japan. By the time the form carried over to poetry in English, it had come to describe a poem of seventeen syllables in a pattern of five, seven, five, often involving an incongruous combination of two images from which a special insight or epiphany emerges, and including a word that indicates the poem is taking place in a particular season. Knowing that Noguchi's poem must live within these conditions helps to prepare us for its intense concentration. It primes us to look out for a word that indicates the time at which the poem is taking place (here, 'clouds', suggesting either spring or autumn) and a point of contrast (here, that between the 'Bits of song' and the poet who somehow gathers or observes them). But it is not just enough to spot that the poem contains these features, as though writing in a particular genre were merely a matter of ticking boxes: we need to consider how it makes something of them. The poem seems aware of its own brevity: it is an example of one of the 'Bits of song' described in the opening line; and that line exploits the poem's brevity in its compressed, ambiguous grammar: 'what else?' may be a question answered in the next line, with the image of the poet; or it could be a weary gesture to the way in which the poem fulfils the conventions of the genre: 'what else were you expecting but a scrap of poetry like this?' (Here it is perhaps significant that Japanese haiku often turn on moments of humour.) Looking for the juxtaposition of images also invites us to wonder about the connection between the poet and these 'Bits of song'. Is his character expressed through these fragments? Do they float free of him? And the image of the poet himself introduces another juxtaposition – between the poet and the natural world which carries him along on its 'stream' but which leaves him 'lone' and unsettled. Approaching the poem with the expectations created by genre in mind allows us to see how skilfully and succinctly Noguchi brings into focus questions about the relationship between the poet, his world, and the art that he produces.

Genre is also a signal of a poem's ambition – it determines the nature and breadth of what a poem will try to show us. Some ways of 'being good' are more significant than others. The scope, and perhaps substance, of a short lyric song, which as Francis Palgrave observed in the mid-nineteenth century, 'tend to turn on some single thought, feeling, or situation',[5] will be lesser than that of an epic poem, a kind of narrative which concerns itself with the myths or stories fundamental to a culture's understanding of itself, and often runs through a compendium of different genres. It would be peculiar to look at a haiku on the page and expect it to deliver a complicated story or extended argument (though haiku can be strung together into sequences). This is not to say that all longer poems are better than all shorter ones: everyone can intend to write something magnificent; achieving it is a different matter – though at the same time a glorious failure may have more to show us than a routine accomplishment.

We have been sailing close, in this section, to the vexed question of a poet's intentions. To think about genre is to realise the practical limitations of sophisticated theories that tell us that the question of what an author meant to do is irrelevant. An understanding of the topic a poet wanted to address, how they wanted to address it, and the traditions in which they are writing is self-evidently of use in coming to terms with a poem. At the same time, it is true that the most productive question to ask of a poem is not 'what was the poet trying to achieve?' (which, after all, an author could presumably just tell us), but 'what have they achieved?' Accomplishments fall short and spread wide of aspirations. Poems may develop new significances in new contexts which a poet has no control over. And writing is a matter of discovery as well as delivery. Like most activities, it involves instinct as well as design. A writer is liable to achieve effects, from local felicities of language to global significances, of which they are only half conscious. The qualities we enjoy in a poem might be things that a poet does innately: a habitual perspective, a particular intensity of perception, a manner of structuring thoughts, a way of handling language that comes naturally but is nonetheless forceful and revealing. The art of reading a poem lies not in recreating a poet's motivations but in judging the nature and significance of what they have put before us.

What Is the Poem about?

To ask what kind of poem we are dealing with is to ask what the poem *is*. The next step is to ask what it is *about*. Often the two questions overlap: a poem's genre can give some indication of its subject. The following lines by Walter Raleigh are sometimes given the title 'Epitaph' (1618), which signals that they are a short memorial to mark someone's death:

Even such is Time, which takes in trust
  Our youth, our joys, and all we have,
And pays us but with age and dust,
  Who in the dark and silent grave,
When we have wander'd all our ways,
Shuts up the story of our days.
But from which earth and grave and dust,
The Lord shall raise me up, I trust.

'Time takes away everything and leaves us with nothing; after life, we end up in the grave; but I trust that from the grave, God will raise me into heaven'. The poem's argument suggests how surprisingly it fulfils the demands of its genre: unusually, Raleigh's epitaph looks forward to his own death and not back on the life of someone else; he is supposed to have written it on a leaf of his Bible the night before his execution. The poem's orientation towards the future, where most epitaphs reflect on the past, underscores Raleigh's hope that the suffering of human life will be redeemed in heaven.

But to describe a poem's argument and its genre is not to pin down all of its concerns. If we ask not 'what is Raleigh's poem saying?' but 'what is it talking about?' we will arrive at a different set of answers: the poem meditates upon time, life, death, and 'trust'. We can, if we like, speak of these concerns as the poem's *themes*. Each has a common human importance that is brought into particular focus by Raleigh's poem. It is not enough, however, just to identify and list a poem's themes, as though a poem were merely an assembly of abstract ideas. What matters is how a writer treats them: how a poem presents its concerns to us and what it has to say about them. It only gives us a vague understanding of Raleigh's poem to say that it 'deals with the theme of death'. But to say that the poem presents us with a mind confronting death, regretting time's capriciousness, but eventually reposing faith in God's redemptive power, gets closer to its heart.

Likewise, we could say of the Noguchi poem above that its themes are poetry, nature, and the self. Or we can say that it presents a sketch of an individual trying to discover the relationship between selfhood, nature, and art – and that the elliptical manner of that presentation in itself suggests the difficulty of coordinating and capturing an understanding of these three elements of life. Identifying a poem's themes or concerns is only ever a platform for more detailed description.

Once we have a sense of what a poem is about – the problems it confronts, the topics it addresses, the wisdom it embodies, the area of life it deals with – it is worth pausing and reflecting: what are our own thoughts, feelings, and associations regarding the issue at hand? Everyone brings their own standpoint to a poem – it is one of the things that enables works of art to mean different things in different situations – and it is worth reminding ourself of our preconceptions about a particular issue, to see how a poem affirms, refines, or surprises them.

We should remember at this point that poems work by showing and not telling. As a result, the question 'what is this poem about?' is liable to splinter into a variety of literal and thematic or conceptual answers. A poem will present us with something concrete – a meditation, a description, a speech, a story – as a way of embodying a larger vision of experience. As the medieval Italian poet Dante said of his *Commedia*: 'the sense of this work is not simple, rather it may be called polysemantic, that is, of many senses; the first sense is that which comes from the letter, the second is that which is signified by the letter.'[6] Reading involves attention to the words on the page and contemplation of what they have to show us. Margaret Cavendish's 'Of a Spider's Web' (1653) is, on the face of it, about exactly what its title suggests:

> The Spider's Housewif'ry no Webs doth spin
> To make her Cloth, but Ropes to hang Flies in.
> Her Bowels are the Shop where Flax is found;
> Her Body is the Wheel that goeth round.
> A Wall her Distaff, where she sticks thread on;
> The Fingers are the Feet that pull it long.
> She's Busy at all times, not Idle lies;
> A House she Builds with Nets to catch the Flies.
> Though it be not so strong as Brick and Stone,
> Yet strong enough to bear light Bodies on.
> Within this House the Female Spider lies,

The whilst the Male doth hunt abroad for Flies.
Ne'er leaving till he Flies gets in, which are
Entangled soon within his Subtle Snare,
Like Treacherous Hosts, which do much welcome make
Their Guests, yet watch how they their Lives may take.

The lines describe the behaviour of a pair of spiders. And one thing that they show us is the value of precise empirical attention to nature. But Cavendish has written a poem and not an entry in a zoological textbook. Her lines prompt us to ask why she is describing the spiders – what significance does she find in them? Cavendish connects the actions of the spiders to the life of human beings. Her account of the spiders' married life implicitly suggests similarities and differences in the relations between the sexes in the animal and human worlds. She seems, for most of the poem, to be holding up the spiders as a model of the craft, industry, and cooperation that humans, too, might deploy in pursuit of survival. Then in the final two lines, what seemed to have been an example of the natural relationship between hunter and prey is presented suddenly in terms of a violation of the bonds between a host and their guest. The terms of the comparison between natural and human worlds are upturned. The spiders, which previously seemed admirably industrious, begin to look more like the Macbeths. The poem brings the sense that nature offers an example to be admired – for its embodiments of hard work, female empowerment, and so on – into conflict with the feeling that natural, instinctive relations alone cannot form the basis for the moral life. The poem is about a good deal more than the spiders it describes.

It can sometimes be tempting to think that reading a poem involves extracting a 'message' or 'moral'. Because poems are ways of showing and not telling, however, they rarely force us to adopt a single viewpoint. Even when a poem seems to give voice to a particular message or instruction, the delivery of that message in the form of a poem puts it into three dimensions and reading is a matter of exploring its presentation and implications. Of course, some poems will do more than others to open up a multiplicity of perspectives. Many of the most immediately stirring poems offer us a motto for living, with which it is assumed we will agree and to which it is easy to surrender. But the appeal of such poems soon wanes. W. E. Henley's 'Invictus' (1888) offers a resounding final announcement:

It matters not how strait the gate,
    How charged with punishments the scroll,
I am the master of my fate,
    I am the captain of my soul.

Yet the words, for all their heartening impact, are too complacently assured of the truth of the 'message' that they offer. There is nothing to go back to here, no sense that the simplicity and conviction of the vision has been won through an awareness of life's complexity. 'We make out of the quarrel with others, rhetoric, but of the quarrel with ourselves, poetry', said W. B. Yeats,[7] and by Yeats's definition, these lines are 'rhetoric', not poetry (and so they have found a happy home in many political speeches, from Winston Churchill to Nelson Mandela). The only 'quarrel' to be found in them is with the world, and it is one in which Henley is sure he has already triumphed. We could, to be generous, say that the poem implicitly places its thoughts in quotation marks, to expose the dangers of self-satisfaction, but those dangers are not something that the poem seems to demonstrate consciously: there is no sense of the self-awareness that would enable us to read the poem as inviting us, at least in part, to adopt an ironical perspective. The most enduring poems often demonstrate the difficulty of coming to an unconflicted position; they show us that life involves maintaining a balance between opposed perspectives and phenomena that are neither wholly right nor wrong, virtuous nor vicious. Cavendish's poem on the spider, though ostensibly on a far less significant subject than Henley's lyric, reaches deeper in its puzzled sense that nature offers both admirable and malicious models for living.

It can be helpful, as F. W. Bateson observes, to think of a poem as 'a miniature drama in which two "sides" meet, come into conflict, and are eventually reconciled'.[8] Approaching a poem by looking for those oppositions, and asking how – and how convincingly – they are reconciled, is always a fruitful way of developing a sense of its concerns. We might think of Raleigh's 'Epitaph' as a struggle between the tragic sense that life just slips through your fingers and the consolations afforded by belief in an afterlife; or of Noguchi's 'Hokku' as a snapshot of the tension between the power of nature, which sweeps humans along on its 'stream', and the impulse of human 'song' to celebrate and resist the flow of time. And if we think back to the list of opening lines we ran through above, it is often the sense that they present two unresolved attitudes that holds our attention:

> A thousand martyrs have I made,
> All sacrificed to my desire . . .

Here speaks a bold, iconoclastic, heartbreaker: on the one hand, we might feel dazzled admiration; on the other, sympathy for those whose lives he or she has trampled over.

What has this bugbear death to frighten man,
If souls can die as well as bodies can?

The speaker's implication that death is nothing to worry about braces itself against the fairly common feeling that death should be feared above everything.

When beauty breaks and falls asunder
I feel no grief for it, but wonder.

Again, stoicism in the face of loss plays off against a sense of the sadness of things falling away.

So, the question 'what is the poem about?' can take us in multiple directions. It can show us the relationship between a poem's literal and thematic concerns. It can take us into the heart of a dilemma that a poem dramatises. It can also help us to realise the ways in which a poem might be about poetry itself. Cavendish admires her spider because it is a creator, and a *she*, who weaves a 'subtle snare' just as Cavendish herself spins a web of lines which take us in and surprise us at the last minute. The poem, from one angle, is a demonstration of how poetry shapes experience. Every poem will show us something – at least implicitly – about the possibilities of poetry as an art, in addition to its more obvious concerns. Every poem is a fresh exploration of the possibilities of what a poem might be and how it should represent experience. Arun Kolatkar's 'Irani Restaurant Bombay' (1963) is a portrait of a café in which the poet liked to work, but it is also a meditation on the possibilities and responsibilities of the imagination:

the cockeyed shah of iran watches the cake
decompose carefully in a cracked showcase;
distracted only by a fly on the make
as it finds in a loafer's wrist an operational base.

dogmatically green and elaborate trees defeat
breeze; the crooked swan begs pardon
if it disturb the pond; the road, neat
as a needle, points at a lovely cottage with a garden.

If we ask what these opening moments of the poem are *about*, we might answer that they are about a rather run-down eatery and its various inhabitants, which include a 'loafer' – perhaps a figure for the poet himself – an entrepreneurial fly, and, in a painting on the wall, the shah – ruler – of Iran. If we ask what they *show us*, we might answer: 'two different ways of looking at the world'. First, there is the loving and humorous attention to life's 'cracked' and dingy imperfections on show in the description of the restaurant; second, there is the 'dogmatic' and life-defeating imposition of an unreal perfection as manifested in the propagandist poster of the shah on its wall. The substance of the poem, we might expect, will turn out to be a dialogue between the belief that art should make orderly, sanitised sense of reality – as embodied in the poster – and the belief that art should illuminate the world's strangeness and disorderliness – as on show in the poem's own style. Yet, in a good poem, the opposition will rarely be so simple or the odds stacked so strongly in favour of its own position – the 'quarrel' has to be genuine. As Kolatkar goes on, he describes how the loafer sees 'the stylised perfection / of the landscape, in a glass of water, wobble.' The poem evolves into a hallucinatory and rather scary daydream which becomes – just as much as the 'perfection' of the painting – an escape from the reality of the social world. The poem holds a distorted mirror up to the cafe, before it ends as the loafer's dream ends:

> tables chairs mirrors are night that needs to be sewed
> and cashier is where at seams it comes apart.

The loafer's surreal, swirling vision spills into the slippery unpunctuated unspooling of the words. But he is brought back from his daydream into a shared reality by the presence of the cashier, who presumably wants paying. Economics triumphs over fantasy. We might feel that this is a shame. But what we might say is that in recognising the need to return from private vision into a social world, Kolatkar's poem behaves differently to the mind of the 'loafer', which in its way shares the escapism of the poster on the wall. Kolatkar's vision is all the more persuasive – all the less 'dogmatic' – for encompassing rather than eluding the inconsistencies of life. The poem shows how an attempt to escape the world through fantasy 'comes apart'; it shows imagination accommodating itself to reality.

What Language Does the Poem Use?

The strangeness of Kolatkar's vision is alive in the strangeness of his language. Phrases such as 'tables chairs mirrors are night' warp our sense of reality by warping ordinary idioms. Likewise, the lifelessness of the poster on the wall is apparent from the trees which are 'dogmatically green', as though imposing a bland ideal of nature, and from the insipid description of the 'lovely cottage with a garden.' A poem's vision is inseparable from its language. And one reason that poetry is central to human life is that its medium, unlike that of, say, painting or sculpture, is one which we almost all use to communicate. But poets handle language, and invite us to contemplate it, with more than ordinary care. Encountering the word 'vale' in a passage from Milton's *Paradise Lost*, Keats scribbled in the margin of his copy the observation that the word seemed to have a sensory reality: 'There is a cool pleasure in the very sound of vale. The English word is of the happiest chance'.[9] Some poets extend their affections to individual letters. The late nineteenth-century poet Ernest Dowson is supposed to have believed that 'the letter "v" was the most beautiful of all the letters, and could never be brought into verse too often' and cherished Edgar Allan Poe's 'The viol, the violet, and the vine' ('The City in the Sea' (1831)), as the 'ideal' poetic line.[10] Not all poets gaze on words and letters with such sensuous involvement as that, but it is hard to imagine a good poet who doesn't think and feel deeply about words. There will always be something to say about how a poet's care over and understanding of language manifests itself, and how it calibrates their vision of the world. The 'cool pleasure' Keats finds in 'vale', has to do, perhaps, with its open vowel sounds (we will turn to the question of sound effects later on); but the word is also shaded by chillier associations – its aural similarity with 'veil' (such as people used to wear in mourning), for one, and its visual and etymological relationship with the Latin word *vale*, meaning farewell.[11] All of these implications colour the sombre opening line of *Hyperion* that we considered above: 'Deep in the shady sadness of a vale'. Keats chooses the word because he values its texture and associations as much as its semantic content (i.e. what it means). The quality of an almost identical line, 'Deep in the shady sadness of a valley', would be different.

Poetry is, among other things, the art of finding the right words. The words of a poem do not need to be particularly special, or ornamental, or to strain after effect. Rather, they need to be true to the situation and the feeling they handle. Here is the opening of a poem by Thomas Hardy (1898), in which a speaker examines their face in a mirror:

> I look into my glass,
> And view my wasting skin . . .

We could hardly put this more simply: 'I look into my mirror and see myself ageing'. Hardy uses no high-flown language. The lack of ornament gives the impression of a poem ready to look facts in the face. Still, flattening the lines out into a paraphrase helps to bring the character of Hardy's words into relief. Why the verb 'view' and not 'see', for instance? One reason might be that 'view' implies a cooler, more distant process of inspection; it banishes the impression you might get from 'see' that the sight of his 'wasting skin' took the speaker by surprise. Why 'wasting' and not 'wasted'? Well, 'wasting' gives the unsettling impression of a process that is ongoing at the very moment Hardy examines himself. Hardy's plainness renders experience with unflinching precision.

A common assumption about poetry is that it involves 'flowery' or 'poetic' language (the assumption often coexists with a notion that poems are merely decorative, tangential to the lives we live). Nobody has scotched this idea more movingly than Wordsworth. In the 'Preface' (1800–1802) to his collection *Lyrical Ballads*, Wordsworth speaks of a conviction that 'Poetry sheds no tears "such as Angels weep," but natural and human tears; she can boast of no celestial Ichor that distinguishes her vital juices from those of prose; the same human blood circulates through the veins of them both.'[12] That is, poetry deals with essential human concerns, and it speaks a human language as it does so. Hardy learned Wordsworth's lesson that the language of poetry must above all be a 'human' one. Here is his poem in full:

> I look into my glass,
> And view my wasting skin,
> And say, 'Would God it came to pass
> My heart had shrunk as thin!'
>
> For then, I, undistrest
> By hearts grown cold to me,
> Could lonely wait my endless rest
> With equanimity.
>
> But Time, to make me grieve,
> Part steals, part lets abide;
> And shakes this fragile frame at eve
> With throbbings of noontide.

One of the striking things about the poem, given its unhappy situation, is that it makes no complaint or appeal for sympathy – it remains content with restrained statement of feeling. And that restraint is a product of Hardy's plain, unsentimental language; what is said and how it is said prove impossible to separate. Few words seem out of the ordinary. 'Would God?' might strike our ears as a little unconventional (it means 'I wish to God'). But it is set in quotation marks, as part of what Hardy presents himself as saying when he looks in the mirror: we might even wonder whether if by using such an urgently compressed phrase he is sending up a slight portentousness in his own immediate response. 'Undistrest' is certainly unusual, but has a quietly bleak impact: the 'un-' formulation suggests the life Hardy dreams of is one defined by its absence of 'distress' rather than by any positive quality; the archaic spelling ('undistressed' would be more contemporary) underscores the sour coincidence of the end of the word's second and third syllables: 'dist'/'rest'. 'Lonely' might also seem to be deployed a little oddly: we usually encounter it as an adjective, describing a character's state of mind, but here it is used as an adverb. The usage strips back the word's emotional implications: to 'lonely wait' is just to wait on one's own – the yearning implication of 'loneliness' is held at bay. 'Abide' is likewise an affecting choice, with its suggestion – not present in an alternative such as 'remain', say – of endurance, or a need for patience. Each of these words carries some expressive character, but none shows Hardy reaching for an idiom that draws attention to itself or is elaborate for its own sake. It is not until the final line that a swell of romantic feeling is allowed into the poem, and it is carried on a word, 'throbbings', which shows how powerfully sudden switches in verbal register can take effect: full with emotional associations, the word seems to surge up through the otherwise placid surface of the language like the emotion Hardy describes.

Hardy shows how poetry need not strain for words which have special meaning, but can rather discover meaning in words. This truth often becomes apparent when a poet puts pressure on a word through repetition. Rebecca Watts's 'The Studio' (2020) draws an apparently sweet picture of a pair of lives lived in a studio flat by listing its contents in a series of couplets which see-saw on the word 'little' to haunting and witty effect. As Watts documents a life's ornaments and necessities ('little apron little jug / little window little rug') her repetitions invite us to take a sentimental view of the scene, as though peering into a doll's house. Then, in the final line, the word 'little' enters to different effect: 'little greedy wanting more'.[13] Suddenly, as it moves from labelling the contents of the flat to judging the character of its inhabitants, the word seems belittling rather than tender, as though spoken by someone higher up the social hierarchy wanting to keep the couple neatly in their place. By calling on the same word, with a slightly different inflection, Watts shows how easily sentimentality slides into condescension. Or are we to take the line at face value, as decrying our materialistic impulse for 'more'? Through its handling of a single common word, the poem opens up a multiplicity of implications.

A similarly skilled use of repetition characterises Watts's pastoral lyric 'After rain' (2016), in which a series of two-line units beginning 'here's' and 'there's' direct our attention to various sights in the aftermath of a rain shower, before, like a piano key being struck out of tune, a single-word line, 'plink', breaks the pattern by describing – and onomatopoeically embodying – the sound of a fish breaching the surface of a pond.[14] As the word's odd musicality shows, simplicity and plainness are not the only poetic virtues. Sometimes poets will invite us to look at life afresh by using familiar words in unusual ways. To read Carol Ann Duffy's description in 'The Christmas Truce' (2011) of a game of football between the World War I trenches on Christmas Eve, during which frost 'treasured' the hair of 'unburied sons', is to feel how a single word can transform our apprehension of the world. The frost 'treasures' the hair by making it sparkle, turning it into a kind of treasure, but also in a sense that implies an active benevolence in the universe, as one would treasure a favourite belonging.[15] The word is so poignantly chosen because this is a benevolence, the description of these soldiers as 'unburied sons' reminds us, only fleetingly afforded in this instance. These 'sons' will become 'buried', as sometimes treasure is, when they become casualties of the war; to feel the need to describe them as 'unburied' is to imply that 'burial' is their default state. Yet the soldiers are 'unburied' in another, warmer sense, too, as they are brought back to life and treasured again in the art of Duffy's poem.

Duffy uncovers new significance in a familiar word. At other times, poets find expressive potential in the furthest nooks and corners of the language. In these lines from *The Seasons* (1730), James Thomson describes some sheep in a frosty landscape:

> The bleating kind
> Eye the bleak heaven, and next the glistening earth,
> With looks of dumb despair; then, sad-dispersed,
> Dig for the withered herb through heaps of snow.

'The sheep look despairingly at the sky, and the ground, then spread out and nibble grass through the snow.' The distance between these lines and their argument is greater than it is in Hardy. Eighteenth-century tastes tended to favour a more elevated poetic language than became common in the wake of Wordsworth. As one of Thomson's near contemporaries, Thomas Gray, said: poetry 'has a language peculiar to itself; to which almost every one, that has written, has added something by enriching it with foreign idioms and derivatives.'[16] Perhaps we disagree. But remembering that one of the things that poetry can do is to open up our sympathies to alien values, let's ask what Thomson's elevated diction (his choice of words) brings to the lines.

First, there is Thomson's rather roundabout word for the sheep. Your walking companion would laugh at you if you turned and pointed out that there was a herd of 'the bleating kind' in the next field. But Thomson is not just being pretentious. To call sheep 'the bleating kind' draws attention to the fact that sheep bleat, and do so most urgently when in distress. A similar effect underlies the slightly arcane verb 'Eye': unlike 'look' – or indeed Hardy's 'view' – 'Eye' calls upon us to visualise a part of the body: to look into the face of the sheep's distress. There is nothing too outlandish in the next line and a half, but we might observe a couple of unusual features. First, Thomson's inverted adjective pairings: ordinarily we would expect the heavens to 'glisten' and the earth to be 'bleak' – here, Thomson suggests by reversing the common associations, is a world turned upside down. Second, the fact that the sheep are 'dumb' (i.e. silent) while they observe all of this: 'bleating' might be second nature to them, but in these circumstances they aren't even 'the bleating kind' anymore; the conditions have stripped them of their nature. 'Sad-dispersed' is a word that Thomson has coined himself. In an earlier version of the lines, he had written 'sad, dispersed': the invented word yokes those two meanings together to trigger a whole cluster of meanings: the sheep might have dispersed in sadness, they might be sad now they have dispersed, or their dispersal might look melancholy to the observer. The coinage serves, too, as a preparation for the fall into starker language in the line that follows, where the effect depends upon the contrast between the 'withered herb' – i.e. the grass, described in terms that remind us that for the sheep the grass is food, and make it sound like a single entity, as though there were only a solitary blade to be seen – and the sturdily no-nonsense description of the 'heaps of snow' under which it is buried.

Hardy's simplicity and Thomson's ornamentation constitute two points on a vast linguistic map. Each poem stays fairly consistently within a particular register. The effect of other poems might depend upon the way they move between different manners of speaking. Amy Clampitt's 'The Cormorant in its Element' (1983) switches dazzlingly between registers to describe the movements of a diving cormorant. As the poem reaches its climax, Clampitt describes how the bird:

   in one sleek involuted arabesque, a vertical
turn on a dime, goes into that inimitable
vanishing-and-emerging-from-under-the-briny-

deep act which, unlike the words of Homo Houdini,
is performed for reasons having nothing at all
to do with ego, guilt, ambition, or even money.

Though Clampitt claims the bird's movements are 'inimitable', her verbal flexibility responds in spirit to its gymnastics. Her lines show how a poet's language can both describe a scene with enhanced precision and vitality and transfigure it into something new. Clampitt shows us the dive, first, as a 'sleek involuted arabesque', a pirouette whose complexities are matched by the elevation of her phrasing: 'involuted' is a botanical term, describing leaves or petals curled in on themselves; an 'arabesque' is an intricate, curling decorative pattern, but also has technical usages associated with ballet, and music – and, fittingly, can be used to describe ornate figures of speech. Clampitt then swoops from this high-flown expression to represent the dive in a more everyday idiom: it is a 'turn on a dime' – suddenly we're in the realm of a football commentary. The words in the third line aren't in themselves unusual, but the hyphens string them together into a new and astonishing compound; Clampitt makes us feel how the bird's behaviour stretches the resources of language. The next three lines, which constitute the ending of the poem, settle back down into a flatter, more run-of-the-mill way of speaking. It is a move at one with their argument: what is remarkable about the bird, as opposed to human beings ('Homo Houdini', always showing off) is that it performs all of this for the sake of it, without hope of reward – so it is appropriate for Clampitt to shift, in saying this, into a register that doesn't call attention to itself. Not that the language here lacks interest: 'even' in the final line introduces a slender irony about human priorities (and the thought of money springs from the 'dime' in the cliché four lines earlier). Clampitt both finds new energy in existing phrases and pushes the language in new directions. The lines show her in her own element.

Do We Need a Dictionary?

Sometimes, as, perhaps, with 'arabesque' in Clampitt's poem, we will encounter a word whose precise meaning – or meanings – we are not sure of. To discover them we need to consult a dictionary. The *Oxford English Dictionary* (*OED*) is the standard choice, and available through most libraries. How can it illuminate our understanding?

The first Canto of Edmund Spenser's *The Faerie Queene* (1590) begins like this:

> A Gentle Knight was pricking on the plaine;
> Ycladd in mightie armes and silver shielde,
> Wherein old dints of deepe wounds did remaine,
> The cruell markes of many a bloudy fielde;

'Pricking', 'Ycladd', perhaps even 'dints': there are some tricky words here. How can we make sense of them? A good edition of the poem might supply a gloss in the margins, explaining that 'pricking' means 'riding briskly', 'Ycladd' means 'clothed', and 'dints', 'dents'. And on a first reading that might be enough: the poem is almost 11,000 lines long – we can't stop to look into every word. But there is scope for investigating the implications of Spenser's language further. Under the entry for the verb *prick* in the *OED* are several familiar senses, among them sense 11a, 'To spur or urge one's horse on; to go on horseback, to ride, *esp.* fast', which is illustrated by a number of quotations from works dating from 1300 to 1940, including Spenser's line. We are told that the sense is 'now archaic', but the examples suggest that it was current when Spenser's poem was written in the late sixteenth century. Consulting the dictionary has confirmed what a gloss might have told us anyway, but the emphasis in the definition on speed is perhaps worth taking note of, at the start of what we will discover to be a lengthy and at times slow-moving poem.

'Ycladd' also looks old fashioned. And if we look the word up, we'll see that while the illustrations of its usage as an adjective run from 1320 to 1812 – including another line from *The Faerie Queene* – it has been archaic since the sixteenth century. This gives us a clue to the linguistic world of Spenser's poem: as we might have deduced already from all the unusual spellings, he is using a language which even for his time was antiquated, redolent of the dreamy realm of chivalrous knights he wanted to evoke. If we look up the noun *dint*, we'll discover that its original sense, 'A stroke or blow; *esp.* one given with a weapon in fighting', is now regarded as obsolete, or to have morphed into a new sense, 'A mark or impression made by a blow or pressure in a hard or plastic surface; an indentation' – a usage for which Spenser's line is given as the first example. Spenser turns the word into a label for the consequence of the blow, rather than the action itself; in reaching into the past, Spenser's lines reshaped the language for the future. He retunes existing words to match his precise meaning.

Given that a quick tour of the dictionary has yielded so much information, we might be tempted to look up a word that seems familiar. Spenser has granted the adjective 'Gentle' prominence right at the start of the poem, so it is worth testing whether it meant the same thing for Spenser as it does for us. Among the various familiar senses of the word listed, we'll find the following, again illustrated with Spenser's lines: 'Of persons. Having the characteristics appropriate to one of good birth; noble, generous, courteous'. While for us, 'gentle' is mostly associated with softness and tenderness, Spenser's usage invokes an older sense that still lingers in words such as 'gentleman'. He is using the word to indicate the Knight's noble lineage as well as his character.

Words have lineages too, known as *etymologies*, and a good dictionary will tell us about them. Part of the reason English is so full and flexibly expressive a language is that its vocabulary flows from several linguistic pools. Two sources dominate: the Germanic languages of the original Anglo-Saxon settlers in Britain and the Latinate, Romance language brought over with the Norman invaders. The result is that English often has two words for the same concept, with contrasting vernacular and courtly, northern and southerly inflections. We look into a farmyard and see pigs, cows, and sheep – all words of earthy Germanic stock; but we eat pork, beef, and (if we have good taste) mutton – on the plate the meat is re-named with more abstract Romance terms (there is no such creature as 'a pork'), because we flinch from considering what we are eating. 'Leave' (Germanic) and 'depart' (Romance), 'stay' (Germanic) and 'remain' (Romance), both mean the same thing, but have contrasting associations. Different etymological groupings give poems a different savour. Compare the following translations of a verse from Psalm 114, describing the mountains turning on the Egyptians as the Israelites fled Egypt. First, that in the Authorized Version (AV) of the Bible (1611):

> The mountains skipped like rams, and the little hills like lambs.

Second, the translation made by Mary Sidney between 1588 and 1599, not published until 1823:

> The mountains bounded so, as, fed, in fruitful ground,
> The fleeced rams do frisking bound.
> The hillocks capreold so, as wanton by their dams
> We capreol see the lusty lambs.

Sidney achieves something more elaborate than the AV – a language which decorates and celebrates the events it describes. And she does so by deploying a more ornate vocabulary, or *diction*. Where the AV uses one verb, the Germanic 'skip', Sidney has the French-derived 'bounded' and the extremely unusual 'capreol', which the *OED* does not even list as a verb, but which is derived from the Latin word for a goat. Though both poems describe the same event, the contrast in the vocabulary is such that it seems one presents a black-and-white pencil drawing and the other a full-colour painting.

Sidney's version of the Psalm ends by warning us to 'quake' at God:

Who in the hardest rocks makes standing waters grow
And purling springs from flints to flow.

The varied textures of the English language allow Sidney to animate the scene by playing words of different registers and etymologies off against one another. Her Germanic 'quake' wields more visceral force than the AV's Latinate 'Tremble', and her lovely-sounding 'purling springs' then 'flow' from the hard-sounding 'flint' with a fuller sense of transformation than the AV's 'turned . . . the flint into a fountain of waters': we feel in Sidney's words the miraculous flow of liquid from the hard stuff of existence which they describe.

'Purling', meaning twisting, or rippled, is probably of north British origin and, the *OED* suggests, is 'perhaps (partly) imitative'. The word, that is, is *onomatopoeic*: it sounds like what it describes. The sense that words are grounded in the reality they describe lies behind the vibrant tradition in English of dialect poetry – poems whose language is attached to a particular region or place. 'Purling' itself, though it was widespread in Sidney's time, is now chiefly a Scottish word. Dialect lends local colour and character; it gives precision; it imbues a poem with a spirit of place. As the Scottish poet Kathleen Jamie says: 'it can do a job that standard English can't do, reach parts that language cannot reach'.[17] Jean Elliot's 'The Flowers of the Forest' (1769), a ballad about the defeat of the Scottish army at the Battle of Flodden in 1513, written down in the eighteenth century, speaks all the more poignantly about loss because it speaks in the voice of the particular community which has suffered:

In hairst, at the shearing, nae youths now are jeering,
The bandsters are lyart, and rankled and gray;
At fair or at preaching, nae wooing, nae fleeching:
The Flowers of the Forest are a' wede away.

In harvest at shearing, no youths now are jeering,
The binders are silvery, rumpled, and gray;
At fair or at preaching, no wooing, no flirting:
The Flowers of the Forest are wilted away.

How much flatter the standard English translation is – how much of the character of a particular way of life is lost in it. The dialect version, in the very texture of its language, expresses grief at once forlornly and fiercely, and there is something redemptive in it, too, since in the very words of the poem the spirit of place is retained.

How Does the Poem Develop?

The verb 'capreold' in Sidney's poem snags the attention. It is a point at which the poem's concentration on the world it describes seems most intense and at which its language is being used most innovatively in response to that concentration. Just as a brilliant splash of colour might be the first thing that catches our eye when we look at a painting, or a snatch of melody might hook our ear when we first hear a piece of music, so when we read a poem for the first time there are likely to be words, lines, images, events, or passages which particularly draw us in. It might be a flash of impassioned emotion, as in the despairing question George Herbert asks in the penultimate stanza of 'The Pilgrimage' (1633):

> I fell, and cry'd, Alas my King!
> Can both the way and end be tears?

It might be a single phrase or image, such as Arthur Hugh Clough's unhappy description of the 'maze of petty life' in 'Blank Misgivings of a Creature moving about in Worlds not realized' (1840–42). It might be an isolated aspect of a poem, such as the voice it is written in. On first encounter with Paul Laurence Dunbar's 'When de Co'n Pone's Hot' (1895), a poem in celebration of the joys of hot cornbread, it is likely to be the rickety energy of the poem's dialect voice and rhythms which strike, and linger in, our imagination, as they embody a terrific vision of a moment unshackled from ordinary routine:

> Dey is times in life when Nature
> Seems to slip a cog an' go,
> Jes' a-rattlin' down creation,
> Lak an ocean's overflow . . .

In a longer poem, it might be that a particular passage or episode draws attention. Charlotte Smith's *The Emigrants* (1793) runs for around 800 lines over two books, but from a first reading it may be that one of the poem's pained questions is all that lodges in the mind:

> What is the promise of the infant year
> To those who (while the poor but peaceful hind
> Pens, unmolested, the increasing flock
> Of his rich master in this sea-fenced isle)
> Survey, in neighbouring countries, scenes that make
> The sick heart shudder, and the man who thinks
> Blush for his species?

All of these features offer a way in: a means of isolating an aspect of the poem in which larger features or concerns are likely to be exemplified, and which might enable us to prise the work open and enjoy it in its entirety. When we re-read the poem to relish the moment or quality over again, we can ask how it brings into focus the poem's broader development or concerns. How does Herbert arrive at and resolve his moment of crisis? How does Clough manifest and negotiate his understanding of life as a 'petty' 'maze'? What place does Dunbar's dialect voice have in giving character to the exhilarating moments he celebrates? Is Smith's question just rhetorical, or does her poem seek to unfold a genuine answer to it?

While there are numerous general questions we can ask to come to terms with a poem, one of the goals of reading is to discover the unique questions raised by each individual work. And following each poem's way of answering those questions involves treating a poem not as a jumble of more or less arresting moments, but understanding how those moments knit together into a coherent whole. With a longer poem, this may take numerous readings. We should be prepared to take our time. Working out how a poem moves from thought to thought, or event to event, may involve returning to it over several days. Reading Smith's *The Emigrants*, for instance, we might ask how the fluid manner of speaking apparent in the lines above (digressing mid-thought as though to catch ideas as they pass across her mind) complicates the challenge of following, and holding in mind, the answers that she formulates. With a long poem, pausing as we read to jot down the central argument of each paragraph can help us to map the poem's larger organisation. But even looking close up at a short passage, it is important to follow a poet's ideas in sequence. Let's think back to the lines from Thomson's *Seasons*. They too would serve as an example of a particular image which might unlock the larger interests of a poem: they invite us to contemplate Thomson's interest in landscape, in the beauties and realities of nature, and in suffering. But part of the reason that they linger in the memory is because of the sequence in which they present things:

The bleating kind
Eye the bleak heaven, and next the glistening earth,
With looks of dumb despair; then, sad-dispersed,
Dig for the withered herb through heaps of snow.

Thomson conducts our gaze, with that of the sheep, from the sky, to the ground, to the earth beneath. His poem consists not just of words, but words in order. Looking at a painting, we can start anywhere (though a painter might seek to draw our attention to a particular spot); reading a poem, it matters that we follow its line of development from the beginning, through the middle, to the end. This is true on a large scale – we know that it will make no sense to start with the last line of a poem and then read upwards – and it is also true, as the example from Thomson shows, of the way information is presented within sentences.

The point might seem obvious, but obvious things are easy to neglect, and they are often fundamental. Henry Howard's 'The Soote Season' (1557) shows the importance of following sense in sequence:

> The soote[1] season, that bud and blome furth bringes,
> With grene hath clad the hill and eke[2] the vale:
> The nightingale with fethers new she singes:
> The turtle[3] to her make hath tolde her tale:
> Somer is come, for euery spray nowe springes,
> The hart hath hong his olde hed on the pale:
> The buck in brake his winter cote he flinges:
> The fishes flote with newe repaired scale:
> The adder all her sloughe[4] awaye she slinges:
> The swift swalow pursueth the flyes smale:
> The busy bee her honye now she minges:[5]
> Winter is worne that was the flowers bale:
> And thus I see among these pleasant thinges
> Eche care decayes, and yet my sorow springes.

The poem depends on the sad shock of the ending – and it might be the final line which most sticks in our mind on a first reading. But the shock that line creates depends on its contrast with the thirteen and a half lines of apparently happy observation that precede it. Other effects of sequencing within the poem are more subtle. It might strike us as slightly unusual, for instance, that the poem notices that 'Summer is come' before it observes that 'Winter is worn': surely the passing of one season precedes the arrival of another? Or are the two lines different ways of looking at one and the same thing? The shift from thinking about the arrival of summer to the withering of winter offers a small foreshadowing of the melancholy of the final lines. In other parts of the poem, the sequencing might seem not to matter at all. The lines about the hart, buck, fishes, adder, swift, and bee could perhaps be re-arranged in any order without losing coherence. But even those lines trace a passage from shedding old clothes to pursuing and producing new food. The poem is about the changes wrought by time, and its own progress through time matters.

[1] sweet [2] even [3] turtle dove [4] skin [5] exudes

Asking what a poem says entails attending to the order in which it says it. We need to follow the shape of its argument. Samuel Taylor Coleridge once entered in his notebook a thought about the kind of concentration a poem demands:

> As late as 10 years ago, I used to seek and find out grand lines and fine stanzas; but my delight has been far greater, since it has consisted more in tracing the leading Thought thro'out the whole. The former is too much like coveting your neighbour's Goods; in the latter you merge yourself in the Author – you *become He* –.[18]

Coleridge's remark shows exactly how poetry enables contact with another consciousness: the more minutely we follow a poem's turns of thought and feeling, the more fully we can inhabit a writer's perspective. It can be easy, on first encountering a poem, to let it wash over us. Its patterns, textures, images, and sounds are all liable to distract attention from the unfolding of its argument. To begin with, this is probably a good thing: initial intoxication with poetry is likely to involve surrendering to the sensuous power of language. But poems are not just washes of sound and imagery. They are more than words arranged in loose association across a 'semantic field'. Poetry pays and communicates precise attention to experience, and part of the value of reading poems is that it trains us to pay similarly precise attention.

How might we put Coleridge's notion of 'tracing the leading Thought' into action? Consider the following poem by Ernest Dowson (1896), whose fondness for the letter *v* we remarked on a few pages back:

Vitae summa brevis spem nos vetat incohare longam

They are not long, the weeping and the laughter,
Love and desire and hate:
I think they have no portion in us after
We pass the gate.

They are not long, the days of wine and roses:
Out of a misty dream
Our path emerges for a while, then closes
Within a dream.

The poem might seem the epitome of poetry as 'grand lines and fine stanzas'. The title translates as 'the brief sum of life forbids us from hope of long endurance'. It is a quotation from the Roman poet Horace, a message that nothing lasts for ever from ages ago; and the sense that the poem expresses the poignancy of life's transience may be all one takes from a first reading. Perhaps a phrase or two might lodge in the head – 'the days of wine and roses', say, as a succinct description of youthful hedonism. Dowson lived an impoverished, bohemian life at the end of the nineteenth century, haunting cafés and absinthe bars; his poem exudes some of the bittersweet, world-weary, *fin-de-siècle* atmosphere he inhabited.

What more can we glean by returning to the poem to describe its precise structure of thought and feeling? The first obvious fact is that the poem is split into two sentences. Both make overlapping observations about the brevity of life; but the second, offering a positive statement about life, not a negative one about what it lacks, seems to follow naturally on from the first. The opening sentence itself falls neatly in two: first a direct statement about the transience of human emotions; secondly, a more vulnerable statement of doubt about their endurance after death, grounded in the phrase 'I think'. If one's first impression is that the poem is mournful, close attention to the emotions that the poem expresses reveals the possibility of a more subtle interplay of moods: that 'laughter, / Love and desire' are transient is of course a cause for sadness; but they are flanked in the sentence by 'weeping' and 'hate': the effect might be to suggest that even these 'negative' human emotions have their value; or it might be to suggest that death brings relief as well as regret.

The second sentence starts with the same words as the first. It might seem merely to say the same thing again in more elevated terms. But the structure of the sentence contains variations. Where the first sentence splits neatly down the middle, the second has an initial statement followed by three lines of description: the warning of life's brevity has itself been cut short. Equally, the fact that the poem circles back to restate its main theme, rather than developing a new idea is itself worth noticing. One of the things that might impress us about Dowson's poem is the direction that it *doesn't* take. If I had been writing this poem, I'd have been tempted to add a moralising *carpe diem* ('seize the day') motto in the second stanza or to offer an effusive response to the tragedy of it all. Dowson's poem is all the more potent for its refusal to moralise or aggrandise. It is content to state a sense of what life is like and leave it at that.

The questions 'what next?' and 'how does this thought follow from the previous one?' will always illuminate a poem. You might even say that knowing what to put next is the whole art of writing poetry – and that the art of reading is to understand the author's choice. Sometimes, as in Dowson's poem, the development feels inevitable: the repetitive quality of the sentences is in harmony with the repeated pattern of the words on the page. But what we often want from poetry is extravagance and surprise as well as inevitability. Think of Bob Dylan's 'Mr Tambourine Man' (1964), which repeatedly departs on wild flights upon a single rhyme before revolving to the home ground of its choruses. Or contemplate the weirdly contorted arguments of Richard Crashaw's 'The Tear' (1646), in which the poet addresses a tear which he imagines 'Weeps for itself, is its own tear' as it falls from the eye of the woman he loves:

Faire drop, why quak'st thou so?
'Cause thou straight must lay thy head
In the dust? o no;
The dust shall never be thy bed:
A pillow for thee will I bring,
Stufft with downe of angels' wing.

Thus carried up on high,
(For to Heaven thou must go)
Sweetly shalt thou lye
And in soft slumbers bathe thy woe;
Till the singing orbes awake thee,
And one of their bright chorus make thee.

There thy self shalt be
An eye, but not a weeping one,
Yet I doubt of thee,
Whether th'hadst rather there have shone
An eye of Heaven; or still shine here,
In th'Heaven of Mary's eye, a tear.

Crashaw asks us to entertain the thought that the tear is sentient and quivers because it is about to fall into the dust. It is a strange idea, and Crashaw develops it along strange lines: he promises to cushion the tear with a pillow made of feathers from angels' wings, before lifting it to heaven where it will sleep before joining in the beautiful music of the spheres (the 'singing orbs' imagined in ancient astronomy as circling the earth). Finally, he suggests that even in that state the tear might be nostalgic for its initial home in Mary's eye. It is not so much the thoughts Crashaw presents us with that make his poem as the path from one thought to another: the turns and extensions are flamboyant and unpredictable, as though Crashaw was intent on making the most extravagant monument to his affection possible, and it is hard in following them not to raise a smile.

Other poems are challenging because they ask us to make sense of elliptical, broken sequences of thought or perception. Michael Ondaatje's 'Driving with Dominic in the Southern Province We See

Hints of the Circus' (2000), for example, depicts a visit to the poet's childhood home in Sri Lanka. Instead of presenting us with a seamless structure of thought and feeling, Ondaatje arranges a sparsely punctuated series of fragmentary half-sentences interspersed with blank spaces, like images whizzing past a windscreen: a 'tattered' circus tent; someone rinsing a trumpet by the roadside; children climbing trees – 'one falling / into the grip of another'[19] – and that's it. Faced with a poem whose argument seems so 'tattered' and fragmentary, we should trust our perceptions. If it is hard to follow a continuous line of thought, the effect is often calculated. We are prompted to seek connections, and to contemplate the nature of and reasons for disconnections. Given Ondaatje's poem's preoccupation with a childhood landscape, it might be appropriate that the poet only apprehends this landscape in fleeting 'Hints': it is a world which he can no longer wholly access or find stability in. The final lines of the poem themselves cause us to wonder about the value of interconnectedness: they show one child 'falling / into the grip' of another – which might be a good thing, if it implies care, or a bad thing, if it implies one person coming under someone else's sway. However we interpret the way the poem skims from image to image – as a delight in freedom or an effort to scrabble together fragments of the past – we should also ask whether there is any sequence guiding the movement from one image to the next. Here the question reveals a drift from age (the 'tattered' tent) to youth (the children at the end of the poem), which might parallel the poet's journey in revisiting his homeland, and which suggests that, even if it tries to reverse it, a poem still has to take place in time.

How Does the Syntax Shape the Sense?

We have established the importance of thinking about how a poem moves between thoughts, images, or sentences; but what about the movement within sentences? Look again at the first line of Dowson's poem: 'They are not long, the days of wine and roses'. Dowson could just have easily written 'The days of wine and roses are short'. The effect would have been more direct. But it would have had nothing of the rise and fall of the line as it is written, nothing of the movement that sees days not in terms of their brevity but of their absence of length, nothing of the delay that creates a small suspense over just what is 'not long'.

The arrangement of words in a sentence is called *syntax*. The tiniest deviations in sequence can affect the quality of expression. When Roberta Flack begins a 1969 song with the line 'The first time ever I saw your face', the care taken to voice the words 'ever I' in their 'correct' rather than idiomatic order (we'd ordinarily say, 'I ever') testifies to the line's sense of wonder. Shakespeare's decision to begin Sonnet 60 (1609) with the lines 'Like as the waves make towards the pebbled shore / So do our minutes hasten to their end' shapes an effect far more vivid than if he had put the sentence the other way round, as 'Our minutes hasten to their end like waves / Which make towards the pebbled shore'. Shakespeare gives us the image first, and it is allowed to hang in our mind, before we know what it is being used to illustrate. Likewise, after the poem has run through a litany of time's destructive effects, the syntax of the closing couplet affects the mood with which it leaves us: 'And yet to times in hope my verse shall stand / Praising thy worth, despite his cruel hand'. Time's 'cruel hand', not the heroic resistance of art, is given the last word. How different the feeling would be had the syntax been re-arranged: 'And yet to times in hope, despite time's hand, / To praise thy worth, my lasting verse shall stand'.

Syntax is in part a matter of punctuation. Near the start of Rosemary Tonks's 'Farewell to Kurdistan' (1967), a poem about leaving behind a life of alienation in London, are the following three lines:

> As my new life begins, I start smiling at the people around me,
> You would think I'd just been given a substantial meal,
> I see all their good points.

There's nothing spectacular about the word order here, but it is striking how often we encounter a comma where the grammar would ordinarily call for a full stop. This is a poem gathering momentum, overflowing the bounds of sentences, refusing to be held back. By the final lines of Tonks's poem, the controlling impulse of the punctuation is almost being run ragged by the impetus of the sentences:

> Oh I shall live off myself, rainclothes, documents,
> The great train simmers . . . Life is large, large!
> . . . I shall live off your loaf of shadows, London;
> I admit it, at the last.

Most striking, perhaps, are the exclamation mark, which underscores an outburst about life's magnitude at the heart of the lines, and the ellipses (' . . . '), which enable the focus of the sentences to flit in and out, as though moving between different planes of expression. Punctuation is also absent or lighter in places where one would usually expect it: no comma after the 'Oh', no full stop after 'documents' – two trains of thought blend instead into a single sentence. The whole arrangement allows words to move with a flair appropriate to a writer who maintained that 'The main duty of the poet is to excite – to send the senses reeling'.[20]

A poem's syntax gives shape to and takes shape from what the poem has to say. It embodies the character and texture of the poem's voice. It can propel or retard our movement towards understanding. Anne Finch's 'A Nocturnal Reverie' (1713) begins with a sentence that leads us to anticipate a resolution that the poem withholds:

> In such a Night, when every louder Wind
> Is to its distant Cavern safe confin'd;
> And only gentle Zephyr[6] fans his Wings,
> And lonely Philomel,[7] still waking, sings;
> Or from some Tree, famed for the Owl's delight,
> She, hollowing clear, directs the Wand'rer right:
> In such a Night, when passing Clouds give place,
> Or thinly veil the Heav'ns' mysterious Face;
> When in some River, overhung with Green,
> The waving Moon and the trembling Leaves are seen;

As we work through this sentence, we sense a promise hanging over it. The first words set up the expectation that the poem is going to tell us what happens 'In such a Night'. But the sentence soon deviates from that purpose: the first three and a half lines pile up a series of sub-clauses which describe what 'such a Night' is like. When we get to the seventh line, the opening phrase returns: the implication is that the poem is finally going to get down to business. But it finds itself distracted again: the phrase is followed by two more subordinate clauses, which document the conditions of the clouds and the river. And so the poem goes on, building an account of the conditions of 'such a Night', but withholding from us what it initially set out to say about it. If we look closely at the phrasing of the opening – 'In' such a night, which suggests immersion, where 'On' might be more usual – there are clues that what the poem is really interested in is communicating the quality of the night itself. Within the individual sub-clauses, more localised details of syntax prove worthy of attention. When 'The waving Moon and the trembling Leaves are seen' in the river, the passive construction ('are seen' by whom?) might seem an awkward adjustment for the sake of the rhyme, but it also has the effect of avoiding mention of an observer: this is a world cleared of the presence of 'tyrant man'. We are told that 'lonely Philomel, still waking, sings', rather than 'lonely Philomel sings, while still awake': the delay of the verb dramatises the ongoing singing the line describes. As when considering a poem's choice of words,

[6] the west wind [7] the nightingale

measuring the phrasing against the syntax of a simpler prose paraphrase is a good way of bringing its effects into relief. The whole poem is an aside to the main clause of its single sentence until, in the final four lines, it at last comes round to its opening phrase again:

> In such a Night let Me abroad remain
> Till Morning breaks, and All's confused again;
> Our Cares, our Toils, our Clamours are renew'd,
> Or Pleasures, seldom reached, again pursu'd.

The poem's syntax has fulfilled its own wish: it has 'remained abroad' in the atmosphere of 'such a Night', and it has proved, too, a point about the wisdom of 'pursuing' ends rather than enjoying the present.

Finch's poem piles clause upon clause in a manner that stretches the length of an ordinary prose sentence, but it doesn't perform too many acrobatics with the order of words within its clauses. By contrast, if we ask how 'After War' (1924) by Ivor Gurney captures so viscerally the experience of unwinding after the fear and exhaustion of battle, then the answer would have a lot to do with the way the words in its meandering single sentence seem to have been roughed up and knocked out of place:

> One got peace of heart at last, the dark march over,
> And the straps slipped, the warmth felt under roof's low cover
> Lying slack the body, let sink in straw giving;
> And some sweetness, a great sweetness felt in mere living,
> And to come to this haven after sorefooted weeks,
> The dark barn roof, and the glows and the wedges and streaks;
> Letters from home, dry warmth and still sure rest taken
> Sweet to the chilled frame, nerves soothed were so sore shaken.

When we attempt to follow the sense closely, we soon realise we are tracing a knotted and elliptical path. Gurney's sentences don't seem so much to reflect on experience as to process it in the moment. His syntax warps and thins out under the stress of experience. Attempting to paraphrase the argument will show the vitality of the mental process. The first three lines up to the semicolon seem just about manageable: 'after battle, you felt peace of heart [giving a jolt to the cliché 'peace of mind'], what with the marching over, the straps of the bag off your back, the warmth and shelter, and the body lying slack on a straw bed'. But the grammar doesn't hold together in any recognisable way: instead, phrases have slumped together, their supporting structure collapsed, much like the soldier's exhausted body.

The semicolon offers a rest, a moment in which it seems the sentence is going to take stock and find a new direction. But instead of moving forwards, it loops back to pick up the list begun at the start of the poem: 'One got peace of heart at last . . . And some sweetness . . . '. In the next line the sentence starts to work towards a resolution: 'And to come to this haven after sorefooted weeks' leads us to anticipate a phrase that is going to round the observation off: something along the lines of 'to come to this haven . . . was a great relief'. This anticipation pulls us through comforts listed in the next two and a half lines – the letters, the warmth, and so on – to the culmination of the sentence: 'To come to this haven after sorefooted weeks', the sentence says, 'nerves soothed were so sore shaken'. The poem's argument, once you iron it out, is simply that 'it was a relief to come to a place of rest after battle'; it is the wrinkles and corrugations which occur as it puts that thought into language that make it feel so exhausting.[21]

Is the Sense Clear?

What does the final phrase of Gurney's poem actually mean? The syntax of 'nerves soothed were so sore shaken' seems shaken up itself. And there are two contrasting ways in which we might unravel it. The most predictable reading is to take the lines as saying: 'to come to this haven soothed the nerves which had been so sorely shaken'; but this involves inserting a 'which' that we would have to understand as having been omitted from Gurney's elliptical syntax. Alternatively, we can discover something more surprising, and more disturbing: 'nerves, which had initially been soothed, were shaken by the shock of the comfort'. The thoughts are contradictory, but the line allows us to hold both in our mind at the same time.

We have put a good deal of emphasis so far on following as precisely as possible the path of a poem's argument. One of the values of reading poetry is that it trains us to follow subtle and complex chains of thought – and perhaps enables us to construct them ourselves in turn. But Gurney's poem shows that there may be times when a sentence seems to take two roads at once. Very often, looking close up at a poem's language, we will find that multiple possibilities of meaning suggest themselves. Individual words can hold many potential significances, as a quick glance at a dictionary will confirm. And sentences can be arranged in ways that suggest branching possibilities. Even the tone in which we are to imagine words being spoken can be uncertain (for more on tone, see page 148). Ordinarily, ambiguity is unwanted. It leads to misunderstandings and is generally a sign of someone insufficiently in control of their language. But a poem attempts something different from an instruction manual, a legal contract, or an invitation to dinner: ambiguity facilitates the nuance, richness, and drama of different perspectives which are central to a poem's grasp on the complexity of experience. And here is another benefit of reading poetry: it trains us to hold multiple ideas in our mind at once.

Nobody has observed the verbal compression characteristic of poetry with more brilliance than William Empson, whose book *Seven Types of Ambiguity* (1930) illustrates how the ways in which 'a word or grammatical structure [can be] effective in several ways at once' operates at 'the very roots of poetry'.[22] Empson shows, for instance, how in the following poem (1880) by Gerard Manley Hopkins, the fact in English we can accentuate different words in a sentence to make it mean different things opens up a variety of possible readings. The poem is about a child's dawning awareness of mortality:

Spring and Fall

To a young child

Márgarét, áre you grieving
Over Goldengrove unleaving?
Leáves like the things of man, you
With your fresh thoughts care for, can you?
Ah! ás the heart grows older
It will come to such sights colder
By and by, nor spare a sigh
Though worlds of wanwood leafmeal lie;
And yet you wíll weep and know why.
Now no matter, child, the name:
Sórrow's spríngs áre the same.
Nor mouth had, no nor mind, expressed
What heart heard of, ghost guessed:
It ís the blight man was born for,
It is Margaret you mourn for.

Empson draws out various possibilities of meaning in a glittering revelation of the economy and intensity of poetic expression. In the line 'And yet you wíll weep and know why', for instance, 'wíll weep' may mean 'you will insist upon weeping, now or later' or 'you shall weep in the future'. Whichever sense one prioritises, 'know' might follow 'will', just as weep does, so that it means 'you insist upon knowing' or 'you shall know'; or we might read it as saying 'you already know why you weep, why you shall weep, or why you insist upon weeping'; or it may be imperative: 'listen and I shall tell you why you weep, or shall weep, or shall insist upon weeping, or insist upon weeping already'. In the lines 'Nor mouth had, no nor mind, expressed / What heart heard of, ghost guessed', the mouth and mind being spoken of may be Margaret's or someone else's (say a sympathetic adult's). 'What heart heard of', as Empson puts it, 'goes both forwards and backwards', so that what the heart has heard may be an unspoken intimation known in the heart but as yet unexpressed by 'mouth' or 'mind' (whether Margaret's or an observer's), or it may be the knowledge expressed in the final two lines: 'Nobody else's mouth had told her, nobody else's mind had hinted to her, about the fact of mortality, which yet her own imagination had already invented, which her own spirit could forsee'; or: 'Her mouth had never mentioned death; she had never stated the idea to herself so as to be conscious of it; but death, since it was a part of her body, since it was natural to her organs, was known at sight as a portent by the obscure depths of her mind.'[23] As we read, we cut a path through this thicket of possibilities. But the language of poetry, because it is often so compressed, often gives us pause to contemplate numerous possibilities of interpretation. Such multiplicity is crucial to the complexity of poetry's grasp on experience and is one reason that poems invite us to take our time, and reward re-readings.

Empson does not say, 'it isn't clear what this phrase means', but rather 'here are several precisely defined and plausible possibilities of meaning'. Richness and vagueness are not the same thing. When faced with lines which seem ambiguous, we should not surrender in the face of apparent obscurity, but patiently set out their range of plausible significances. In this way, we can come to terms with difficulty. We can bring complexity into focus, spot moments where we need to refine our understanding, and even determine where a poem has left unsatisfying loose ends. Consider the ambiguities that riddle the following lyric by William Blake, an effort to explore the possibilities of communication and miscommunication between lovers:

Never pain to tell thy love
Love that never told can be
For the gentle wind does move
Silently invisibly

I told my love I told my love
I told her all my heart
Trembling cold in ghastly fears
Ah she doth depart

Soon as she was gone from me
A traveller came by
Silently invisibly
O was no deny

The first line might mean 'never struggle to say something that can't be articulated, you'll never succeed', or it might mean 'never try to articulate feeling if you find it is bringing you pain'. In the second line the 'Love' that can never be told might stand for 'those aspects of love which are too intense to be articulated', or 'those aspects of love that are best kept to yourself', or 'love in its entirety' (there may even be a flicker of ambiguity at the end of the first line about whether to 'tell thy love' means to 'express emotion' or 'to tell something to one's lover'). Another kind of ambiguity arises in the third and fourth lines, surrounding the relation of 'gentle wind' to the first part of the sentence. The lines seem to offer an explanation of why one should never try to 'tell thy love'. Presumably the wind functions as an image for the way love makes itself felt without conscious effort or articulation – but, given that love's ability to make itself felt prior to explanation is the central thought at this point in the poem, it is fitting that we have to work out this warning against excessive explanation for ourselves.

At the start of the second group of lines, an ambiguity arises about the situation of the poem as a whole. Is the voice that starts up here that of someone else, responding unhappily to what is said in the first sentence? Or is it the same speaker, reflecting on the lessons of personal experience? Either is possible, and the ambiguity allows us to read the poem in two different ways: we can see it as a conversation in which one voice answers the advice of another too late, or as a single speaker offering us wisdom drawn from regretful experience. Another ambiguity depends upon the syntax of these lines: who is it that is left 'Trembling cold in ghastly fears'? The speaker as a result of what he has to tell his lover? Or the lover as a result of what she hears? The line hangs between both possibilities.

The third group of lines is arguably the most mysterious in the whole poem. They shift from a verbal to a more situational ambiguity. Who is the 'traveller' and where is he heading? Is it the wind, 'Silently invisibly' haunting the poet with a reminder of what he has lost? Is it someone else, on their way to the poet's lover with a better understanding of the way love works? The ambiguity here is not so much a function of the fullness of the poem's phrasing as of the sparseness of its detail. What a poem leaves out is often just as significant as what it includes. We might even feel that Blake's writing becomes too elusive to offer any coherent sense. But how we interpret the lines colours how we interpret the whole mood of the poem: as these possibilities jostle in our mind, the outlook see-saws between the hopeful and the tragic.

Blake's poem is especially riddling. It seems so irresolvable in part because Blake left it unpunctuated in a notebook (Blake probably wrote the poem in the early 1800s, but it was unpublished until 1863), lending the phrasing and sentences an unresolved quality and failing to supply some of the contexts (a title, relationship with other poems, prefatory explanation) that we often rely on for eradicating ambiguities (in ordinary speech, it is often clear from the nature of the speaker, the intonation, the person they are addressing, and the situation in which they are speaking which of a range of possible meanings is intended, and poems can do more than Blake's does to indicate these circumstances). We might judge the result to be intolerably ambiguous, to the extent that it is impossible to pick out a continuous thread of thought; or we might think that Blake's ambiguities – whether by accident or design – are appropriate, given the poetry's preoccupation with the complexities of communication. As Empson warns: ambiguity 'is not satisfying in itself, nor is it, considered as a device on its own, a thing to be attempted; it must in each case arise from and be justified by the peculiar requirements of the situation'.[24] Poets don't produce ambiguity for its own sake. It is a product of their sense of the complexity of a given situation. Likewise, our awareness of the ambiguities in Blake is a result of our search for precise meaning. Reading a poem involves being alert to ambiguities but is not a matter of hunting them out obsessively or of wrenching a meaning from the words that cannot be sustained. A student once argued that when Keats imagines in 'To Autumn' (1820) that the bees are tired of the summer because it has 'o'erbrimmed' the 'clammy cells' of their hive with honey, the adjective 'clammy' directs us to think of shellfish. There is no way of disproving this possibility, but it is hard to see how the point could be plausibly or profitably made; the same student, hearing her friend observe that her hands were 'clammy', wouldn't assume that they had become like bivalve marine molluscs, and in reading a poem there is no reason to abandon the judgement one wields to make sense of all statements in their particular contexts.

Equally, there are times when unambiguous precision is just as much a virtue as abundant suggestiveness. It is possible to admire the flowering complexities of Blake's lyric alongside the exactness of writing such as the following question and answer by James Henry (1866), which negotiates the complicated situation of God's justice with a studious avoidance of ambiguity:

> Who's the great sinner? He, who, being Omniscient,
> Forsees all sins, and, being Omnipotent,
> Can, if he please, prevent them and does not –

Nay, not alone does not, but punishes;
And – one tic farther still, one farther tic
Incredible – when punishment's no use.

The writing leaves no room for doubt. We might even feel in that repeated 'farther' (thanks to its proximity to 'father') something like an inverse ambiguity, or one being resisted: what Henry describes is the most 'unfatherly' behaviour imaginable. It is not that the poem is without drama but that the drama comes from the intensity with which the poem braces itself against the implied opposed perspective – belief. The meticulous accumulation and extension of the second sentence, neglecting the opportunity to reach an end until every detail of the case has been assembled, achieves an unambiguous force.

How Is the Sense Organised into Lines?

What is it about that last clause of Henry's poem that means that it doesn't just state its exasperation, but dramatises the process of an individual reaching the limits of his patience? The answer has to do with the difference that exists between the words 'one farther tic incredible –' as they appear in their prose order and as they are arranged on the page:

one farther tic
Incredible –

It is a difference that literally pushes understanding over a limit and edges emphasis onto 'Incredible'. And it is a difference that is crucial to the distinction between verse and prose.

Almost every point we have considered so far could apply to prose as well as verse. But it is trickier than we might first think to distinguish between the two. What is *verse*? T. S. Eliot gave a helpful definition when he said that 'verse, whatever else it may or may not be, is itself a system of *punctuation*'.[25] That is to say, verse is a means of organising words on a page – a resource for forming and controlling meaning that operates in combination with the usual resources of grammar. Verse shapes our experience of the sense of a poem. Any successful poem will yield answers to the questions of how it controls, realises, or expands the expressive possibilities of verse. The devices that first spring to mind as being fundamental to such 'punctuation' are probably rhyme and rhythm. But any attempt to distinguish between verse and prose along those lines soon collapses: not all poems rhyme (and sometimes prose rhymes), and prose has rhythms, too. (Though it is true that rhyme and rhythm tend to function more systematically in verse than they do in prose.) In the end, it is the line that is essential: in prose the lines run on to the end of the page, in verse the ending of the line is under the poet's jurisdiction.

This might seem a tiny and even a disappointing distinction, but then reading poetry involves noticing the significance invested in minutiae. This small distinction makes poems, and poems make something out of it. Consider what a difference exists between these two versions of the opening of John Milton's epic *Paradise Lost* (1667), printed first as verse, and then as prose:

> Of man's first disobedience and the fruit
> Of that forbidden tree, whose mortal taste
> Brought death unto the world, and all our woe,
> With loss of Eden, till one greater Man
> Restore us, and regain the blissful seat,
> Sing Heav'nly muse . . .

> Of man's first disobedience and the fruit of that forbidden tree, whose mortal taste brought death unto the world, and all our woe, with loss of Eden, till one greater Man restore us, and regain the blissful seat, sing Heav'nly muse . . .

Discarding the lineation (and the capitalisation that reinforces it) is like unwinding a piece of string from a taut loom: the sentence pools shapelessly. Lineation directs emphasis: gone from the versified version is the prominence afforded to the word 'fruit' at the end of the poem's opening line, for instance – a prominence which underscores Milton's pun on the word as both literal 'fruit' (he is about to tell the story of Adam and Eve) and 'consequence' (you might even be tempted to say that word hangs at the end of the line just like the apple Eve eventually plucks). Lineation also provides structure: this is a very long sentence (it goes on even after the point at which I've broken it off), and its meaning doesn't become clear until the verb 'Sing' falls into place at the start of the sixth line (the Victorian poet Matthew Arnold said that Milton wouldn't let a sentence 'escape him until he had crowded into it all he can').[26] The ambitious span of the sentence matches the ambitious span of the poem it begins, but such scope is only possible because of the way the lineation paces our reading and builds anticipation.

The 'punctuation' done by a poem's lines shapes energy, clarity, and emphasis. And the support and direction lineation affords can often be demonstrated simply by taking it away. Another example will prove the point in reverse. Here are two sentences from Elizabeth Barrett Browning's *Aurora Leigh* (1857), arguing that poets should take the contemporary world as their subject:

> Nay, if there's room for poets in this world a little overgrown (I think there is), their sole work is to represent the age, their age, not Charlemagne's, – this live, throbbing age, that brawls, cheats, maddens, calculates, aspires, and spends more passion, more heroic heat, betwixt the mirrors of its drawing-rooms, than Roland with his knights at Roncevalles. To flinch from modern varnish, coat or flounce, cry out for togas and the picturesque, is fatal – foolish too. King Arthur's self was commonplace to Lady Guenever; and Camelot to minstrels seemed as flat as Fleet Street to our poets.

This is very bad prose. Try to read it aloud, and you'll see what I mean: there's little sense of the thought being measured out with the breath, of the scope for pause and emphasis, of the sentences building up ideas with a shape of their own, of the ebb and flow of passion and argument. All that work is done, in Barrett Browning's poem, by the verse:

> Nay, if there's room for poets in this world
> A little overgrown (I think there is),
> Their sole work is to represent the age,
> Their age, not Charlemagne's,[8] – this live, throbbing age,
> That brawls, cheats, maddens, calculates, aspires,
> And spends more passion, more heroic heat,
> Betwixt the mirrors of its drawing-rooms,
> Than Roland[9] with his knights at Roncevalles.
> To flinch from modern varnish, coat or flounce,
> Cry out for togas and the picturesque,
> Is fatal – foolish too. King Arthur's self
> Was commonplace to Lady Guenever;
> And Camelot to minstrels seemed as flat
> As Fleet Street to our poets.

This is much easier to give voice to. The effect is like an untuned radio being brought to the right frequency. And the clarity is a result of the structure, support, and pacing afforded by the division into lines. Verse provides a framework for longer sentences that would otherwise be flaccid. Just as one example, consider how the lineation supports and counterpoints Barrett Browning's description of the 'sole work' of the poet. First, we get a line that distils the argument into a neat slogan:

[8] eighth-century European ruler [9] early medieval military leader who died in battle at Roncevalles

> Their sole work is to represent the age,

Then, in the next line, a refinement of that position:

> Their age, not Charlemagne's, – this live, throbbing age,

This line also begins to define what the qualities of 'this age' are; but the qualities include a vibrancy and vitality which overspill its limits:

> this live, throbbing age,
> That brawls, cheats, maddens, calculates, aspires,
> And spends more passion . . .

And the argument goes on.

Just because verse is arranged into lines doesn't (or doesn't usually) mean that it forgoes other forms of punctuation. The commas, dashes, and parentheses in the lines above all contribute to the dynamics of the argument (see page 51). And there is a neat wit at work in the way the parenthesis at the end of the second line quoted just manages to find space to squeeze itself into the line: 'if there's room for poets in this world / A little overgrown (I think there is)'. But it is always worth asking how the 'punctuation' created by arranging poems into lines intersects with marks of punctuation familiar from prose. Sometimes the two simply fall in with one another, as in Chaucer's description of the Cook in the *General Prologue* to the *Canterbury Tales* (c. 1400):

> He coude rost, and seeth,[10] and broil, and frye,
> Maken mortreaux,[11] and well bake a pie.
> But greet harm was it, as it thoughte me,
> That on his shin a mormal[12] hadde he.
> For a blankmanger,[13] that made he with the best.

When lines correspond with grammatically complete units like this (usually it involves line endings coinciding with a mark of punctuation, as they do above) they can be described as *endstopped*. Chaucer's vignettes of his various pilgrims in the *General Prologue* often use successively endstopped lines for a rapid-fire listing of details. He enjoys the possibilities they afford for a jumbling of incongruous attributes: the cook's blancmange sounds distinctly less appetising following on from the description of the open sore on his shin, but the diverse characteristics are all thrown in as part of the mix.

[10] boil [11] stew [12] open sore [13] blancmange

Endstopping emphasises the integrity of the individual line. Chaucer delights in its power to create discord as divergent lines pile one on top of another, but in the hands of another poet, endstopping might support an effort to impose order, as in these thoughts on a rejected suitor by Elizabeth I (1582):

> I grieve and dare not show my discontent,
> I love and yet am forced to seem to hate,
> I do, yet dare not say I ever meant,
> I am stark mute but inwardly do prate.
> I am and am not, I freeze and yet am burned,
> Since from myself another self I turned.

The Queen's emotions may be muddled, but the verse gets feeling into line. Each line holds contradictory emotions alongside one another – grief and composure, love and hate, silence and inward torment – before the passage reaches a climax as *two* pairs of conflicting impulses are crowded together in its penultimate line: being and not being, freezing and burning. The verse, then, clarifies feeling: whether this constitutes a triumph over the Queen's turmoils or brings them into more intense focus is left open to question.

It is a question which we can feel the poet revolving within each individual line. Speak the lines aloud and we find ourselves pausing at the end of each one – a tendency encouraged by the punctuation. But we will also find ourselves pausing for a breath – perhaps a slightly lighter one – in the middle of each line, in response to its movement back and forth between conflicting feelings: 'I love [*pause*] and yet am forced to seem to hate', 'I do, [*pause*] yet dare not say I ever meant', and so on. These pauses are known as *caesuras* and are another way in which division into lines gives shape and definition to a voice. As these examples show, caesuras need not fall directly in the middle of a line and need not be marked by punctuation (though punctuation might encourage a heavier pause). Elizabeth sets up a pattern by repeatedly positioning a caesura early, so that each line see-saws, only just getting started before pausing and pursuing a contrary path as the Queen's consciousness swings between extremes: 'I feel this – but I'm acting in a contrary way'. The first three lines we looked at by Barrett Browning show a slightly more even dispersal of pauses:

> Nay, if there's room for poets [*pause*] in this world
> A little overgrown [*pause*] (I think there is),
> Their sole work is [*pause*] to represent the age . . .

The impact here is less dramatic – there's no particular expressive point we would want to attribute to the pauses, beyond observing how they divide up the sense of the sentence – but they are no less important to the way that verse shapes a voice.

Does the Sense Flow over the Line Endings?

Queen Elizabeth's poem allows sense to unfold in step-by-step blocks. If all poems moved in so orderly a fashion, verse would be a rigid and repetitive medium. In most poetry, there is a more fluid interaction between line and syntax; meaning flows across line endings, a process known as *enjambment*. That is what occurs, for instance, as Barrett Browning observes that this is a 'world / A little overgrown'; it is what animates the voice's exasperation in the example from James Henry; and it is what creates an ambiguity about whether the 'fruit' Milton has in mind is a literal one or a moral consequence at the end of the first line of *Paradise Lost*.

The word *verse* derives from the Latin word to describe the turning of a plough as it reaches the end of a field and goes back on itself, and the notion of the lines of a poem as so many furrows through which the words travel before wheeling back remains a helpful image. Sense seldom develops in conveniently stackable line-by-line units. As syntax and lineation start to operate in tension, reading becomes a more complex matter, more demanding of concentration. Wordsworth's long autobiographical poem *The Prelude* (1805) contains some lines which describe Wordsworth's response to a formative episode from his childhood. Finding a boat on a lakeside, Wordsworth rowed out into the middle of the lake. As he got further from the shore, it seemed, thanks to a trick of perspective, that a mountain 'black and huge' was rising up behind the bank of the lake that he was facing, and looming larger the further out he rowed, as though it were a 'living thing' (think of how moving up close to a building may obscure a taller one behind it). Terrified, Wordsworth rowed back to the shore – which meant being brave enough to move *towards* the entity apparently looming over the hill. Reflecting on this disturbing experience from the perspective of adulthood, Wordsworth needs a suppler medium than regularly endstopped verse supplies – one responsive to the fluid development of his thoughts and feelings:

> after I had seen
> That spectacle, for many days, my brain
> Worked with a dim and undetermined sense

Of unknown modes of being; o'er my thoughts
There hung a darkness, call it solitude
Or blank desertion. No familiar shapes
Remained, no pleasant images of trees,
Of sea or sky, no colours of green fields;
But huge and mighty forms, that do not live
Like living men, moved slowly through the mind
By day, and were a trouble to my dreams.

The flow of Wordsworth's thought plays off against the regular structure of the lines. The enjambments encourage us to pursue the momentum of the sentence over the end of each line, pausing only as the punctuation directs. So, we might hear the lines above as though they had been printed like this:

after I had seen That spectacle,
for many days,
my brain Worked with a dim and undetermined sense Of unknown
  modes of being

The phrases elongate as they contemplate the operations of Wordsworth's mind. And yet, because of the poem's arrangement into lines, the 'familiar shapes' of the individual lines remain as an intuited presence. Even in the most fluently enjambed of poems, the division marked by the ending of the line encourages a slight pause – if only as a result of the physical process of looping one's eye from the end of one line to the start of another. As Wordsworth himself put it: poetry's lines make it 'physically impossible to pronounce the last words or syllables of the lines with the same indifference, as the others, i.e. not to give them an intonation of one kind or another, or to follow them with a pause.'[27] So what one hears as one reads the lines aloud, or imagines them read aloud, is:

after I had seen [*slight pause*] That spectacle, [*longer pause for punctuation*]
for many days, [*longer pause for punctuation*]
my brain [*slight pause*] Worked with a dim and undetermined sense [*slight pause*]
  Of unknown modes of being

The two systems of organisation – punctuation and lineation – work in tandem and in tension.

Enjambment often causes a sentence to move through time in a manner related to its meaning. The slight pauses that Wordsworth's line endings open up within his enjambed phrases dramatise the mental activity they describe – the mind's response to an 'undetermined sense / Of unknown modes of being'. The effort of mental endeavour is recreated in the slight hesitation that paces 'my brain / Worked', for instance; while the enjambment of 'No familiar shapes / Remained' grasps out for the familiar shape of a line whose distinctive 'shape' is now diminished. Such effects of enjambment are more frequent in poems which emulate a speaking voice – indeed, enjambment is one of the resources through which the impression of natural speech is created. Enjambment is rarer in song (though listen to Neil Young's 'Alabama' (1972) and 'Powderfinger' (1979) for instances of how it can be used surprisingly and expressively).

Another effect of the pauses is to introduce ghosts of alternative meanings. A potent example occurs when Wordsworth describes the natural 'forms, that do not live / Like living men'. The pause opens up different possibilities of interpretation: is it that these 'forms' do not live at all? Or is it that they do live, but in a different way to 'living men'? The arrangement of sentences across line endings, causes us to experience the words of a poem differently. To say, 'my heart was full / of clear dark water', as Judith Wright does in response to a beautiful scene in her poem 'Egrets' (1962)[28] is not the same as saying simply, 'my heart was full of clear dark water': the idea that the heart is full of emotion, as well as of the scene, is introduced. Elinor Wylie in 'Cold Blooded Creatures' (1923)[29] wonders how man imagines:

> That he alone is sentient
>
> Of the intolerable load
> Which on all living creatures lies

Here the enjambment, this time across the gap between groups of lines, diffracts the syntax into two possible meanings: first, the implication is held out that man assumes 'he alone is sentient'; this resolves into an accusation that is at once more specific and in its way implies a greater solipsism – that man imagines that he alone is conscious of suffering. Back among Wordsworth's contemporaries, Thomas Lovell Beddoes uses enjambment to spring a sinister and grotesque surprise in this tiny excerpt from a speech in his play *Death's Jest-Book* (1829):

> I could not wish him in my rage to die
> Sooner . . .

The first line feints as though to say something generous: 'However furious I am, I couldn't wish death upon him.' But lurking round the corner of the line is the word 'Sooner', which creates a last-minute twist of the knife.

Endstopping can help clarify feeling and vision; careful enjambment can have the opposite, disorientating effect. The following description of a bird-filled hedgerow by another of Wordsworth's contemporaries, John Clare (1832), shows how run-on lines can play tricks of perception:

Tweet pipes the robin as the cat creeps bye
Her nestling young that in the elderns[14] lie
& then the bluecap tootles in its glee
Picking the flies from blossomed apple tree
& pink the chaffinch cries its well known strain
Urging its mate to utter pink again
While in a quiet mood hedgsparrows trie
An inward stir of shadowed melody
While on the rotten tree the firetail mourns
As the old hedger to his toil returns
& chops . . .

The movement of this is somewhere between Wordsworth's fluency and the steady unfolding of line upon line we saw in Chaucer and Queen Elizabeth. Each line is almost – but never quite – a self-contained unit: the writing apprehends each image momentarily in isolation before gathering it into a larger picture. The opening line could quite happily stand alone: 'The robin tweets as the cat creeps by'; but the cat doesn't just 'creep by', but creeps by 'Her nestling young'. Or, in a later line, the firetail 'mourns' on a rotten tree; but what the poem really wants to draw our attention to is that the bird sings at just the same moment as the old hedger (someone who mends hedges) returns to his work. Clare is fascinated with the way individual components of a landscape knit together, just as his enjambments sew individual lines together into a completed poem. The enjambments conduct a continual play of suspense and revelation – the scene is introduced a segment at a time, sometimes with abrupt transitions, sometimes with one scene melting into another. Each line ending involves a tiny guessing game over whether there will be more to come.

How Do the Lines Move?

Clare's lineation harnesses the interconnected energies of an ecosystem. It arranges life's endless sequence of one thing after another into a pattern which orders without stifling it. In the prelude to *Faust, Part One* (1808) by the German poet Goethe, the character of the Poet describes a similar process as the basis of all poetic art:

While Nature, blandly turning, feeds
Thread on the spindle without end;
When a mass of messy voices

[14] elder bushes

Sings out harsh, annoying sounds;
Who'll measure out life's ever-flowing line
So that it lives in rhythm? Who'll call
Each separate thing to join
The glorious harmony of all?

It is hard to imagine a better account of the way the poetic imagination discovers patterns in the disordered flow of experience, and of the importance of verse to that process. Lineation orchestrates the chaos of life. It 'measure[s] out' the 'ever-flowing line' of thought, feeling, and perception, into an achieved whole which 'lives in rhythm'. As another Romantic poet, Percy Bysshe Shelley, wrote: poetry 'makes us the inhabitants of a world to which the familiar world is a chaos'.[30] In Clare's verse the rhythms that re-organise the world are steady: the lines are all of equal length, and as we read, we slow in anticipation of the line ending at regular intervals, before the enjambment causes us to pick up the pace again (how to measure the length of lines, beyond just using our eyes, is something we'll come on to). The rhythmical impact of lineation becomes more obvious in poems which shift between lines of different lengths. John Betjeman's 'I. M. Walter Ramsden' (1954)[31] begins with two lines that move very differently to the poems by Clare and Wordsworth:

Dr Ramsden cannot read *The Times* obituary to-day
He's dead.

The first line plods on its way, recording what seems an unremarkable observation; the second line gives us a shock. There is something jaunty about the suddenness of the transition from one very long line to a very short one. Having waited so long for a pause in the first instance, our ear is surprised when another arrives so soon: 'He's dead'. The sense of comic imbalance is obviously a risk in a poem about someone's death, but the abruptness of the second line, after the wandering ordinariness of the first, is what makes it so potent: death can intrude abruptly.

Sometimes poems will allow us to become used to lines of a certain length before switching. Here is another set of opening lines (c. 1774), this time by the eighteenth-century poet William Cowper. Cowper believed that he was damned to suffer in hell, and the rhythm established by the movement of these lines dramatises his foreboding:

Hatred and vengeance, my eternal portion,
Scarce can endure delay of execution,
Wait, with impatient readiness, to seize my
Soul in a moment.

'Hatred and vengeance' are made to wait, with a sense of impending doom, as the syntax unwinds through the first three lines, before the shorter final line allows us finally to digest the meaning of the sentence – much as Cowper fears his soul is going to be gobbled up. The enjambment into the final line leaves us in suspense about what is going to be 'seized', a suspense that mimics the divine 'vengeance' Cowper feels is hanging over his head (the feeling of anticipation is accentuated by the way Cowper slows down his penultimate line by inserting an extra caesura: 'Wait, [breath] with impatient readiness, [breath] to seize my . . . ').

In both examples, the shape and movement of the poem are not just decorative but expressive. The lines pace our apprehension of the poem's argument. Anne Carson discovers a similar interdependence of rhythm and vision in her poem 'Lines' (2005). The lines in question are both those of the poem and those that it talks about: the telephone lines connecting the poet with her seemingly dying mother, the lines of snow that fall as the conversation goes on, the lines into which the speaker arranges paper clips as she talks:

> Out
> the window snow is falling straight down in lines. To my mother,
> love
> of my life, I describe what I had for brunch. The lines are falling
> faster
> now. Fate has put little weights on the ends (to speed us up) I
> want
> to tell her – sign of God's pity. She *won't keep me*
> she says, she
> *won't run up my bill.* Miracles slip past us. The
> paperclips
> are immortally aligned.

The recurrent expansion and contraction of its lineation is the most immediately obvious thing about the poem. In moving between lines which reach longingly across the page and lines of a single word, Carson spins a web which captures the coexistence of the most absent-minded of activities (the trivialities that occupy the conversation and her attention) and the most emotionally weighty of situations (the approach of death). Carson's sentence negotiates that structure sensitively. Enjambments catch moments where the voice threatens to break – as when the poet reports her mother's poignantly ambiguous promise not to 'keep her' – or suggest, as the sentences fall vertically through them, an ominously increasing speed: 'falling / faster / now.' Across the passage, the longer lines get shorter, suggesting time is running out – on the call, and on life. We can bring trivial things, like paperclips, into 'immortal' alignment, but can't, the poem's arrangement suggests, escape the apparent acceleration of time. Lineation shapes vision and tracks feeling.

Poems are rhythmical structures. Movement is at the core of their significance; it gives them shape and dimension. To ignore it would be like trying to appreciate a sculpture from a two-dimensional drawing or to conceive of the words of a song without their melody. Many things have a rhythm: a beating heart, the lumbering of a charging rhino, the tumbling of a gymnast across the floor. Rhythm embodies character. It is the sound of life. It is innately captivating, as you will know if you have ever been lulled by the shunting of a train, or stood mesmerised by the repeated rolling and breaking of waves on the shore, or watched a body moving to music, as Sarojini Naidu does in 'Indian Dancers' (1905):

Their glittering garments of purple are burning like tremulous dawns in the quivering air,
And exquisite, subtle and slow are the tinkle and tread of their rhythmical, slumber-soft feet.

Now silent, now singing and swaying and swinging, like blossoms that bend to the breezes or showers,
Now wantonly winding, they flash, now they falter, and, lingering, languish in radiant choir;
Their jewel-girt arms and warm, wavering, lily-long fingers enchant through melodious hours,
Eyes ravished with rapture, celestially panting, what passionate bosoms aflaming with fire!

Naidu is struck by the cascading eloquence of the dancers she watches, and finds in their performance a model for how she wants her own verse to feel; she translates the movement of the dancers into the rhythm of her voice. She does so, most immediately, through her lineation: the lines are so extended that they seem to move without joins, the words 'singing and swaying and swinging' in uninterrupted flow. Because it takes so long to get from the start of one line to the end, the movement of the poem is 'subtle and slow', and yet the pent-up energy and expectation of a pause for breath means that the lines themselves become the expression of 'passionate bosoms aflaming with fire!'

What Are the Rhythms within the Lines?

The rhythm of the human voice – and consequently of a poem – is a matter not just of pacing but of stress. It depends on how quickly or slowly we speak a run of words, but also on the fact that we accentuate the syllables of certain words more than others. The words written on a page might seem to have little control over how quickly we speak them, but many of the technical aspects we have considered so far have an influence: shorter lines zip past more quickly than longer ones; shorter, more heavily punctuated sentences, impede momentum; longer ones can eventually lose it. A higher proportion of more lightly stressed syllables causes a line to come more trippingly on the tongue, while a dense clustering of heavy stresses slows the pace. But what do we mean by 'stress'? And how do we measure the length of a line? It is a thorny issue. We'll try, in the next few sections, to come to terms with these questions as methodically and as lucidly as possible.

Hearing the rhythms of a poem means not only listening to it but *listening in* to it. The sound that a clock makes is simply a succession of *tick – tick – tick* noises, but as we process those sounds in our brain, we hear an alternating sequence: *tick – tock – tick – tock*. And we should be primed to discover a similar organisation of sounds in a poem: we should read with an ear ready to attune itself to a regular pattern. By listening carefully to Naidu's poem, we can hear that the dancing, musical effect is down not only to the way the lineation paces the movement from one line to the next, but to the way the words within the lines are arranged along a regular pattern of emphasis. Read the lines slowly, trust the natural emphases of your voice, and you will hear that they have a pulse. There is a regular intensification and depression of emphasis through each line:

Their **glit**tering **garm**ents of **purp**le are **burn**ing like **trem**ulous **dawns** in the **quiv**ering **air**,
And **ex**quisite, **subt**le and **slow** are the **tink**le and **tread** of their **rhyth**mical, **slumb**er-soft **feet**.

Now **sil**ent, now **sing**ing and **sway**ing and **swing**ing, like **bloss**oms that **bend** to the **breez**es or **show**ers,
Now **want**only **wind**ing, they **flash**, now they **fal**ter, and, **ling**ering, **lang**uish in **rad**iant **choir**;
Their **jew**el-girt **arms** and warm, **wave**ring, **li**ly-long **fing**ers en**chant** through me**lod**ious **hours**,
Eyes **ra**vished with **rap**ture, ce**lest**ially **pant**ing, what **pass**ionate **bos**oms a**flam**ing with **fire**!

The pulse brings the voice to life, it gives a regular impetus to the poetry's movement through time. The writing's ability to match the 'the tinkle and tread' of the dancers' movements depends upon the way the words and phrases wreathe themselves around this pattern. Each line rises to regularly spaced points of emphasis and intersperses its eight more heavily emphasised syllables with a regular arrangement of lighter ones: der-der-DUM, der-der-DUM. We can also hear a slight quickening or slowing of the rhythm dependent upon whether the more lightly stressed syllables run within or across the gaps between words, and upon how the sentences are punctuated. While the pattern of stresses throughout 'Now **sil**ent, now **sing**ing and **sway**ing and **swing**ing' and 'And **ex**quisite, **subt**le and **slow** are the **tink**le' are the same, the latter is 'subtler' and 'slower' thanks to the way the punctuation interrupts the momentum of the voice immediately before the second stress and to the obligation to bring the stress in 'exquisite' forward in order to keep the beat (we will return to such effects below); the phrase 'Their **jew**el-girt **arms** and warm, **wave**ring, **li**ly-long **fing**ers' captures the length and fluency and 'wavering' movement of the dancers' limbs and fingers thanks to the way the phrasing runs over the caesura which in most lines divides the rhythms into balanced four-beat units, and thanks to the comma before 'wavering', which stalls the crescendo of the 'der-der-DUM' pattern. Naidu's response to the music involves a complex rhythmic artistry of her own.

Don't worry if, on a first reading, the details of the previous paragraph seem puzzling. The point to take on board, for now, is that poetry creates rhythm not just through its division into lines, but by arranging the words within those lines in sequences of heightened and decreased emphasis. We can measure the length of a line by counting out the number of emphasised or accentuated syllables – the number of beats – it contains. In a good deal of poetry, as in the example from Naidu, that pattern will consist of beats arranged in sequences of four (or factors or multiples of four). As we read, we can time out these beats at regular intervals: 'Now **sil**ent, now **sing**ing and **sway**ing and **swing** || ing, like **bloss**oms that **bend** to the **breez**es or **showers**' (the caesura splits the eight beats of the line into two four-beat units). There is also a vast body of poetry which moves to a less emphatic five-beat pattern. In almost all metrical poetry (i.e. poetry with a regular pulse) we can count out sequences of four or five peaks of emphasis running along the line before renewing themselves. Just by tapping out those sequences we can start to sense the character they bring to expression:

One – Two – Three – Four
One – Two – Three – Four

Or:

One – Two – Three – Four – Five
One – Two – Three – Four – Five

The first is emphatic, balanced, readily chanted; the second has a quieter pulse, pliable to variation, more easily attuned to the patterns of speech. It is possible to vary the intensity with which each beat is struck, and it is possible to vary the number of syllables between the peaks of emphasis, as we shall see; but the beats will still fall at regular intervals, underpinning the unique rhythmical identity of each line.

How can we hear this rise and fall of emphasis in an actual line of verse? How do we know when a syllable is stressed? When we speak, we naturally apply more pressure to some syllables than to others. Speak the following sentence aloud and you will notice that the pressure naturally rises and falls as indicated:

This **eve**ning we will **walk** by the **ri**ver, **eat din**ner, and then **go** to the **gall**ery.

Because these patterns of emphasis come naturally to native speakers of a language, they can sometimes be so familiar that we don't notice them. But if we try to pronounce the sentence stressing different syllables, as in the version below, we will find that it sounds awkward and unnatural:

This eve**ning** we **will** walk **by the** ri**ver**, eat din**ner**, **and** then go **to** the gall**er**y.

Alternatively, try to pronounce the sentence without any variation in emphasis at all, and we find that we start speaking slowly and mechanically, like a Dalek. Variation is the sign of an expressive speaking voice.

It takes time and practice to tune our ear to these patterns of emphasis; it is tricky to become self-conscious about things that we do naturally. Usefully, for all that these patterns emerge as a matter of instinct, there are principles determining which syllables take stress and which ones don't. Words with more than one syllable are easiest: each polysyllabic word in English has a primary stressed syllable, and wrenching emphasis away from it sounds odd. So, in the sentence above, for instance, we say, '**ri**ver' and not 'riv**er**', '**gall**ery' and not 'gall**er**y' or 'galler**y**'. Sometimes, shifting the stress from one syllable to the other even changes the significance of a word: I can be 'con**tent**' with the '**con**tent' of an essay; '**in**cense' is burnt in churches and students' rooms, but if I 'in**cense**' you, I make you angry; we 're**ject**' a job application, but when our application is rejected it joins the '**re**ject' pile, and so on. Sometimes polysyllabic words have one or more secondary stresses, too, which take a slightly lighter emphasis than the main syllable: '**un**be***liev***a**ble**', 'phe***nom***e**non**', '**app**a***ri***tion'. Finally, there are words such as 'evening' which we can pronounce with a varying number of syllables: we say, 'eve-ning' in the common flow of conversation, but sometimes 'ev-en-ing' when speaking more formally. The pronunciation of such words in verse often depends upon the patterns we need them to uphold: we read 'To **me** the **mean**est **flower** that **blows**' (Wordsworth, 'Ode' (1804)), but 'With **flow**ers, **gar**lands, **and** sweet-**smell**ing **herbs**' (Milton, *Paradise Lost* (1667)).

Monosyllables (words made up of one syllable) are shiftier. Speak any monosyllable aloud by itself, and it is almost impossible to tell how much stress we are affording it, since stress is relative, and we are lost without adjacent syllables for comparison ('almost impossible' because the four-letter word you roar when you stub your toe against the bedpost evidently takes emphasis, while the same word sighed in resignation as your team concedes in the last minute for the third week in a row gains world-weary expressiveness from your refusal to grant it too much force). But as soon as we put monosyllabic words into a sentence, some come under greater pressure than others. As a rule, stresses fall on those words which carry important information. Nouns, verbs, adjectives, and adverbs usually take more stress than articles, conjunctions, and prepositions: so, in the above sentence, the monosyllabic verbs 'go' and 'eat' take emphasis, as does the noun 'walk'.

Stress is a matter of emphasis, and, consequently, a third governing factor in accounting for whether a syllable is stressed is whether the context demands that we give it special prominence. Usually this means giving force to a word which would not normally take a heavy stress ('we're having fish and chips *and* a curry?' a friend once asked me with a mixture of incredulity and greedy anticipation, misinterpreting a message about a change of dinner plans). In the sentence above – This **eve**ning we will **walk** by the **ri**ver, **eat din**ner, and then **go** to the **gall**ery – we would put heavier stress on 'then' if we were speaking the words in response to someone who had proposed reversing the order and visiting the gallery before eating.

All speech, therefore, has rhythm, a rise and fall of emphasis. Because speech is generally unpremeditated, its rhythms fall naturally. The rhythms of written language, however, are always to some degree consciously arranged by the author. In prose, those rhythms are free to develop irregularly, to no fixed pattern. In the majority of verse in English, the natural rhythms of speech are arranged into sequences. They are given a regular pulse; they are brought to life. The system of arranging these patterns of emphasis is known as *metre*. 'Metre', as Timothy Steele says in one of the most helpful surveys of the subject, is '*organized* rhythm'.[32]

'So what?' we might think. Let's pause over a short example to think about what metre – the organisation of stress into patterns of rising and falling emphasis – actually does. Below is an impish little poem by

Matthew Prior (1718), arranged according to the four beats to the line pattern we mentioned above:

A True Maid

'No, **no**; for **my** vir**gin**ity,'
'When **I** lose **that**,' says **Rose**, 'I'll **die**:'
'Be**hind** the **elms**, last **night**,' cried **Dick**,
'Rose, **were** you **not** extr**eme**ly **sick**?'

The stressed and unstressed syllables fall into a regularly alternating sequence. What does this regularity bring? First, it tells us that we are reading a poem. Metre is a way of priming us to respond to the writing in a certain way: the words are not presenting themselves as a historical record but as an imagined conversation; they have been elevated out of the randomness of everyday speech into artistic order. That order purges the extraneous detail which might characterise prose: the above exchange is so funny because it is so snappy – we are presented with two voices cutting against one another, and no other supporting information; the metrical framework makes the voices self-sufficient; it shows, rather than tells us, that Dick's witty retort was promptly delivered and perfectly matched. We are left to imagine, too, the various actions or utterances prior to the beginning of the poem which Rose's 'No's might answer to. In disciplining the language into a regular pattern, the metre also intensifies its suggestiveness. Empson writes well about this: 'a metrical scheme imposes a sort of intensity of interpretation upon the grammar', he says; 'the demands of metre allow the poet to say something which is not normal colloquial English, so that the reader thinks of the various colloquial forms which are near to it, and puts them together; weighting their probabilities in proportion to their nearness'.[33] Nobody would naturally say, 'No, no; for my virginity, when I lose that, I'll die'. Various more idiomatic expressions play around the lines: 'you must pay due consideration to my virginity'; 'I'm resisting you for the sake of my virginity', 'we can't do this because of the importance of my virginity' (and so the compression enabled by writing in metre is often a source of ambiguity). Metre also offers a guide to how we should hear particular lines. Because the presence of metre is something we discover as we *listen in* to a poem, it can cause us to grant words a different emphasis than we would in ordinary speech. And immediately a difficulty arises, since describing the rhythm of a line involves a judgement about how far the patterns of emphasis might be wrenched beyond ordinary pronunciation. In the prose order of the final line, for instance, we might be inclined to stress 'Rose' over 'were' – and the pause occasioned by the comma further encourages us to do so; but the pressure exerted by the metre tells us to place emphasis on 'were' (which points a question to which Dick already knows the answer), accentuating the coy irony of Dick's reply. Neither reading is wrong: metre invites us to hear regularity but doesn't impose it upon us; and as we shall see, the laws of metre enable a degree of expressive variation. Such flexibility is a source of metre's difficulty, but also of its fascination.

How Can We Describe the Rhythms?

Before we get on to variations, let's establish the standard patterns. There are several metrical schemes which verse can assume. And there is a technical terminology associated with metre which describes these patterns and helps us to hear them. The terminology supplies a way of describing both the length of a particular line and the pattern of stresses within it. It describes the number of beats a line contains and the way in which the syllables are arranged around those beats. The process of describing patterns of metrical stress in a poem is known as *scansion*. In *scanning* a line of verse, we are describing its shape and not its sense. We are asking how it might be divided up into units of rhythm, not meaning (though we may go on to consider how the two interact). Each unit of rhythm is known as a metrical *foot*, and each foot consists of a heavily stressed syllable – one of the beats in the line – in combination with an associated number of more lightly stressed syllables (I will refer to these as 'unaccented', rather than 'unstressed' syllables, since, as we shall see, the speaking voice may still place stress on syllables which don't constitute one of the line's peaks of emphasis). Sometimes the divisions between feet will fall between words, sometimes they will fall within them. The most common metrical feet take the following shapes (where / equates to an accented syllable, and x to a lighter, unaccented one):

trochee: a foot in which the first syllable is more heavily stressed than the second (/ x)
iamb: a foot in which the second syllable is more heavily stressed than the first (x /)
dactyl: a foot in which the first syllable is more heavily stressed than the last two (/ x x)
anapaest: a foot in which the third syllable is more heavily stressed than the first two (x x /)

We should note straight away that any division of language into 'stressed' and 'unstressed' syllables is a simplification. In practice, the gradations of emphasis we might place on a syllable are almost infinite, and the leaps between the accented and unaccented syllables in a foot may be large or small: all that is required in a trochee is that emphasis falls from the first to the second syllable, and all that is required in an iamb is that emphasis rises from the first to the second. The beats will fall at regular intervals along a line, but they might land with differing intensity. We will return to this point in due course. In addition to the above terms, you might also encounter the terms *spondee* (describing a foot of successive heavily stressed syllables of equal emphasis (/ /)) and *pyrrhic foot* (describing a foot of two successive lightly stressed syllables of equal emphasis (x x)). In practice, such occurrences are rare: it is seldom that one syllable in a foot doesn't take slightly more emphasis than another, even if both seem very heavily or lightly stressed. Spondaic and pyrrhic feet never form the basis of any metrical poem in English – they are best reserved for describing interruptions to a prevailing metrical pattern and are perhaps most usefully thought of as positions to which iambic or trochaic feet might tend when the difference in emphasis between the syllables in a foot is very slight, and not phenomena which commonly occur in their ideal form.

Even in the abstract, we can begin to see how different metrical patterns open up different possibilities of expression. Tap out a sequence of trochees –

DUM-der | DUM-der | DUM-der . . .

– and a sequence of anapaests –

der-der-DUM | der-der-DUM | der-der-DUM . . .

– and you will hear the rhythms wreathing themselves around the beats with differing pace and texture.

To calculate the length of a line, we count the number of metrical feet – and consequently the number of beats – it contains. The names for describing these lengths are derived from Greek, and are as follows:

monometer – one foot
dimeter – two feet
trimeter – three feet
tetrameter – four feet
pentameter – five feet
hexameter – six feet (sometimes known as an *alexandrine*)

heptameter – seven feet
octometer – eight feet

Differing lengths of line, as we have seen, open up different possibilities of movement and expression. Shorter lines tend to give a rapid, staccato feel, leaving little space within the line to expand beyond a single phrase or image and little scope to vary the metrical pattern; four-foot lines tend to create an emphatic regular beat – you find them often in popular song and ballad forms – and they are well suited to witty poems, like the example from Prior above; five-foot lines dampen that beat, and allow more flexibility and variety of modulation. Lines of six feet tend to snake along, and feel elongated, even dragging – they are sometimes insinuated into pentameter poems, often as the closing line of a stanza. By the time a line extends out to seven feet, either you have to dampen the rhythmical emphasis so the line starts to sound like prose, or it risks collapsing under the weight of its own stresses and resolving into separate three- and four-foot units (but see Chapman's translation of Homer's *Iliad* on page 21 for a rare handling of the form that marries fluency and impetus, escaping the sing-song tendencies of the line). A fluent but regular eight-foot line, such as Naidu's in the example above, is a rare accomplishment.

To describe the metre of a line, we combine the label for its metrical pattern with the label for the line's length. Since the lines above by Prior follow an iambic (x /) pulse, and there are four of those iambic feet in each line, we can describe them as being in *iambic tetrameter*.

We observed above that most poems fall into either four- or five-beat rhythms. How can we square this with the various line lengths I have just described? The answer is that, aside from pentameters and the hexameters (which are rare in English), most line lengths can be heard in terms of a four-beat sequence. However many feet in a line, and however many unaccented syllables within those feet, our ears seem predisposed to hear rhythms in sequences of four evenly spaced beats. Poems entirely in monometers are understandably rare. And when they do occur, there is not much rhythm to hear *along* the line – the ear naturally groups lines into longer chains. The example always given is Robert Herrick's 'Upon His Departure Hence' (1648):

Thus I
Pass by,
And die:
As one
Unknown

And gone:
I'm made
A shade,
And laid
I' th' grave:
There have
My cave,
Where tell
I dwell.
Farewell.

Herrick finds a way of extending his phrases beyond units of two syllables while retaining the punchiness of the single-foot lines. If we read the poem aloud, slowly, we will notice that the punctuation causes us to group the fifteen lines into segments of three, three, four, four, and then one line. We might also hear that the pause after the groups of three lines is naturally weightier than that after the groups of four: it is as though there is a 'missing' fourth beat:

Thus **I** / Pass **by**, / And **die**: / BEAT
As **one** / Un**known** / And **gone**: / BEAT

When the sentences start to run over four lines and not three, our ear naturally fills this 'missing' fourth beat in. The stand-alone final line then serves so well as a 'Farewell' because it forestalls the sequence before it can get going for a fifth time, functioning like a rhythmical full stop.

Thanks to our predisposition to hear things in sequences of four, dimeter lines naturally pair off with one another to form four-beat units. Trimeter lines often feel as though they have a missing foot, just like the groups of three in Herrick's poem. We sense the absence when we read a poem that alternates between tetrameter and trimeter lines, such as Phillis Wheatley's 'A Farewell to America' (1773):

In **vain** | the **feath** | ered **warb** | lers **sing**,
In **vain** | the **gard** | en **blooms**, [BEAT]
And **on** | the **bos** | om **of** | the **spring**
Breathes **out** | her **sweet** | per**fumes**. [BEAT]

We hear that the trimeters are a beat shorter than the tetrameters, and we count that beat in at the end of the line for balance. The prevalence of the four-beat pattern means that it is rare to read heptameter lines without hearing how they might resolve themselves into this 4 – 3 – 4 – 3 sequence, too. At the end of each heptameter line of Felicia Hemans's 'The Indian

Woman's Death Song' (1828), for instance, we can hear a similar missing beat that would balance out the stresses either side of the caesura:

She **bears** thee **to** the **glor**ious **bowers** || where **none** are **heard** to **weep**, [BEAT]
And **where** th' un**kind** one **hath** no **power** || a**gain** to **troub**le **sleep**; [BEAT]
And **where** the **soul** shall **find** its **youth**, || as **wak**ening **from** a **dream**, – [BEAT]
One **mom**ent, **and** that **realm** is **ours**. – || On, **on**, dark **roll**ing **stream**! [BEAT]

But though the movement is similar to the form Wheatley adopts, the impact is different. The seven-foot line, where a caesura and not a line ending marks the renewal of the four-beat count, flows with a momentum sympathetic to the longing for oblivion that Hemans's singer expresses. The different ways in which the heptameters, tetrameters, trimeters, and monometers above thread themselves around the four-beat sequence indicates why we need the separate metrical terms to describe them.

Acquiring the technical language of metre is less important than developing an ear for the actual rhythms of a poem: rhythm is real; metre is the abstract ideal that underpins it. Yet having the technical vocabulary to hand can sharpen our attention to what we hear. Let's try to determine the metre of the following lines in tribute to her husband, by Anne Bradstreet (1678):

My head, my heart, mine eyes, my life, nay more,
My joy, my magazine of earthly store,
If two be one, as surely thou and I,
How stayest thou there, whilst I at Ipswich lie?

We'll begin on this occasion with the patterns of emphasis, rather than the number of beats. We can tell after a few readings that the lines follow the same stress pattern as those by Prior we examined above: they are written in iambic feet. There is a regular rise and fall of emphasis, the pressure increasing and then decreasing as we move from one syllable to the next. There are a couple of ways in which we can confirm or test this hypothesis. First, we might try reading the lines according to an alternative pattern, as though the metre were trochaic, for instance:

My head, **my** heart, **mine** eyes, **my** life, **nay** more,
My joy, **my** mag**az**ine **of** earth**ly** store,
If two **be** one, **as** sure**ly** thou **and** I,
How stayest **thou** there, **whilst** I **at** Ip**swich** lie?

This is patently unnatural. But read the lines with an exaggerated emphasis on the second syllable in each pair, and while things might sound a little odd, it doesn't feel as though we are pushing against the grain of the language. Secondly, if we're struggling to hear the rhythm naturally, then we can take our cue from the principles governing emphasis that we ran through above. Take the polysyllabic words first: '**mag**a**zine**', '**ear**ly', '**sure**ly', and '**Ips**wich'. We know that stresses have to fall on the syllables in bold, and that helps to set the pattern for the rest of the line. Next the monosyllables. The first line is a string of them, and the nouns – the various features with which Bradstreet associates her husband – all require a stress if the line isn't to sound manically possessive. Elsewhere, in the third line, 'thou' and 'I' mark out the protagonists in the relationship; while in the final line the important verbs 'stayest' (one syllable) and 'lie' seem to require emphasis, too. ('[T]hou' appears again in the final line, on this occasion seemingly unstressed: monosyllables are useful on account of how flexibly they may be accommodated within a metrical pattern.) The information gives us enough to begin to mark out a pattern through the lines if we haven't been able to detect one already. Calculating the metrical length of Bradstreet's lines is simpler: there are five iambic feet in each line, so we can speak of them as being written in *iambic pentameter*.

Bradstreet's lines also demonstrate an important point about metre in poetry: it is only ever an abstraction, a simplified model of the actual rise and fall of emphasis we hear or perform when the lines are read. The more time we spend tuning our ear to poetic rhythms, the more we come to hear that classifying syllables as either 'stressed' or 'unstressed' flattens out a whole range of nuances. Stress is not binary – a matter of turning emphasis on or off – but a matter of degree. Try to voice every stressed syllable with equivalent emphasis, and each more lightly stressed syllable with equivalent lightness, and your voice will sound mechanical. It would be an insensitive reader who went through Bradstreet's opening line, for instance, without registering the increasing urgency as the comparisons accumulate: 'My head, my heart, mine eyes, my life, nay *more*' ('eyes' seems oddly out of sequence). There are questions, too, over how strongly to stress the first syllable of '*sure*ly' in the third line: if you stress it lightly, it implies an assured confidence in the lovers' intimacy, if you stress it more urgently it betrays a hint of desperation – either is possible. In the final line, meanwhile, a sensitive reading would need to register a heightened pressure of stress on '*Ip*swich' to register the speaker's discomfort at being left behind in the provinces (it is Ipswich, Massachusetts, that Bradstreet means, but the lines will speak to the heart of any love-lorn denizen of the Suffolk town, too). As we have said, it is helpful to think of a metrical line not as one in which a series of syllables, some taken from a pool marked 'stressed' and some from a pool marked 'unstressed', are arranged in alternation with one another, but instead, as Timothy Steele suggests, as a sequence in which emphasis fluctuates between regularly spaced, but differently elevated, peaks and troughs. Some peaks will rise to greater heights of emphasis than others, and some troughs may be shallower than others. The art of writing in metre is to orchestrate these variations. Describing a poem as being written in a particular metre is not to say that it will sound identical to another poem in the same metre. Identifying the metre of a poem is only a starting point: it is a platform for measuring the expressive variations a poet plays on the underlying pattern in order to realise a distinctive rhythm.

Do the Lines Play Variations on the Metre?

Metre is the foundation of rhythm. Reading metrical verse involves reading with an ear to the way in which the words might be keyed-in to the different patterns we described above, and listening for moments of resistance as well as concord. A poet may choose to build a rhythm squarely on top of the metre, as Abraham Cowley does at the start of 'The Motto' (1668):

> What **shall** | I **do** | to **be** | for**ev** | er **known**,
> And **make** | the **age** | to **come** | my **own**?

The lines are composed almost entirely of monosyllables. The alternation of emphasis is evenly paced, and the peaks and troughs of emphasis are fairly even, too. Cowley allows the shape of the underlying metre to show through his lines, suggesting that one thing you can do to ensure immortality is to discipline your voice to a regular impersonal structure. But life is chaotic and irregular, and in most metrical poems (including Cowley's, when it gets going), we will feel a greater tension between the natural rhythms of the language and the artificial order of the metre. Sometimes this will be a matter of the ways in which the sentences interact with the metrical pattern. Count out the beats through the following lines from Isabella Lickbarrow's 'The Pilgrim' (1814), for instance, and what we hear is a regular, iambic, four-beat pattern: der-DUM, der-DUM, der-DUM, der-DUM (the main deviation, appropriately, is the stress on the word 'Lost' – an effect we shall come on to). But the sentences run irregularly across that regular sequence:

Sometimes (along some desart strand
  Lost and bewilder'd) as I stray'd
O'er the drear view, the gloom of night
  Approaching, threw a deeper shade,
I heard the howling of the storm,
  The wind breath'd sullen on mine ear,
The rising surges of the main,
  With dreadful sound, seem'd rushing near . . .

The sentences meander across the boundaries of the line like the pilgrim searching forlornly for happiness that they describe. Then towards the end of the passage the clauses fall in again with the metre, beating out the approach of the coming storm. We have already remarked on this phenomenon when we thought about lineation and enjambment; considering the tension between the two 'systems of organisation' in relation to metre allows us to see the sources of those effects in richer terms.

Just as the syntax of a sentence can pull away from a poem's lineation, so the rhythms of a sentence can pull against the regular rise and fall of metre. The words 'What **shall** I **do** to **be** for**ev**er **known**' follow the same alternation of stresses whether we read them in verse or prose. But encounter a line such as Naidu's 'Their **jew**el-girt **arms** and warm, **wave**ring, **li**ly-long **fing**ers en**chant** through me**lod**ious **hours**' in prose rather than verse and the pattern of emphasis falls slightly differently: 'Their **jewel**-girt **arms** and **warm**, **wave**ring, **li**ly-long **fing**ers en**chant** through me**lod**ious **hours**'. Read outside of its verse context, the line starts with an iambic pulse, before rippling out into anapaests. As we *listen in* to Naidu's poem, primed to discover a regular pulse, the momentum of the surrounding lines enables us to read the words with a more regular beat, and as we do so, we can feel the verse rhythms pulling against the more natural emphasis of the prose. There is often a gap such as this between the rhythms of a line as we would read it in prose and the regular pulse of stresses encouraged by verse. It is one of the sources of difficulty in thinking about metre, since it requires us to make a judgement about how far the rhythms of a sentence can be pulled out of their 'natural' order without sounding excessively strained, or even invited to hold two plausible readings in our mind at once. Yet the sense that the syllables of a line have to be imbued with regular order or want to spring free from their metrical shackles is often a source of expressive life and energy. Enjoying metrical poetry involves observing how the looser cadence of a prose reading and the disciplining impulse of metre are in negotiation.

Metre imposes order on language, but there are various ways in which the voice of a poem can push back against its regularity. A poet can shift the stresses out of their usual place, thus disturbing the regular rise and fall of the metrical pulse. They can vary the number of more lightly stressed syllables between the main stresses: crowding in more to hurry a line along, reducing the number to slow a line down (however many syllables between the stresses, their beats will still fall at regular intervals). And, as we have begun to observe in the example from Bradstreet, they can vary the weight of emphasis on both the accented and unaccented syllables, in accordance with the emotional intensity and significance of the words being spoken – not all stressed syllables rise to equal peaks of intensity.

Consider the following lines by Ben Jonson, from 'Still to be neat, still to be dressed' (1609):

> Give me a look, give me a face,
> That makes simplicity a grace;
> Robes loosely flowing, hair as free:
> Such sweet neglect more taketh me
>   Than all th'adulteries of art:
> They strike mine eyes, but not my heart.

It might seem a contradiction for these lines to be written in metre at all, given that they express delight in disorder. But they begin to show how metre can accommodate rhythmic variety. Jonson makes use of the first and last of the three options above. Take the line 'Robes loosely flowing, hair as free'. If we stress it according to the prevailing iambic pulse of the rest of the passage, we get the feeling, at the start of the line, of the natural rhythms of speech being wrenched awkwardly for the sake of regularity: 'Robes **loose** | ly **flow** | ing, **hair** | as **free**.' To pronounce the line without strain, we need to switch the stresses in the first foot, loosening the metrical shackles: '**Robes** loose | ly **flow** | ing, **hair** | as **free**.' Consider, too, where the pause, or caesura, comes: not, as in lines one and six, right in the middle of the line, with two metrical feet either side, but in the middle of the third foot. The division means that the two important nouns in the line take a heavier emphasis than the other stressed syllables, from their position at the start of their individual unit: '***Robes*** loose | ly **flow** | ing, || ***hair*** | as **free**.' The rhythm of the line flows and falls naturally, against the orderly metrical backdrop. Then consider the final line: to read it in a way that carries the sense, we need to put a contrastive emphasis on 'They', which turns the first foot into a trochee and again pulls against the regularity of the metre: '**They** [i.e. 'th'adulteries of art'] strike | mine **eyes**, | but **not** | my **heart**'. The iambic metre of the line (and the lines that surround this line) provides an ideal regularity against which the expressive irregularities of Jonson's actual rhythms come into relief.

Jonson, like Lickbarrow with her seemingly out-of-place stress on the word 'Lost', is taking advantage of the freedom poets have when writing in metre to *invert* certain metrical feet, so that they disrupt the regular alternation of accented and unaccented syllables. It is a common tactic to invert the opening foot of a line, to give punch and impetus. The blind Samson, in Milton's *Samson Agonistes* (1671) complains of his fate in iambic-pentameter lines:

> **Blind** a | mong **en** | em**ies**, | O **worse** | than **chains**,
> **Dunge**on, | or **begg** | ary, **or** | de**crep** | it **age**!

Try to read the first foot of each line as an iamb and it sounds unnatural. Inversions in the first foot of two successive lines give kick to the exclamations of despair. The device can be used to accentuate detail. Thomas Carew's 'The Spring' (1640) describes how:

> Now **that** | the **win** | ter's **gone**, | the **earth** | hath **lost**
> Her **snow-** | white **robes**, | and **now** | no **more** | the **frost**
> **Cand**ies | the **grass** . . .

The inverted stress on '**Cand**ies' draws attention to the strange, precise beauty of the word. Or consider the bluecap '**Pick**ing | the **flies** | from **bloss** | omed **app** | le **tree**' in the lines from Clare we looked at a few pages back, where the inverted foot picks out the bird's eager action.

Inversions in the middle of lines are also possible. They often enable a line to shape itself to the events or feelings it describes. Charles Johnston's translation of the Russian poet Alexander Pushkin's *Eugene Onegin* (1829; tr. 1977),[34] contains the following thought about death and leaving a legacy:

> it **would** | be **pain** | ful **to** | de**part**
> and **leave** | no **faint** | **foot**print | of **glor**y . . .

The fear of leaving no 'footprint' by which you might be remembered is brought to life by the unexpected trochaic inversion in the third foot of the second line: having already placed a reasonably solid emphasis on 'foot', in the first syllable, it is a surprise to find the emphasis not rising, but falling away, as the 'footprint' of the metrical foot itself is switched around.

In Christopher Marlowe's *Hero and Leander* (1598), the god Jupiter raises the beautiful Leander up from the depths of the ocean to stop him from drowning:

> He **heaved** | him **up**, | and **look** | ing **on** | his **face**,
> **Beat down** | the **bold** | **waves** with | his **tri** | ple **mace**,
> Which **mount** | ed **up**, | in**tend** | ing **to** | have **kissed** him,
> And **fell** | in **drops** | like **tears**, | be**cause** | they **missed** him.

Try to sustain an iambic pattern through 'Beat **down** | the **bold** | waves **with** | his **trip** | le **mace**' without any modulation of emphasis and it sounds forced. To preserve the sense of a speaking voice, we have to read the line with an inverted third foot (and perhaps even a spondee in the first), and doing so bunches stresses in a manner that animates Jupiter's battle with the ocean: '**Beat down** | the **bold** | **waves** with | his **trip** | le **mace**'. To say that it is possible to shift the stresses from the position that the metre would normally demand in this manner might seem inconsistent, since I said above that the prose reading of a line will often sound different to the verse one, as though metre were a way of wrenching syllables into order. But the rhythm of natural speech will only submit to so much metrical discipline, and there always comes a point (which is admittedly sometimes a matter of interpretation) when the natural stresses of a line refuse to yield to the regular metrical order.

Both Johnston's and Marlowe's lines illustrate another technical point about metre, which is that any line can carry an extra lightly stressed syllable at its close. Johnston's final foot, 'of **glor**y', ensures his line ends on a falling cadence, in keeping with its glimpse of oblivion; Marlowe's endings 'have **kissed** him' and 'they **missed** him' cause the lines to end on a downward cadence in sympathy with the action of the waves. Such leeway enables lines to end on words that have an unaccented final syllable, and means that many lines of iambic tetrameter will have nine syllables, many lines of iambic pentameter eleven, and so on, creating a falling effect. Lines with extra unaccented syllables are known as *hypermetrical* (since we are not adding any extra beats to the line, the metrical length of the line does not change). The downcast pentameters of Cowper's 'Lines Written During a Period of Insanity' (see page 69) feel like they are limping to a close thanks to their hypermetric final syllables:

> ***Him*** the | vin**dic** | tive **rod** | of **an** | gry **just**ice
> Sent **quick** | and **how** | ling **to** | the **cent** | re **head**long
> ***I***, fed | with **judge** | ment, **in** | a **flesh** | ly **tomb**, am
> **Bur**ied ab | ove **ground**.[35]

The dimeter final line sounds all the snappier because it denies the forlorn falling pattern our ear has come to expect.

In lines shorter than pentameters, hypermetric syllables are often inserted within the lines (such insertions are rare in pentameters, since it is already such a pliable metre – though they are not unheard of: see David Ferry's translation from Virgil on page 122). William Blake's 'Auguries of Innocence' (c. 1803) begins with some famous, but rhythmically unstable lines, whose movement owes to the way in which Blake varies the number of syllables in between the principal stresses:

To **see** | a **World** | in a **Grain** | of **Sand**
And a **Heav** | en in a **Wi** | ld **Flower**:
Hold | In**fin** | ity in the **palm** | of your **hand**
And E**ter** | nity **in** | an **hour**.
A **Rob** | in **Red** | breast **in** | a **Cage**
Puts | all **Heav** | en **in** | a **Rage**.
A **dove** | house **filld** | with **doves** | & **Pig**eons
Shud | ders **Hell** | thr' **all** | its **reg**ions.
A **dog** | starvd **at** | his **Ma** | ster's **Gate**
Pre**dicts** | the **ru** | in **of** | the **State**.

These lines are difficult to scan. The dominant metre is iambic tetrameter, but it is not until the ninth and tenth lines that we get two successive lines which follow that pattern without any deviation. The lines seem to discover this steady rhythm as they go. There is a noticeable break – in sense and rhyme scheme as well as rhythm – between the first four lines, which we'll return to in a minute, and the ones that follow. From the fifth to the eighth line, the metre seems at first sight to alternate between an iambic and a trochaic pattern. In the sixth and eighth line, there are only seven syllables – a more lightly stressed syllable has been lost from the front of the line, and the resulting falling rhythm means that it is tempting to scan the lines not as I have done above, but like this:

A **Rob** | in **Red** | breast **in** | a **Cage**
Puts all | **Heav**en | **in** a | **Rage**

Rhythmically, the two ways of scanning the line are identical. But since the remainder of the passage is iambic, and since the syllable has been lost from the front of the line, then it makes sense to think of an iambic metre as prevailing here. The difference is simply a matter of categorisation – just as in one musical key we might describe a note as B-flat and in another we might describe the same note as A-sharp, despite the fact that they are both the same pitch. The technique at work here is known as *catalexis*. Catalexis allows poets to lop off the more lightly stressed syllables from the feet at the beginning or end of a line, and, like the addition of unaccented syllables enables greater fluency and flexibility of expression.

What is going on in Blake's first four lines? Not one is perfectly iambic, and the second and fourth are trimeters not tetrameters. They sound more meandering and meditative than the snappy, proverbial couplets that follow, and part of the reason for that is the way Blake inserts extra unstressed syllables into the lines. The third foot of the first line is an anapaest; so is the first foot of the second, while the second foot of that line has three lighter syllables prior to its stress; the third line is catalectic, and again has three unaccented syllables prior to the stress in its third foot, before a final anapaest (cramming syllables in appropriately); the fourth rolls to a satisfying conclusion with two anapaests and a closing iamb. Without abandoning a regular pulse, Blake takes liberties with the numbers of unstressed syllables between the beats, causing the pace and emphasis of the lines to ebb and flow, and achieving the seductive music which is one reason that the lines are so haunting. Such effects are common in four-beat lines, where the pulse is so emphatic that it can take the strain of the variation. The deceptively complicated trimeters and tetrameters of Rudyard Kipling's 'We and They' are a good example:

> **All** | good **peop** | le ag**ree**,
>   And **all** | good **peop** | le **say**,
> **All** | nice **peop** | le, like **Us**, | are **We**,
>   And **ev** | ery **one** | else is **They**:
> But **if** | you cross **ov** | er the **sea**,
>   Ins**tead** | of **ov** | er the **way**,
> You may **end** | by (**think** | of it!) **look** | ing on **We**
>   As **on** | ly a **sort** | of **They**!

For all it trips off the tongue, the verse wobbles so frequently between an iambic and an anapaestic pattern that it is impossible to say which is predominant – a technique appropriate, we might think, to the poem's fascination with mirrored perspectives.

On occasion, a poet might vary the number of syllables between the stresses in a way that upsets the regular pulse of a line to the point at which the dominant metre seems to get left behind entirely. Langston Hughes's virtuoso performance 'The Weary Blues' (1926)[36] achieves a music and movement akin to the song of the blues musician that it describes from the way it trims and augments the numbers of unstressed syllables along its swaying anapaestic tetrameter lines to achieve a syncopated jazzy effect. At times, Hughes pulls against the anapaestic norm so completely that it seems momentarily as though he is writing a completely improvised rhythm, as when, observing the musician, he describes how:

With his **eb** |ony **hands** | on each **iv** | ory **key**
He **made** | that poor pi**a** | no **moan** | with melo**dy**

The first line quoted is a regular anapaestic tetrameter, as we can see. But to read the second line as a tetrameter requires a certain amount of strain: 'He **made** | that poor pi**a** | no **moan** | with melo**dy**'. A sequence of four anapaests has been shuffled into two iambs and two feet of four syllables. The line scans much more readily as a series of iambs: 'He **made** | that **poor** | pi**a** | no **moan** | with **me** | lo**dy**'. Hughes faces us with a choice. We can preserve the dominant four-stress metre of the poem as a whole, 'demoting' syllables which would normally take a stress ('made', 'poor', and 'mel'), hurrying some extra unstressed syllables into some feet and leaving them out from others to preserve the four-beat-to-the-line movement. Doing so makes the line itself 'moan' as we voice it as far as possible in keeping with the demands of the metre. Or, by raising the emphasis a touch on certain syllables, we can temporarily abandon the metrical norm, and give the line a plinky-plonk iambic regularity. It is an example of the sometimes irresolvable negotiations between the speaking voice and the metrical frame.

In the line 'With his **eb** |ony **hands** | on each **iv** | ory **key**' we might notice that the syllables 'hands' and 'key', taking up a full word to themselves, are struck with greater emphasis than 'eb' and 'iv', which are no sooner sounded than they trail off into the rest of their words. The second of Hughes's lines moves so readily into a sequence of iambs because the second of the more lightly stressed syllables in the second and fourth feet are almost as heavily weighted as the stresses themselves. As we observed in our discussion of Bradstreet's lines on page 81, not all stressed or 'unstressed' syllables take equal weight. A metrical line, it is worth restating, is not a sequence of syllables in which some are stressed and others receive no stress at all. It is one in which stress rises and falls at regular intervals, but to differing peaks and troughs. When, in Marlowe's poem, we speak the line 'He **heaved** | him **up**, | and **look** | ing **on** | his **face**', the key verb, 'heaved', and the key noun, 'face', rise above the other stresses. Reading a line, we need to allow the voice to add its layers of tone and emphasis as it negotiates the metrical path. And the way in which a poet varies the peaks and troughs of emphasis is crucial to the expressive force of their writing. The effect can be subtle. It would sound unnatural, in reading Thomas Gray's line 'The **paths** | of **glo** | ry **lead** | but **to** | the **grave**' ('Elegy, Written in a Country Church-Yard' (1751)) to give 'to' the same weighting as 'paths' or 'grave'. The syllable is still in a stressed position – it takes more emphasis than 'but', the other word in its foot – but the emphasis rises to a lower peak than other more important words in the line. The effect is to create a slight lull before the bleak crescendo of the line's ending. Or take two lines from the start of George Herbert's 'Artillery' (1633):

As **I** | one **eve** | ning **sat** | be**fore** | my **cell**
Me**thought** | a **star** | did **shoot** | in**to** | my **lap**.

Here the heavier stresses are scored by the alliteration: 'sat', 'cell', and then with heightened emphasis matching the speaker's astonishment, higher peaks on 'star' and 'shoot' in the second line. Because we determine whether a syllable is stressed or not only by weighing it against the other syllables in its foot, it is possible for a syllable which is unstressed on one foot to carry more weight than a stressed syllable elsewhere in the line. Steele gives the example of Robert Frost's description of a desiccated riverbed in 'Hyla Brook' (1916):

Its **bed** | is **left** | a **fad** | ed **pap** | er **sheet**
Of **dead** | leaves **stuck** | to**geth** | er **by** | the **heat**.

In speaking the second line, 'leaves', though unaccented, receives more weight of emphasis than 'by', which is the stressed syllable of the fourth foot. The line remains conventionally iambic, since it follows the requisite sequence of rises and falls, but as the voice runs through the words 'dead leaves stuck', the stressed and unstressed syllables clump together.

We need not think only in terms of heightened emphasis. The critic James Smith once wrote beautifully of the verse of Wordsworth's poem 'Michael' (1800) as a pentameter that has 'almost ceased to beat, and seems maintained only by the flutter of tenuous hopes and sickening fears'.[37] He quotes the following lines, which describe the protagonist's response to having to use his savings to cover a debt incurred by his nephew:

This | un**looked**- | for **claim**,
At **the** | first **hear** | ing, **for** | a **mom** | ent **took**
More **hope** | out **of** | his **life** | than **he** | sup**posed**
That **an** | y **old** | man **ev** | er **could** | have **lost**.

So muted are the stresses in these lines that the distinction between stressed and unstressed syllables at times seems almost non-existent. The opening of the second line feels especially frail: the stressed syllable in the first foot is weaker than the unstressed syllable in the second foot, as though the line cannot bring itself to deliver its news. But listen carefully, and you will hear that the iambic pulse does sustain itself – the second syllable in each foot is stronger than the first (an iambic metre only requires a movement from lighter to more heavily stressed syllables within its individual feet, so it is entirely possible, if rare, to end up with a sequence of four increasingly stressed syllables like this). And the need to uphold the metre in the final line shapes our reading as it puts affectingly restrained emphasis on 'old' rather than 'man', adding a touching note of modesty to Michael's supposition.

Not all poems that we encounter will make use of metre: some twentieth-century poets felt that metre's expressive possibilities had been exhausted and tried to leave it behind, as we will see. But in those poems that are composed in metre, it serves as one of poetry's crucial principles of organisation. Metre directs emphasis and underscores feeling. It is a response to our basic pleasure in rhythm and to the desire of art to order and to organise the randomness of experience. It controls and elevates the voice, situating it within an impersonal structure and tradition, and making us aware that we are dealing with something distilled from the irregularity of the everyday world. It acts, in the words of F. W. Bateson, as 'a continual reassurance to the reader' that care has been taken over the poem's creation: "Here is the cosmos of mind and not the chaos of phenomena."'[38] But what the observations and examples above also demonstrate is that metre, as it organises the rhythms of the speaking voice, also establishes an abstract framework against which the language of a poem can achieve expressive variety. As Claude Rawson says: 'No one with an ear for the English language would read . . . strictly according to the stresses indicated by the presumed iambic beat. At the same time no natural reading . . . is free of an unspoken relation to this presumed beat, and the unceasing silent conversation between the prescribed and the actual or natural cadences is an essential element of the vitality of poetic expression.'[39] Metre shows that freedom and individuality take root in order and convention.

How Does the Metre Give Character to the Poem?

Metre is among the most challenging concepts for new readers of poetry to grasp. In books, in the classroom, and in the lecture hall, it is presented as one of the few abstract sets of rules that we have to learn in order to understand poetry. And so, having been introduced to the idea, on finding that we can't immediately apply it, the temptation is to throw our arms up in the air and lament our shortcomings. But to learn the basic principles of metre is not to cross the threshold to a new world of understanding, any more than being told the rules of cricket, or American football, is to immediately understand those sports, without going through the experience of watching or playing some games. An ear for the rhythms and patterns of poetry is something we develop through practice rather than simply switch on.

One source of difficulty is the expectation that metre 'creates' meaning or that different metres are encoded with different significances. Students often want to say that lines of iambic pentameter mimic a heartbeat, for instance. But, as we have seen, metre is only ever an abstract model of a poem's actual rhythms. It is a foundation upon which variations in stress, intonation, pacing, syntax, and significance are layered. Those rhythms are themselves meaningful and worth taking pleasure in for their own sake. Our aim should not be to 'translate' the metre, but by attending to it to bring a poem's rhythms into sharper relief. Coleridge's lines in 'The Eolian Harp' (1795) describing a landscape 'Where the breeze warbles, and the mute still air / Is Music slumbering on her instrument' achieve their own music, whose nature and beauty becomes more apparent when we consider how Coleridge plays upon the iambic pentameter to realise it. As we read them, the lines seem to 'warble' unsteadily like the breeze – the stresses of the first line in particular drift and cluster together: 'Where the **breeze warb**les, and the **mute still air**' – but analysis shows the lines to keep to an iambic pattern:

> Where **the** | breeze **warb** | les, **and** | the **mute** | still **air**
> Is **Mus** | ic **slumbe** | ring **on** | her **inst** | ru**ment**.

The emphasis increases in the second syllable of each foot. The swelling and falling impression owes to the way the unaccented syllables of some feet take a heavier emphasis than the accented syllables of those that precede them, so that through a run such as 'Where **the** | breeze **warb**' (a very lightly stressed iamb, tending towards a pyrrhic foot, followed by a strongly stressed one, tending towards a spondee) the pressure continually builds; likewise with the manifestation of stillness created by the tiny increments of stress through 'the **mute** | still **air**'. Then, as Coleridge describes the soothing sound of '**Mus** | ic **slumbe** | ring', the sense of soporific laziness is enhanced through the way the words are made to fall over the divisions between metrical feet.

While different metrical feet and line lengths might suggest various expressive shapes and possibilities, metrical patterns in themselves have no inherent character and come with no pre-packaged associations or effects. No two poems in anapaestic trimeter, for example, will be entirely alike – each will realise its possibilities differently. The same metre that Edward Lear uses in his limericks (1846) –

There **was** | an Old **Man** | of White**hav**en,
Who **danced** | a quad**rille** | with a **Rav**en;
But they **said** – | 'It's ab**surd**, | to en**cou** | rage this **bird!**'
So they **smashed** | that Old **Man** | of White**hav**en.

– Algernon Charles Swinburne deploys in his languorous hymn of besotted love, 'Dolores' (1866):

By the **rav** | enous **teeth** | that have **smit**ten
Through the **kiss** | es that **bloss** | om and **bud**,
By the **lips** | inter**twist** | ed and **bit**ten
Till the **foam** | has a **sav** | our of **blood**,
By the **pulse** | as it **ris** | es and **fal**ters,
By the **hands** | as they **slack** | en and **strain**,
I ad**jure** | thee, res**pond** | from thine **al**tars,
Our **Lad** | y of **Pain**.

Each moves around a four-beat structure. Lear is quirky, tripping, comic; Swinburne is heavy, sensuous, lulling. Lear gets the rhythms to jog along, at first in step with the dance and then horribly out of step with the man's fate; Swinburne harnesses the momentum of the metre as a way of channelling and heightening feelings of intoxicated erotic abandon, capturing, literally, 'the pulse as it rises and falters'. The lightness of Lear's limerick owes, admittedly, to the way he quickens the pace of the third line by pivoting on an internal rhyme that makes the tetrameter sound like two dimeters and foreshortens the first feet of the first two lines (making use of catalexis); both poets deploy falling endings (finishing the line on a spare unstressed syllable), though Swinburne achieves more hypnotic effect by modulating back and forth between lines ending in stressed and unstressed syllables in a more regular manner. The movement of the two poems has a common root, but they grow to very different ends.

A poet's choice of metre determines the character of their poem, but that character is better seen in terms of an expandable range of options than as a fixed quality. A good way to observe how different metres afford different expressive possibilities is to think about how translating a poem from a foreign language into different metres might result in different effects. Here is John Milton's translation of the Roman poet Horace's Ode 1.5:

What slender Youth bedew'd with liquid odours
Courts thee on Roses in some pleasant Cave,
    Pyrrha for whom bindst thou
    In wreaths thy golden Hair,

Plain in thy neatness; O how oft shall he
On Faith and changed Gods complain: and Seas
    Rough with black winds and storms
    Unwonted shall admire:

Who now enjoyes thee credulous, all Gold,
Who alwayes vacant, alwayes amiable
    Hopes thee; of flattering gales
    Unmindfull. Hapless they

To whom thou untry'd seem'st fair. Me in my vow'd
Picture the sacred wall declares t' have hung
    My dank and dropping weeds
    To the stern God of Sea.

Milton uses an iambic metre, moving between lines of five and three stresses (pentameters and trimeters). The feeling this pattern creates of something shifting endlessly back and forth – an impression reinforced by the extra unaccented syllable lingering at the end of the first line, and occasional inverted first foot – suits Milton's enjoyment of the precarious, unstable relationship between Pyrrha and the 'slender youth' and is a fitting vehicle for the winding, unpredictable syntax in which he describes that relationship (read the sentences slowly and notice how they seem to change shape and meaning before your eyes). The qualities of the poem's voice, and its vision of the love affair it describes, are grounded in its choice of metre. The unvarying iambic pentameter which Anna Seward used to translate Horace's poem roughly a century later, by contrast, lacks the seductive grace of Milton's version:

Where roses flaunt beneath some pleasant cave,
    Too charming Pyrrha, what enamour'd Boy,
Whose shining locks the breathing odors lave,
    Woos thee, exulting in a transient joy?
For whom the simple band dost thou prepare,
That lightly fastens back thy golden hair?

That is Seward's version of the opening stanza (1799) and in its regular, endstopped progress, it has a more stately, distanced quality to it than Milton's translation, as though being spoken by someone eager to keep any involvement in the emotions they describe at bay. Seward earns the rewards of that potentially tedious regularity in her poem's final lines, in which the metre trembles as her speaker describes her gratitude to the God who 'Snatch'd me to shore, from an o'erwhelming sea', rescuing her from the dangers of Pyrrha's charms. It is hard to read that line as a regular pentameter: 'Snatch'd' demands an inverted stress, underscoring its urgency, and as we try to uphold the iambic pulse through 'from **an** | o'er**whelm** | ing **sea**' it is drowned out by the relative weakness of the stresses on 'an' and 'whelm', so that the voice gropes for a stability which is not there (compare Milton's technique of dampening the stress in the initial foot of his final line, so that while the metre of 'To **the** | stern **God**' remains iambic, the emphasis increases through each word, rising to a crescendo which underscores the God's sternness). A more recent rendering of the poem (1911) by Bert Leston Taylor shows how different characters take root in different metres:

I've dipped. The wet ain't fine.
Hung on the votive line
    My duds. The gods can see
    I'm free.
        Eh, Pyrrha!

Three lines of iambic trimeter, followed by an iambic monometer and an amphibrach (a foot in which the most heavily stressed syllable has a lighter stress on either side: x / x). This version is lighter on its feet. The language is slangy, the attitude is breezy, and the staccato brevity of the metre is an appropriate accompaniment.

One thing made apparent through these examples is that metre always has its impact in combination with other aspects of versification: it rarely makes sense to ask about the impact of metre alone. A crucial virtue of thinking about metre is that it encourages us to look close up at a poem, and in doing so we may notice other things. In 'Reapers' (1923), Jean Toomer achieves a sharp and sensitive portrait of rural labour through his subtle arrangement of sense and syntax around the metrical frame:

Black reapers with the sound of steel on stones
Are sharpening scythes. I see them place the hones
In their hip-pockets as a thing that's done,
And start their silent swinging, one by one.

Black horses drive a mower through the weeds,
And there, a field rat, startled, squealing bleeds,
His belly close to ground. I see the blade,
Blood-stained, continue cutting weeds and shade.

Eight lines of iambic pentameter. Four sentences. Two points of focus: reapers, working in the fields, and the animal life that accompanies them. The first sentence, unpunctuated, takes us almost to the midpoint of the second line. Before the line break, an image of the reapers, making a sound; over the break, and an explanation of their activity. The rhythm holds steady to the iambic metre:

Black **reap** | ers **with** | the **sound** | of **steel** | on **stones**
Are **sharpe** | ning **scythes**.

We might be tempted to turn the first foot into a spondee – certainly 'Black' would seem to take as much emphasis as 'with' in the following foot – but otherwise the pattern is steady. The metre ensures that the stresses fall on a series of alliterating words, the emphasis of the voice striking down like the steel on the stones that they describe. The next sentence is two and a half lines, taking us to the mid-point of the poem. The iambic pulse keeps going for the remaining three feet of the second line ('I **see** | them **place** | the **hones**' – here the verbs and nouns take the stresses), but what of the third line? Try reading it to a regular iambic pulse, and all of a sudden you can hear the natural speech rhythms coming under a little more strain. The prose rhythm would be something like –

In their **hip-pock**ets as a **thing** that's **done**

– with only four stresses bunching and then expanding; so to string the line out along an iambic pentameter feels unnatural:

In **their** | hip-**pock** | ets **as** | a **thing** | that's **done**

The metre has to work hard to discipline a line whose rhythms are rather indistinct. Why has Toomer done this? One answer might have to do with the casual phrasing at the end of the line, 'a thing that's done', which suggests – and manifests – an activity performed by rote. The line itself, drawing prose rhythm together into an awkward pentameter order, mimics the struggle between human movement and the grim routine into which the workers are coerced. By the fourth line, the iambic pulse has returned, along with its emphasis on *s*-words: one can catch an echo of the blades swinging through the air. But notice how the metre and the syntax intersect so that both '**sil**ent' and '**swing**ing' straddle metrical feet (i.e.

the words run across the break between feet), giving impetus to the lines' movement through the metre. Very often, attention to metre begins in technical observation before expanding out into a question of the whole atmosphere and significance of the poem.

The second half of the poem starts with another two-and-a-half-line sentence, extending three feet into the poem's penultimate line. It also begins with the word 'Black', but this time our attention is directed towards the horses in the field: Toomer leaves it unsaid whether he wants us to see these animals in contrast to the workers or as an emblem of the condition to which their work has reduced them. How do the metre and rhythm of the fifth and sixth lines compare?

Black **hor** | ses **drive** | a **mow** | er **through** | the **weeds**,
And **there**, | a **field** | rat, **start** | led, **squeal** | ing **bleeds**

The metre of both is identical: a steady iambic pentameter. But the rhythm is very different. The first line rolls smoothly and uninterruptedly along, just as the horses drive their mower; we might detect a slight pause for breath and a caesura in the middle of the fourth foot, but nothing drastic. But the rhythmic landscape of the next line is far bumpier. Partly, again, this is to do with the intersection of words and feet: because the line's most prominent words '**field** | rat, **start** | led, **squeal** | ing' all straddle metrical feet, the sense of easy accommodation between voice and metre is disrupted. Punctuation also impedes fluency: commas after 'there' 'field rat' and 'startled' give the line its own startled quality, enacting the shocked and damaged predicament of the rat. The sentence limps on for another three iambic feet but can't get itself through the next line in its entirety.

The final sentence extends, like the first, across a whole line and two further metrical feet. Like the second sentence of the first half of the poem, it begins with the words 'I see': the metre enables Toomer to look steadily at a bleak scene. The rhythm, for the most part, again holds steady to the iambic pulse. But what about the phrase at the opening of the final line, 'Blood-stained'? These words bear much of the horror of what the poem describes and seem to demand a weight of emphasis: they read more naturally as a spondee than an iamb. In the phrase's wake comes a comma, creating an early caesura, which underscores the violence of the image. But then across the remaining four feet of the line, the iambic rhythm plays out serenely, in harmony with the cool indifference with which the blades 'continue cutting weeds and shade'. The metrical regularity steadies the poem's gaze, refusing to let it flinch from the unpleasantness to which it bears witness.

Does the Poem Rhyme?

Some of the stressed syllables in Toomer's lines sound the same. At the end of successive lines we have 'stones' and 'hones', 'done' and 'one', 'weeds' and 'bleeds', 'blade' and 'shade'. The lines rhyme, and more than that, the rhyme pairs themselves have an aural similarity: the second and fourth rhyme pairs sound like withered versions of the first and third pairs. We might even notice that the climactic image in the poem, the 'Blood-stained' 'blade' that has cut through the rat, is itself underscored by something that approaches a rhyme, as 'Blood' and 'blade' whet themselves against one another – though if we wanted to call this a rhyme, it would not be in a position where our ears have been primed to listen out for one, at the end of a line. These harmonies and discords all work in sympathy with the lines' concerns, and hint at various ways in which rhyme connects words together, suggests relations between sound and sense, and creates a formal architecture. We'll get round to these matters in due course, but it's a good idea to start with a basic question.

'What is rhyme?' asks a character in a dialogue by Gerard Manley Hopkins: 'Is it not an agreement of sound –?' 'With a slight disagreement, yes', another character breaks in, wittily demonstrating the principle at stake.[40] Rhyme occurs when the vowel sounds and one of the consonantal sounds of two stressed syllables are the same as one another. It might be easy to spot a rhyme; it is less obvious to know what to make of rhyme's presence in poetry, beyond the observation that this poem rhymes, this one doesn't. Even that can be a useful distinction to start with, though. Some poets make a point of rejecting rhyme. John Milton objected to rhyme on the grounds that it causes poets 'to express many things otherwise, and for the most part worse then else they would have exprest them'. Milton presented his refusal to deploy rhyme (or at least any regular system of rhyme) in his epic *Paradise Lost* (1667) – whose opening lines we encountered in our discussion of lineation – as an example of 'ancient liberty recover'd to heroic Poem from the troublesom and modern bondage of Rimeing'. The crux of Milton's argument is that rhyme paints you into corners. Once you have chosen to rhyme on the word *love*, say, then you limit the directions that the line you are going to rhyme it against might take: somehow, the poem is going to have to come round to one of *above*, *clove*, *dove*, *glove*, *shove*, *of*, or maybe, at a push, *you've* – each offering various degrees of usefulness and plausibility (there's a reason why doves appear so often in love songs, while it's difficult to imagine a poem pairing *love* and *clove* unless it was a versified recipe for mulled wine). Alongside this little squadron are *move* and *prove*, and words that rhyme with them, which, although they don't 'agree' exactly with 'love' to the ear, have come to be accepted as rhymes by convention – perhaps to afford poets more options, perhaps on account of altering standards of pronunciation. But still, you can see how rhyme narrows a poet's options. Milton felt such constraints inappropriate to a poem concerned with liberty, choice, and free will.

A common complaint against rhyme when badly handled, which might fall under the umbrella of Milton's objection, is that it makes the progress of a poem all too predictable. 'Whilst seeking to please our eare, we inthrall our judgement',[41] the Renaissance critic Samuel Daniel observed, meaning that rhyme enables a kind of poetic autopilot, a dull procession from one cliché to the next. The point is made with witty weariness by Alexander Pope in his *Essay on Criticism* (1711), as he complains of poets who 'ring round the same unvaried chimes / With sure returns of still expected rhymes':

> Where'er you find 'the cooling western breeze',
> In the next line, it 'whispers through the trees':
> If 'crystal streams with pleasing murmurs creep',
> The reader's threaten'd (not in vain) with 'sleep'.

Pope is not objecting to rhyme *per se*, rather to an unimaginative use of it – he is after all rhyming himself. Still, a poet wanting to avoid falling into the trap of 'expected rhymes' might well shy away from the device altogether.

Just as damaging as instances where a poem glides unthinkingly from one rhyme to the next are those moments where the words of a poem contort themselves to meet the demands of a rhyme scheme. It is hard to imagine gathering much consolation from the following greetings-card verse, mainly because whoever wrote it sacrificed all other considerations to the need to stick to their plan for a rhyme between 'express' and 'distress':

> Sometimes words are inadequate
> Our feelings to express
> When someone who we hold so dear
> Is in such great distress.

Somehow you don't get the feeling that the 'adequacy' of words has been put to the test. The imprecise grasp on feeling goes hand in hand with clumsy technique, and we can be grateful for the small mercy that the writer at least wasn't moved to wrench a closing rhyme on 'unhappi*ness*' instead (remembering rhyme is usually a coincidence of stressed syllables).

Listen, too, to how awkwardly the rhythms of the lines jar against the metre: either you have to say, 'Some**times** | words **are** | in**ad** | e**quate**', which imposes an unnatural iambic pulse upon the language; or you go with '**Some**times | **words** are | in**ad** | e**quate**', whose rhythms, two trochees followed by two iambs, sound deadened, lacking the life brought by metrical identity.

So, rhyme sets traps which poets might wish to avoid. And yet English poets have found rhyme to be a rich resource. Oscar Wilde, observing that rhyme is not a common feature of classical poetry, said that it was 'the one chord we have added to the Greek lyre'.[42] Rhyme shows how words can be brought into harmonious relationship with one another. Rhyming can lend punch, elegance, and memorability. It simply sounds more forceful to say:

> All human things are subject to decay
> And when Fate summons, monarchs must obey.

Than:

> All human things are subject to decay
> And when Fate summons, monarchs must submit.

It is as though the rhyme finds a natural order and harmony in the language; the second line 'obeys' the terms set by the first. Here is a way for verse to 'call / Each separate thing to join / The glorious harmony of All' in Goethe's words (where the rhyme in the translation has one word 'calling' across the line endings to another and gathering 'All' into harmony). Rhyme gives expression the ring of truth.

For Milton's contemporary, John Dryden, from whose poem *MacFlecknoe* (1682) those lines come, rhyme's value lay precisely in the discipline and constraint that Milton rejected: 'imagination . . . is a faculty so wild and lawless that, like a high-ranging spaniel, it must have clogs tied to it, lest it outrun the judgment'. Unrhymed poetry, argued Dryden, is undisciplined poetry, it 'renders the poet too luxuriant'.[43] Dryden's disparagement of 'wildness' and 'luxuriance' is hardly a view that feels in sympathy with the contemporary way of looking at things – just as (I hope) nobody now is going around tying clogs to spaniels; but the discipline that rhymed couplets in particular instil makes them the fitting medium for poems which emphasise the importance of restraint and realism. Here, for instance, is George Crabbe decrying falsified idylls of rural life in his poem *The Village* (1783):

the Muses sing of happy swains,
Because the Muses never knew their pains.
They boast their peasants' pipes, but peasants now
Resign their pipes and plod behind the plough;
And few amid the rural tribe have time
To number[15] syllables and play with rhyme . . .

Crabbe's rhymes drive a tough-minded truthfulness. Their force depends not only on the rigid order they impose on the sentence as they parcel it into two-line units, but on the way rhyme encourages us to seek correspondence or contrast between the meanings as well as the sounds of the words they bring together. So, the idyllic world of rural 'swains', is brought into contact with the 'pains' of realities unimagined by 'the Muses'; 'now' and 'plough' exist in parallel, rather than opposition, sharpening focus on present actualities; the final rhyme on 'time' and 'rhyme', one of the commonest pairings in English, nevertheless makes its point forcefully: there is no time, the rhyme implies, for the frivolity of conjuring up surprising rhymes – just find one that does the job. And yet, the way in which the hackneyed rhyme coincides with that point is itself inventive. 'I paint the cot / As Truth will paint it, and as bards will not', Crabbe remarks later, where 'not' snaps home crossly against the slightly poeticised word 'cot' (meaning cottage) with which it is paired. Crabbe's rhymes might be predictable, but they are deliberately and effectively so.

For other poets, rhyme exerts a pressure that invigorates, rather than disciplines, imagination. 'I wish to write such rhymes as shall not suggest restraint but contrariwise the wildest freedom', Ralph Waldo Emerson once wrote in his notebook.[44] A sense of how rhyme can energize thought is alive in the work of the medieval poet John Skelton, one-time tutor to Henry VIII, who wrote poems which tumble through hectic cascades of consecutive rhymes, hammering away on a single sound until its possibilities are exhausted. The following run of lines from 'Colin Clout' (c. 1531), in which Skelton imagines how an audience might attack the satirical nature of his writing, catches the technique's raucous energy:

Say this and say that
His head is so fat,
He wotteth[16] never what
Nor whereof he speaketh;
He crieth and he creaketh,
He prieth and he peeketh,

[15] count, arrange in metrical order [16] knows

He chides and he chatters,
He prates and he patters,
He clitters and he clatters,
He meddles and he smatters,
He gloses[17] and he flatters;
Or if he speak plain,
Then he lacketh brain,
He is but a fool;
Let him go to school,
On a three footed stool
That he may down sit
For he lacketh wit . . .

The impact is visceral, a manifestation of 'wildest freedom' in words. The effect is like a soldier rattling on until his ammunition runs out, picking up a new clip, and going again; with the added impact in these lines from the way Skelton's rhyme sounds, on 'that', 'chatters', and 'sit', intermittently stage their own aural collisions. It is a fine way of expressing fury, and in this case, of intimating how anger can all too easily become carried away with itself. Skelton made the style so much his own that this kind of verse, 'Skeltonics', is named after him.

Other poets defending rhyme might find wriggle room in Milton's statement that rhyme's imperative to express things 'otherwise' is only 'for most part' to express them 'worse'. Rhyme can paint a poet into corners, yes, but that pressure can make it an agent of discovery as well as constraint, a means of 'waking a new mood', as Oscar Wilde put it, 'or stirring a fresh train of ideas, or opening by mere sweetness and suggestion of sound some golden door at which Imagination itself had knocked in vain'.[45] Primo Levi makes a similar point: 'The restriction of rhyme obliges the poet to resort to the unpredictable: compels him to invent, to "find"; and to enrich his lexicon with unusual terms; to bend his syntax; in short, to innovate'.[46] English poetry is full of moments of verbal ingenuity which turn rhyme into a moment of surprise as well as expectation. To take one brief example, Andrew Marvell begins 'The Garden' (1681) with a reflection on the vanity of poetic ambition (palm, oak, and bay leaves are awards for civic, military, and literary achievement):

How vainly men themselves amaze
To win the palm, the oak, or bays . . .

These lines might themselves seem too contrived to come near earning any poetic laurels: the natural syntax would be 'How vainly men amaze

[17] falsifies, flatters

themselves'. But it is fitting that the necessity of meeting the rhyme should cause the word order to get a bit tangled up, just like the ambitious individuals Marvell has in his sights.

Marvell's couplet makes a virtue of its entanglement in rhyme; other poets may brandish the apparent ease with which they negotiate rhyme's artificial constraints. Lord Byron was a master of this approach: Byron boasted a famously suave and debonair personality – and his most characteristic poetry uses its nonchalant rhyming as a way of cutting a similar dash on the page. Here are some lines Byron scribbled in the margins of his masterpiece *Don Juan* (1819):

> I would to heaven that I were so much clay,
> As I am blood, bone, marrow, passion, feeling –
> Because at least the past were passed away –
> And for the future – (but I write this reeling,
> Having got drunk exceedingly today,
> So that I seem to stand upon the ceiling)
> I say – the future is a serious matter –
> And so – for God's sake – hock and soda water!

The poem is a cry to live in the moment, free from the consciousness of past and future. Its improvisatory verve allows it to fulfil that wish. There is an intricate rhyming structure at work here (the abababcc rhyme scheme follows a pattern known as an *ottava rima* – we will come to the larger structures rhyme enables a poet to build up in due course); at the same time, the rhymes themselves often seem to fall into place just by chance. Let's focus for now on the chain of rhymes that flows from 'feeling'. The word is given prominence at the head of a list of earthly things Byron wants to rid himself of. It is also not the easiest word to rhyme on; but for Byron this difficulty becomes an opportunity for showing his skill. That he meets the word with two rhymes that come in a parenthetical aside might seem a sign of a poet driven to digression; but the digressive, off-the-cuff air is exactly what Byron is after. And those rhymes carry expressive flair: 'reeling' puts the skids under any temptation to ascribe inflated significance to 'feeling' – and offers an apt description of what the verse does as it wheels from line to line; the next rhyme, on 'ceiling' is even more audacious, revelling in the outlandishness with which it upturns any potential self-regard. Byron's rhymes ensure that the voice of the poem seems always to be operating at the limits of a precarious control; artifice is put to the service of apparent spontaneity.

What Kinds of Rhyme Does the Poem Use?

Rhyme, as Hopkins says, is an 'agreement of sound', but there are different ways and degrees to which sounds may 'agree'. Looking back at the rhymes in Byron's stanza, we can see three different rhyme sounds in operation. The first set of rhymes – 'clay', 'away', 'today' – involve the coincidence of the final accented syllable of each word. Rhymes of this sort are known as *masculine* rhymes. In Byron's stanza they serve as a counterpoint to the more extravagant rhymes we looked at above: their sound is picked up in 'I say' at the start of the couplet, as if to steady the ship before the poem's final outcry. The second set, by contrast – 'feeling', 'reeling', 'ceiling' – all of which sport an unaccented syllable after the stressed vowel, are known as *feminine* rhymes (feminine rhymes may trail any number of unaccented syllables behind the rhymed syllable). Where Byron's masculine rhymes strike home firmly, without drawing too much attention to themselves, his feminine rhymes brandish their ingenuity, lending an improvisatory flamboyance: they sound chancy, even surprised by the harmonies that they discover.

At the end of Byron's stanza is another feminine rhyme, but this time one that rings less brightly, rather in the same manner as the chime between 'blade' and 'Blood' at the end of Toomer's 'Reapers': 'matter' and 'water' make what is known as a *half-* or *off-rhyme*. Rhymes of this sort set their vowels at a slant to one another, so that the words are almost in agreement, but not quite. The effect, in Byron's pairing, is to give the end of the stanza a slightly tipsy feel, and to dilute the portentousness of the claim that 'the future is a serious matter', by underscoring how the cry for wine and sparkling water (a popular hangover cure) cuts through it.

Rhyming skilfully is a matter of uncovering the varied expressive power of these different kinds of rhyme, and their intimations of harmony and discord. There is no set effect that comes from rhyming in a particular way; each poet will uncover unique possibilities in the phenomenon. Byron's friend Percy Bysshe Shelley interlaces masculine, feminine, and off-rhymes beautifully in his lyric 'To Jane' (1822):

> The keen stars were twinkling,
> And the fair moon was rising among them,
> Dear Jane.
> The guitar was tinkling,
> But the notes were not sweet 'till you sung them
> Again –
>
> As the moon's soft splendour
> O'er the faint cold starlight of Heaven

Is thrown –
So your voice most tender
To the strings without soul had then given
Its own.

The stars will awaken,
Though the moon sleep a full hour later
Tonight;
No leaf will be shaken
Whilst the dews of your melody scatter
Delight.

Though the sound overpowers
Sing again, with your dear voice revealing
A tone
Of some world far from ours,
Where music and moonlight and feeling
Are one.

The poet recalls how, on a starlit night, a woman sang to the tune of a guitar. Just as the moonlight softened the cold light of the stars, so her voice gave soul and feeling to the melody of the strings. He calls on her to sing again and endow the world with splendour once more.

Appropriately in a poem about music, the lines take special care over their own sound effects. They pedal with simple beauty between masculine and feminine rhymes. The first two rhymes in each stanza are feminine; they resolve onto a single masculine rhyme, which marries the two halves of the stanza. In the first stanza 'twinkling' and 'tinkling' are closely matched: the sound of the music harmonises the light of the stars. To close the stanza with a rhyme on 'again' reminds us that rhyme itself is a process of repetition, of hearing things 'again', both intensified and altered. 'Splendour' and 'tender' in the second stanza are more distant: they play out the process through which Jane's voice adds soul and feeling to the night's cold grandeur. With 'later' and 'scatter' in the third stanza, the rustlings of off-rhyme start to intrude: it is the same discrepancy Byron's couplet made use of, but here it draws attention to the potential for music to create renewed inspiration. The play of harmony and discord is even more potent at the poem's close, as the writing perpetuates its attractive rhyming effects but offers a heightened consciousness of the potentially illusory beauty they create. Rhyming on 'tone' and 'one' brings rhyme into the forefront of our mind, since rhyme itself is a question of matching 'tones' and is also an effort to make them 'one'. Jane's voice reveals 'A tone / Of some world far from ours', and Shelley's agile sestets (groups of six lines) show that poetry might do the same. Yet the stanza's musicality also makes all the more audible the subtly discordant 'music' of its final rhyme, where 'tone' and 'one' do not quite become one tone to the ear: the rhyme grounds the poem's awareness that poetry may aspire towards but can never wholly abandon itself to a 'world far from ours'.

Shelley's lyric might seem to prove the argument once made by Algernon Charles Swinburne that 'Rhyme is the native condition of lyric verse in English; a rhymeless lyric is a maimed thing, and halts and stammers in the delivery of its message' (disagreement with Swinburne might start with a consideration of how Milton's 'rhymeless' translation of Horace on page 95 achieves musical effects through its far from 'stammering' syntax).[47] But it may be that such halting and stammering is just the effect a poet is looking for: not all poems find order and harmony in the world. Shelley's off-rhymes are tentative, suggesting tender, precarious connections. But the extent to which words 'agree' with one another, to use Hopkins's word, is a matter of degree. Just as speaking of a syllable as either 'stressed' or 'unstressed' flattens nuance, to imagine only three possibilities of 'rhyme', 'off-rhyme', and 'no rhyme' simplifies an aural spectrum. Off-rhyming often carries a sense of something gone wrong. Jarvis Cocker sings in Pulp's 'The Fear' (1998) of an anxious state in which you've given up hoping for the grand things such as 'beauty or love', just want a life 'with the edges taken off', and can't even say what your fear is 'of'.[48] The diminishment of 'love', with all its promise, into 'off' and then 'of' (with another almost-rhyme, 'life' drifting into the aural distance) takes the edge off the word and blurs it into a morass of less consequential rhyme partners in a manner evocative of the state of lassitude the lines envisage. The song shows how a writer might do something original with this most hackneyed of rhyme words.

Off-rhyming can be cacophonous, as in the First World War poetry of Wilfred Owen, where discordant rhymes answer to the clutter and clatter of battle:

> I am the enemy you killed, my friend.
> I knew you in this dark; for so you frowned
> Yesterday through me as you jabbed and killed.
> I parried; but my hands were loath and cold.

The 'Strange Meeting' (1920) of this poem's title is between the poet and the ghost of a soldier he has killed; but it is also between the words that recount that meeting, which refuse to form a harmonious accompaniment. Again, it pays to think of the meanings of the words that the rhymes bring into contact: there is an appalling pathos as the heartbreaking address from the dead soldier, 'my friend', is matched against the poet's 'frown'.

For a contrasting effect, in which rhymes embody fraying harmonies, rather than angry collisions, compare the clangour of Owen's off-rhymes with those in the opening stanza of W. B. Yeats's 'The Second Coming' (1919). Owen's rhymes pitch us into the thick of battle; Yeats's rhymes, matching his poem's more panoramic scope, establish fragile relationships between words which answer to a fragile sense of order more generally:

Turning and turning in the widening gyre
The falcon cannot hear the falconer;
Things fall apart; the centre cannot hold;
Mere anarchy is loosed upon the world,
The blood-dimmed tide is loosed, and everywhere
The ceremony of innocence is drowned;
The best lack all conviction, while the worst
Are full of passionate intensity.

The rhymes in the first four lines enact a precariously sustained harmony: 'gyre'/'falconer', 'hold'/'world': you can hear the lines spiralling further and further apart. As the poem proceeds, rhyme falls away altogether, via one last look back to the 'gyre'/'falconer' rhyme in the fifth line's 'everywhere': as the poem describes a collapse of order, its rhyme scheme collapses in turn, and it finds a disharmonious medium for its disharmonious vision.

Yeats's poem's spiral of despair is brought to a halt by a pair of lines in which rhyme seems to stutter in entirely the opposite way:

Surely some revelation is at hand;
Surely the Second Coming is at hand:
The Second Coming!

The repetition here, in the position where one has been led to expect a rhyme, stops the voice in its tracks, as though stunned by the moment of revelation. The phenomenon is sometimes known as *autorhyme* and depends for its effect on the denial of the expectation that rhyme will always offer a step forward, as well as a glance back. We have come across autorhyme in some of the poems we have looked at already. One reason that the final four lines of Dowson's 'They are not long' open and shut as completely as the life they imagine is the way they move out from and return back to the word 'dream': 'Out of a misty dream / Our path emerges for a while, then closes / Within a dream.' Autorhyme is also integral to the curious flatness of tone with which Lear's limerick on page 94 reaches its end. The limerick form sets up the expectation of a surprising punchline, but Lear's limericks rarely supply this satisfaction, returning instead to their opening rhyme word: when 'There was an Old Man of Whitehaven' is answered by 'So they smashed that Old Man of Whitehaven', the predictability of the repetition provides an unflinching context for the surprising violence of the verb 'smashed'.

Such effects have to do with an already-rhymed poem stuttering, or falling flat. But autorhyme can create seductive effects in otherwise unrhymed poetry, where it shapes the haunting effect of a rhyme being aspired to but not quite attained. Edward Thomas's 'March' (1918) autorhymes evocatively on the word 'silence':

> Not till night had half its stars
> And never a cloud, was I aware of silence
> Stained with all that hour's songs, a silence
> Saying that Spring returns, perhaps tomorrow.

Thomas describes listening on a March evening to a 'silence' that seems to promise that Spring is on its way, and the reiteration creates that silence for us in the very texture of the verse. But the way the rhyme hovers disconcertingly between perfection and blankness brings into focus the doubtfulness underpinning the lines: *is* the 'silence' saying something hopeful, or is it just a hollow absence? Letitia Landon's 'Change' (1829) describes two childhood friends who meet again later in life, and evokes through autorhyme the puzzlement each feels at the mismatch between remembered and present personalities:

> They met again, – but different from themselves,
> At least what each remembered of themselves.

The effect is akin to a double take. The repetition has a dumbstruck blankness which marries with the lines' holographic syntax: each man is different from how the other remembered them, and that difference has also opened a gap between the two formerly matched characters.

The effect is not always so lyrical or tongue-twisting. At the start of Ted Hughes's hallucinatory narrative poem *Gaudete* (1977) is a scene of ritualistic violence in which a changeling spirit takes the place of the vicar of a rural parish, Reverend Lumb. In a weird initiation ceremony, the guts of a bull are spilled over the changeling before he assumes the Reverend's identity. Hughes's successive use of autorhymes channels the writing's violent impulses, recreating in the textures of the verse the suffocation the new Lumb experiences as he

> pushes his head clear, trying to wipe his eyes clear.
> Curtains of live blood cascade from the open bull above him.
>
> Wallowing in the greasy pulps, he tries to crawl clear.
> But men in bloody capes are flinging fresh blood over him.

Where Thomas enjambs his autorhymed lines, so 'silence' is both the ending of the line and the point from which it opens out, in Hughes, each line is endstopped, causing the words to stick even more stubbornly in the throat: 'clear' – 'above him' – 'clear' – 'over him'. Rhyme is often an agent of suggestion and forward movement (think back to the lines by Skelton), but at this moment of Hughes's poem it is as though the words themselves can't get 'clear' from the horrors they are documenting.

The possibilities of rhyme are so various that it is difficult to generalise about them. Used well, rhyme enables poets to discover effects unique to a particular poem. But as one final way in which rhyme might go awry, the absence of rhyme where one expects to find it is always disconcerting. Wendy Cope registers the fact with deadpan acumen in this stanza from 'An Attempt at Unrhymed Verse' (2008):

> Writing verse is so much fun,
> Cheering as the summer weather,
> Makes you feel alert and bright,
> 'Specially when you get it more or less the way you want it.

The surprise here is down to the way that we think the poem is falling into the same sing-song predictability aspired to in the greetings-card verse we looked at above, before it then defies those expectations. The words at the end of the second and fourth lines are not, as the rhyme leads us to expect, 'sun' and 'get it right'; and wrapped up in the awkwardness of the phrasing is a joke about how getting it right is often a matter of working against as well as with the framework of rhyme and metre, and the knowledge that while rhyme and metre impose order and harmony, perfection and conformity are not always the most desirable or most interesting outcomes.

How Does the Poem Sound?

Rhyme and rhythm are not the only ways in which a poem can address our ears. Sometimes it is the sound of individual words and letters that bewitches us. Richard Lovelace's 'La Bella Bona Roba' (1649) begins with a discordant stanza whose off-rhymes inhabit a larger echo chamber of vowels through which the poem's unsettling sexual confidence reverberates:

I cannot tell who loves the skeleton
Of a poor marmoset,[18] nought but bone, bone,
Give me a nakedness with her clothes on.

The voice sounds darkly attractive, even before we get round to considering what it says. In lingering over the word 'bone', Lovelace isn't just dwelling on the line's chilly vision but drawing attention to the long 'o' sound that sits askew with the shorter 'o' in 'skeleton' and 'on' in the other rhyme positions, and pricks our ears to the whole variety of tones that he wrings from the vowel. The lines square up to us in a voice simultaneously lust-filled and death-haunted, and Lovelace creates a verbal music appropriate to its haunting sense of the skeleton beneath the skin.

The following lines from Shakespeare's *King Lear* (c. 1606), in which the loyal Kent describes the sycophantic Oswald, likewise discover a potent eloquence rooted in the texture of individual letters and syllables:

Such smiling rogues as these
Like rats, oft bite the holy cords a-twain
Which are too intrise t'unloose.

The first line is a series of *s* sounds, insinuating themselves through the sentences like the sneers of the 'smiling rogues' it describes. Then, a litter of *t* sounds, tasted by the tongue at the front of the mouth, where biting takes place. Last, in 'too intrise t'unloose' comes a knotting of the two, as the words are entangled in our ears like the intricate social bonds Kent cherishes. Sound and sense themselves seem 'too intrise t'unloose' in Shakespeare's words. In both examples, the vision and attitude of the lines is woven through the aural fabric of the language.

However hard it is to follow the sense of a poem, there will always be something to say about the way it sounds. Some poems are challenging because they seem to present us with little more than sounds. Early in the twentieth century, Gertrude Stein's pursuit of what she called 'exact words' resulted in poetry which seems to forgo the conventions of grammar, syntax, and expression in favour of a language which does not so much describe a thing as embody it in its sounds. Stein's response to the fictional Flamenco dancer Susie Asado (1922)[49] begins like this:

Sweet sweet sweet sweet sweet tea.
Susie Asado.
Sweet sweet sweet sweet sweet tea.
Susie Asado.
Susie Asado which is a told tray sure.

[18] i.e. a 'wanton' woman

There is little in the way of sense to be encountered here. The poem rolls words and names around the mouth for the sheer pleasure of it. Sentences assume the posture of coherent sense before sliding away (it is impossible to be 'sure' what a 'told tray' is). 'This is a please this is a please there are the saids to jelly', runs a later line, whose syntactical legs seem to have turned to jelly, but which communicates a sense of pleading desire all the more effectively for that. Erotic attraction is conveyed, appropriately, through the language's sensuous and not its conceptual qualities. In a manner similar to the Lewis Carroll poem we discussed at the start of the book, the lines deflect, rather than fulfil, our expectations that language will offer coherent meaning, encouraging us to take pleasure and draw significance instead from what Stein called the 'melody of words'.[50]

Stein's is an extreme case. Few poems sacrifice sense so absolutely to the pleasures of sound. But the way a poem sounds is always an important signal of its character. Tom Paulin has suggested that you can divide up English poetry between 'a high, melodic, vowel-based tradition' which 'looks south to the Romance languages for its essential inspiration' and a counter-tradition whose 'fricative, spiky, spoken texture' is 'northern and consonantal' with its roots 'in the people, rather than in the court'.[51] Set the gruff, rhythmically hobbled verse of a poet such as Thomas Wyatt alongside the jewelled delicacy of Alice Meynell, say, and we can see what he means. Wyatt, in a poem like 'Mine Own John Poins' (c. 1540), writes in a voice whose fractured staggering abrasive progress decries its own eloquence:

I am not he such eloquence to boast,
        To make the crow singing as the swan,
        Nor call the liond of cowardes beasts the most
That cannot take a mouse as the cat can:
        And he that dieth for hunger of the gold
        Call him Alexander[19] . . .

'I can't sugar-coat the truth to make crows sing like swans, describe lions as cowards, present greedy men as great leaders', these lines say; and as we read them aloud we can feel in their alliterative cacophony and rhythmical stumbles a roughness that makes its own assault on conventional notions of 'eloquence'. The syntax always seems to be taking the most awkward route through the sense; the metre seems an impediment rather than a platform. Meynell, meanwhile, in a poem such as 'Chimes' (1901), finds in the ringing lucidity of her lyric voice an echo of the church bells she describes:

[19] i.e. a great military leader

Like birds from the cote to the gales,
        Abrupt – O hark!
A fleet of bells set sails,
        And go to the dark.

Sudden the cold airs swing.
        Alone, aloud,
A verse of bells takes wing
        And flies with the cloud.

Sense almost dissolves as we voice Meynell's stressed monosyllables aloud. The sequence through 'Alone, aloud, / A verse of bells takes wing / And flies' sends the voice ricocheting in a rise and fall between deeper and higher vowel sounds: 'lone'–'loud'; 'verse'–'bells'; 'wing'–'flies'. Meynell's voice itself becomes 'a verse of bells'.

'A good poem is a love affair of sound and sense', says Ruth Padel.[52] The remark holds true so long as we understand that love affairs can involve distance, discord, and friction as well as harmony. Some poems ask us to hear a melody that contradicts their sense. Wyatt's love poems deliver their expressions of vulnerable tenderness in the same fricative edgy voice as characterises the letter to John Poins quoted above, suggesting through their sounds a nervousness at the heart of affection. Or consider the following song that Ariel sings to the shipwrecked Ferdinand in Shakespeare's *The Tempest* (c. 1611):

Full fathom five thy father lies;
Of his bones are coral made;
Those are pearls that were his eyes:
Nothing of him that doth fade
But doth suffer a sea-change
Into something rich and strange.
Sea-nymphs hourly ring his knell.
                Ding dong!
                Ding dong bell!

It is hard to imagine a more bewitching marriage of syntax, sound, and rhythm in combination with a more painful message: 'your father has drowned'. (The message turns out to be a lie, but still.) It *sounds* lovely. The song begins like a tongue-twister, switching back and forwards between 'fa' and 'fi' sounds. The next line rearranges words to create a curious beauty: the line means 'coral are being made out of his bones', but it does so by reconstructing the more ordinary syntax 'His bones are made of coral' into something richer and stranger. The wandering syntax of the next line straddles a similar ambiguity: it elides the senses, 'those things that used to be his eyes are now pearls' and 'those pearls used to be his eyes'. All the while the rhythm spirals and wanders, refusing to settle into any consistent metrical pattern, while the rhymes play a simple alternating *abab* accompaniment. Translated into song, even the most painful of experiences undergoes a 'sea-change'.

What Is the Poem's Form?

The resources of lineation, metre, and rhyme are all aspects of a poem's *form*. To speak of the form of a poem at large is to think about the ways in which these technical aspects exist in combination. Why do poets give form to their words? To ask that question is to realise immediately that it needs rephrasing, since it is impossible to imagine a series of words – written or spoken – which doesn't have some form, however loose or random the arrangement. Why, then, do poets give their words such regular and orderly forms? The answer takes us back to the question of what a poem is: a struggle in words to clarify experience, to find order amid the randomness of life, to redeem the transience of existence by giving it lasting shape. A tension between the haphazard flow of experience and what Coleridge called the 'shaping spirit' of the imagination ('Dejection: An Ode' (1802)), between the energy of life and the monumentality of art, lies at the heart of all poems. The patterns of lineation, metre, and rhyme are ways of endowing language with aesthetic significance, so that the words of a poem present to us not just a detachable meaning but a meaning inseparable from the order they create. In a stimulating old book called *The Critical Sense* (1956), James Reeves asks us to imagine the difference between a prose story for children, which includes the sentence 'the death of the robin caused great unhappiness among the other birds' – a way of putting it that lacks formal distinction – and the opening lines of the nursery rhyme 'Cock Robin':

> All the birds of the air fell a-sighing and sobbing
> When they heard of the death of poor Cock Robin

'There is a shift in the reader's emotion when he turns from one version to the other', observes Reeves: 'the pathos shifts, as it were, from the event to the form: in the prose version the pathos is in the event, in the poetic version it is in the words'. And to support his point, Reeves draws attention to the rhythm, 'which is always associated with heightened emotion', the varied alliterative effects of the lines, the 'suggestion of universal woe' in the phrase 'All the birds fell', and the thought that 'the rhyme strengthens the feeling, since it places emphasis on the final word "Robin".'[53] To think about form, then, is to think how a poet has shaped language expressively. And while thinking about form is no simple matter of translating a poem's patterns into a direct verbal equivalent (wanting to find in every iambic-pentameter line the rhythms of a heartbeat, say), the subtlety and complexity of a poem's arrangement do generally attest to a subtlety and complexity in its apprehension of experience. The mechanical beats that come thudding from a car at the traffic lights communicate a blunter vision of life than the poised and swirling movement of a Schubert string quartet.

Whether a poet chooses to write in an established form or to develop their own shapes and patterns, form is a way of disciplining expression. It draws the individual and ephemeral voice of the poet through the lasting and impersonal structures of verse. That is not to say that when a poet writes in a particular form they simply replicate an ideal pattern. It can be tempting to think of form as a kind of container into which the words of a poem are poured: so many abstract rules and requirements regarding rhyme and metre which a poem needs to fulfil. But that would be to imply that all sonnets, all limericks, all blank verse poems, and so on, are fundamentally the same. Instead, 'form', as Stephen Spender says, 'does not lie simply in the correct observance of rules. It lies in the struggle of certain living material to achieve itself within a pattern.'[54] And that struggle, as we have seen when contemplating enjambments, metrical variations, different shades of rhyme, and so on, results in moments of irregularity and imperfection, moments where the 'living material' of the human voice deviates expressively from the ideal order towards which it aspires. Form can be a monument of failed aspiration as much as of artistic command. What matters and what fascinates about a poet's handling of form is how they fulfil the demands of an ideal order in an individual way. And, as we shall see over the next few pages, fully understanding a poet's handling of a particular form involves being aware of what previous poets have done with that form. A form is made afresh each time it is attempted.

Let's take one of the most common poetic forms, the sonnet, as an illustration. There are, of course, rules that govern what a sonnet is like. The classic sonnet is a fourteen-line poem in iambic pentameter. It is usually broken up into smaller units according to the patterns of either a Shakespearean (or 'English') rhyme scheme (abab cdcd efef gg) or a Petrarchan (sometimes 'Italian') one (abbaabba cdecde). A final distinguishing feature is the presence of a turn in the argument, or *volta*, which in the Shakespearean form usually occurs before the final couplet, and in the

Petrarchan form in the break between the first eight lines (the octet) and the last six lines (the sestet). Even in the abstract we can see that the formal shape of the poem carries implications; the structural possibilities it affords affect the kind of argument or expression that the poem might develop. The sonnet wouldn't be the form you would choose if you wanted to write a long narrative, for instance (though it is amenable to being strung together as a series of mini-episodes in a larger sequence, as many poets have found); but it is appropriate, perhaps, to the working out of an idea that evolves, or can be contemplated, in stages, or that hinges on a transition from one state of understanding to another. In choosing to write a sonnet, then, a poet is selecting not just an artistic pattern, but engaging with a particular structure of argument; as the poet Don Paterson describes it, the sonnet is 'one of the most characteristic shapes human thought can take'.[55]

Our notion of the sonnet is a product of all the poets who have already written in and developed the form. There is no ideal sonnet locked away in a vault somewhere. Instead, it is built up anew each time a poet writes one. Imagine that you are the Renaissance poet Fulke Greville, a near contemporary of Shakespeare's. You have an idea for a poem about the way at night-time all your problems and troubles seem worse – perhaps a poem which puzzled out an answer to why this might be and what it might suggest about the human imagination. Thinking that you'd probably need somewhere in the region of fourteen lines to work through your ideas (this isn't a problem that'll need a whole book to contemplate, and perhaps having a definite limit on the number of lines will encourage focus), you decide to attempt a sonnet (1633). The form should help bring order and coherence to this abstract idea. And all of your friends are writing them, after all. You might begin by seeing whether there was enough room to establish the problem in the opening four lines, perhaps by setting the scene with some description:

In night when colours all to black are cast,
Distinction lost, or gone down with the light;
The eye a watch to inward senses plac'd,
Not seeing, yet still having power of sight,

This sums up the scenario powerfully enough, with the further virtue of finding balance within the two-line structure: the first two lines describe the onset of darkness with night; the second two describe the consequent loss of vision. But there is a problem, which is apparent from the fact that we've halted the quotation on a comma: we've got to the end of the first quatrain before the sentence is over; we still haven't arrived at the main verb. The contours of the form are not matched by the structure of the sentence. Still, there is no rule to say that they should be, and this is a poem about confusion and blurring of distinctions – perhaps it is appropriate that the breaks between formal units should not be too clear-cut: the verb can wait for the next set of lines. But what are those lines going to say? They'll need to establish more clearly what the troubles are that arise out of the eye's inability to see the world properly in darkness. So, 'The eye':

> Gives vain alarums[20] to the inward sense,
> Where fear stirr'd up with witty tyranny,
> Confounds all powers, and thorough self-offence
> Doth forge and raise impossibility:

Without a clearly apprehensible external reality to cling on to, the mind starts imagining all sorts of troubles and problems. Again, the sentence could stop here, cutting its cloth according to the bounds of the conventional sonnet. We'd have a self-contained octet and the satisfaction of form and content neatly tailored to one another. The illusory terrors of the dark have been described well enough as 'fear stirred up with witty tyranny' – that is, fear generated by the imagination's own overactive processes – and the lines have captured, too, a sense of how 'fear' conjures up dangers we know to be 'impossible'. Alternatively, we could push on in a more experimental way, refusing to let syntax be determined too strongly by the form itself. After all, the point of adopting the form is to have something that enables rather than constricts argument. There doesn't need to be a turn until the closing couplet, so what if we persisted in our effort to classify the nature of these 'vain alarums' the eye sends to our 'inward sense'? 'The eye gives vain alarums':

> Such as in thick-depriving darkness
> Proper reflections of the error[21] be;
> And images of self-confusedness,
> Which hurt imaginations only see;

This has moved us on to an understanding of the sources of our unease: our fears are the product of 'hurt imaginations'. They are like images of our own sin we might be faced with in hell; they are projections of our own tormented inner state. Developing the argument through the sonnet's internal units has allowed us to evolve towards a moment of revelation; we've arrived at a rational understanding that our fears are really

[20] calls to arms/signals of danger [21] original sin

a projection of our own flaws. Still, it feels like the sentence needs a snappy finish, something that gives point and punch to its calm, exploratory progress. Fortunately, there are two lines left for us to bring things to a conclusion. Too sharp a change in direction, of a sort that might dismiss the argument, or offer a flippant alternative, would be out of keeping with the methodical unfolding of the poem's syntax, however (compare the use Byron makes of his couplet in the example on page 104). What we need is something which rejects the opportunity for a final twist or punchline afforded by the couplet, in favour of something that underlines the poem's mode of calm judgement:

> And from this nothing seen, tells news of devils,
> Which but expressions be of inward evils.

Presenting the couplet in this isolated way raises a question about the poem's syntax: what is the subject of 'tells'? If we work back through the poem, we'll see that the most obvious contender is 'The eye', at the start of the third line. As the syntax of the poem's single sentence has travelled over the points of its various colons and semicolons, it has become harder and harder to keep track of its main verb, to distinguish between dominant and subordinate clauses; as the lines of the sonnet have accumulated, the construction of the sentence has started to mimic the blurred sense of 'Distinction' we experience in the dark. Gathering up the main thread of the poem's thought once again, the final pair of lines ties up the poem's central realisation. Formally, the couplet is neat without being self-satisfied. Rhyming 'devils' against 'inward evils' means that the poem doesn't snap shut in too clear-cut a manner (to the ear, it is a slight off-rhyme), and the pairing makes audible and visible how easily one's perception of the external world can mingle with perception of one's inner nature: we can see the word 'devils' hidden in 'inwar*d evils*'.

There is scope for more minute investigation of the way the form of Greville's poem shapes and is shaped by its expression. We could talk about the control of the iambic pentameter, for instance, or the dynamic relationship between the lineation and the syntax. But this worked example begins to show that writing in a given form is not a single decision, but a dynamic series of negotiations with the possibilities afforded by any given structure. Like any other sonnet, Greville's poem achieves a unique realisation of what a sonnet might be.

Is the Poem Composed in Blank Verse?

The sonnet is popular among poets because it combines intricacy and brevity with relatively flexible formal demands. It affords a happy balance of freedom with constraint; it is patterned without being unduly elaborate; it structures rather than strangles argument. Form should be expressive as well as extravagant. Purely technical achievements soon seem hollow. There is a reason why the wild pyrotechnics of luridly clad 1980s lead guitarists, while superficially impressive, soon become tiresome. Formal accomplishment is not an end in itself but a means of expression – a way of *giving form* to an idea, feeling, or vision which could not be expressed otherwise. As Stephanie Burt says, a poem is not a 'stunt': 'If it doesn't sound like something is at stake – like there's some reason to read *besides* achieved form – then you are not likely to reread.'[56]

Alongside the sonnet, the most enduring forms in English have been those which offer the simplest framework and the most scope for variation within that framework. Across the next few sections, we'll take a small sample of these forms as models for thinking about how poets achieve a distinctive voice within a traditional structure.

What might be thought of as the standard form in English poetry over the last half millennium is blank verse: unrhymed lines of iambic pentameter arranged into verse paragraphs (or sometimes stanzas) of indeterminate length. The very plainness and simplicity of blank verse's demands are at the core of its adaptability. Being unbound by any elaborate recurring pattern beyond the shape of the pentameter line, blank verse is suited to a range of styles and purposes, from narrative to description, to declamation, to discursive elaboration of argument or feeling. On a local level, it affords scope for playing off syntax against lineation, for modulating rhythm against metre, and for sustaining the most elevated and the most quietly spoken of registers. Here is a sample of the possibilities, beginning with some lines from the poem in which the form was first used in English, a translation of Virgil's *Aeneid* composed by Henry Howard (c. 1540). Howard presents the death of the Trojan king Priam at the hands of the son of the Greek hero Achilles, Pyrrhus:

At the altar him trembling 'gan he draw,
Wallowing through the blodshed of his[22] son:
And his left hand all clasped in his heare,
With his right arme drewe fourth his shining sword,
Which in his side he thrust up to the hilts.

[22] i.e. Priam's

Of Priamus this was the fatal fine,[23]
The wofull end that was allotted him
When he had seen his palace all on flame,
With ruin of his Troyan turrets eke,[24]
That royal prince of Asia, which of late
Reigned over so many peoples and realmes,
Like a great stock now lieth on the shore;
His head and shoulders parted been in twain:
A body now without renown and fame.

There is a certain relentless impressiveness to this: each endstopped line piles one new piece of information on to the picture, and the metre seldom yields to variations of rhythm or emphasis. The regularity gives the narration a stately impassivity. But to a contemporary ear, the lines probably feel rigid, and deaf to the possibilities of the medium. Part of the reason that they do so is that we are usually introduced to blank verse through reading Shakespeare, who, seventy years after Howard, was able to do something more jagged and vibrant:

How blest am I
In my just censure, in my true opinion!
Alack, for lesser knowledge – how accursed
In being so blest! There may be in the cup
A spider steeped, and one may drink, depart,
And yet partake no venom, for his knowledge
Is not infected; but if one present
The abhorr'd ingredient to his eye, make known
How he hath drunk, he cracks his gorge, his sides,
With violent hefts. I have drunk, and seen the spider.
Camillo was his help in this, his pander.
There is a plot against my life, my crown;
All's true that is mistrusted.

This is the jealous Leontes convincing himself of his wife's infidelity in *The Winter's Tale* (c. 1611). Shakespeare uncovers a far richer range of expressive possibilities than Howard: look for the metrical variations, shortened lines, enjambments, varied sentence lengths, and effects of rhyme and repetition which give colour and character to Leontes's speech. In Shakespeare's hands, blank verse becomes a medium for embodying the rhythms of consciousness. As we read the lines above aloud, they cause our voice to change. They start with a series of abrupt exclamations, exploding one after another in a chain reaction – the sound of a mind eagerly confirming its own worst suspicions. Then a convoluted image, rounded off by a short, half-line sentence whose

[23] end [24] also

accent trembles between horror and self-satisfaction: 'I have drunk, and seen the spider'. Then two lines whose rhythms are near identical, tracing the contours of a mind which is now complacent in its convictions. Finally, a culminating statement which seems to lift itself out of its dramatic situation and speak on behalf of the play as a whole, as though Shakespeare himself were stepping into the speech: 'it might seem as though I'm offering you a catalogue of fantasy, but there's truth in it'.

As a form develops a history, it gathers associations. Blank verse acquired an implication of grandeur from its associations with epic and tragedy; to write in the form became implicitly to make a claim about your status as a poet and the dignity of your subject matter. 'What we mean by blank verse is verse unfallen, uncurst; verse reclaim'd, reinthron'd in the true language of the gods', declared Edward Young in his *Conjectures on Original Composition* (1759).[57] So when Anna Laetitia Barbauld, in 'Washing Day' (1797), uses blank verse to describe the communal laundry days she participated in with her mother as a child, she develops a tension between her topic and the exalted associations her form had acquired. The poem is pulled between mocking the idea that such mundane occurrences could become the subject for poetry and making a claim for the dignity of ordinary lives. It begins with an amused depiction of the Muses descending from high-flown concerns:

> The Muses are turned gossips; they have lost
> The buskin'd[25] step, and clear high-sounding phrase,
> Language of gods. Come, then, domestic Muse,
> In slip-shod measure loosely prattling on
> Of farm or orchard, pleasant curds and cream,
> Or drowning flies, or shoe lost in the mire
> By little whimpering boy, with rueful face;
> Come, Muse, and sing the dreaded Washing-Day.

The verse turns aside the opportunity for 'high-sounding phrases'. The opening line offers no grand pronouncement, but rather a throwaway reflection which is finished before the line is over; the prose rhythms of the line ('The **Mus**es are **turned gos**sips; they have **lost**') want to pull away rather than receive emphasis from the underlying metrical order. The syntax of the sentence as a whole is loosely strung, its last clause, 'Language of gods', hangs limply over the line ending, rather than marking any achieved finale. But for all the lines seem to speak about creative decline (read as a stand-alone unit, the opening line sounds like it is announcing a defeat), the verse settles into a cadence which starts to discover the virtues of the 'domestic Muse',

[25] a fine, knee-high boot or stocking worn by actors in classical tragedy

'prattling on' fluently through its accounts of a rural scene and flowing naturally through the iambic 'measure' without any disruptive metrical events. Barbauld inhabits her blank verse with an amused self-mockery, as though in fancy dress, as when in the poem's final verse paragraph, she describes how she used to 'sit me down, and ponder much / Why washings were'. And yet, in coming back down to earth, the poetry discovers an authentic accent in sending up its own poetic pretensions. 'Earth, air, and sky, and ocean hath its bubbles, / And verse is one of them – this most of all', the poem ends, looking scornfully at its own accomplishment. The final line discovers a punctured shape. You can feel a discrepancy between the natural emphasis of the prose rhythm, 'And **verse** is **one** of them – **this most** of **all**', where the first phrase withers to a close and the heavily stressed final clause turns finally on the poem's own imaginative liberties and the more regular spacing of stresses required by the metre: 'And **verse** | is **one** | of **them** – | this **most** | of **all**'. Either we tilt our voice towards the prose reading, ending the poem on a shrug, or we uphold the metre to the end of the line, as though fulfilling a contractual obligation.

Blank verse endures because of the vocal and tonal pliability which Barbauld demonstrates. It affords a huge range of possibilities. The question to contemplate is how a poet's handling of the medium marries with the subject matter. Here is the same passage of the *Aeneid* as Howard translates, in a version by David Ferry (2017):

> And as he says these words he drags old Priam,
> Trembling and shaking and slipping in the blood
> That was pouring out of the body of his son,
> To the high altar; and there he clutches him by
> The hair with his left hand and with his right hand
> Raises his glittering sword, and plunges it in,
> Up to the hilt, into his side.

These lines show Ferry's feeling for blank verse as a medium which allows 'room for syntactical manipulation, room for – and a susceptibility to – tonal variation, variations in the degrees of pressure of emphasis on the "weak" syllables in the iambic feet and on the "strong" syllables as well, often subtle, sometimes introspective, while continuing to be regular iambic pentameter events'.[58] Ferry deviates freely from the iambic norm. '**Tremb**ling and **shak**ing and **slip**ping **in** the **blood**', for instance, moves with a predominantly dactylic cadence, skidding across the iambic pulse that we expect. The next line, 'That was **pour**ing **out** of the **bod**y **of** his **son**', expands iambs into anapaests, achieving a fluidity in accordance with

Ferry's sense of the pentameter as a line in which 'iambic events naturally dominate, with anapaestic events as naturally occurring'[59] and in mimicry of the horror it describes. Ferry defies our expectations that there will be a strong stress at the end of a line as he describes how Pyrrhus 'clutches him by / The hair', where one can almost feel the flimsiness of Priam's bending neck in the ease of the enjambment. The next enjambed line coincides with an inverted stress that lends dramatic power to Pyrrhus' sword 'Raised' for the slaughter. Enjambments also allow Ferry to discover rhythmic subunits within the iambic grid. The three phrases at the end of the sentence are given remorseless symmetry: '**plung**es | it **in**, / **Up** to | the **hilt**, | **in**to | his **side**.'

Is the Poem in Rhyming Couplets?

Another common form in English is the rhyming couplet. Couplets are sequences of paired rhyming lines. Again, the form's simplicity is at the heart of its adaptability, and in reading poems in couplets it pays to ask the same questions as one might of blank verse: how has the poet achieved a distinctive pattern of syntax, rhythm, and lineation within the demands of the form? Couplets are common in tetrameters and pentameters, and to compare the impact of the two is to feel how metre affects the shape and possibility of poetic expression. Consider the use to which Winthrop Mackworth Praed puts tetrameter couplets in dramatising the attempts of a tedious poet to woo the heroine in 'Laura' (1820) alongside Lucy Hutchinson's appeal for divine inspiration at the start of her epic retelling of the book of Genesis, *Order and Disorder* (1679). Here is Praed:

> 'Laura – I perish for your sake,' –
> (Here he digress'd, about a lake);
> 'The charms thy features all disclose,' –
> (A simile about a rose);
> 'Have set my very soul on fire,' –
> (An episode about his lyre);
> 'Though you despise – I still must love,' –
> (Something about a turtle dove) . . .

And here is Hutchinson:

> In these outgoings would I sing his praise,
> But my weak sense with the too glorious rays
> Is struck with such confusion that I find
> Only the world's first Chaos in my mind,

Where light and beauty lie wrapped up in seed
And cannot be from the dark prison freed
Except that Power by whom the world was made
My soul in her imperfect strugglings aid,
Her rude conceptions into forms dispose,
And words impart which may those forms disclose.

Praed finds in the tetrameter couplet a form suitable for joking. His lines bounce between the overblown statements of a lover and snapshots of his predictable, clichéd behaviour. In Hutchinson's pentameter meanwhile, the rhymes feel less noticeable, since they are spaced out by an extra foot. The more fluid and elastic movement of her syntax shapes the lines' effort to clarify the 'confusion' of the 'world's first Chaos', until the endstopped final lines afford more prominence to the shaping structure of the couplet, as though the prayer to God to give form to her 'rude conceptions' were already starting to be answered. We feel in Hutchinson's lines the parallels between divine and poetic creation. This is not to say that all tetrameter couplets will produce the levity characteristic of Praed's verse, nor that all pentameter couplets will move with Hutchinson's winding grandeur, but the comparison does begin to suggest something of the innate tendencies and directions of each form. It is hard to imagine pentameter couplets skipping along like Praed's tetrameters, and it's likewise hard to imagine the tetrameter achieving the searching dignity of Hutchinson's lines.

Rhyming couplets may be *closed*, where the syntax is contained within each couplet pair (as in Praed's lines), or *open*, where the sense overspills the bounds of the rhymes (the enjambment through the second to fourth lines of Hutchinson's poem would be a good example of this). Like the individual pentameter line in blank verse, the couplet is a structure which a poet can accentuate or work against. Closed couplets emphasise the epigrammatic potential of the form – its ability to shape language into snappy, memorable, self-contained units. Often – as in Praed – this entails a sense of balance, or call-and-response, between endstopped lines. But even within enclosed couplets there is ample scope for expressive variation, as Robert Herrick shows in his tiny poem 'Dreams' (1648):

Here we are all by day; by night we're hurl'd
By dreams, each one into a sev'ral world.

Rather than balancing one line against the next, Herrick has three phrases, of three, three, and then four metrical feet fill his couplet:

Here we are all by day;
by night we're hurl'd By dreams,
each one into a sev'ral world.

The first clause keeps its feet on the ground ('Here we are all . . . '); then comes a pause with the semi-colon and the caesura, after which the sentence stretches out, unfurling across the enjambment and skipping over a lighter, earlier caesura as it soars into 'a sev'ral world'.

Open couplets tend to propel rather than contain expression. Wordsworth, for all the fluency of his blank verse (see page 65), disliked the technique: 'Reading such verse produces in me a sensation like that of toiling in a dream, under the night-mair. The Couplet promises rest at agreeable intervals; but here it is never attained – you are mocked and disappointed from paragraph to paragraph.'[60] But restlessness might be just the effect a poet wants. Think of the 'confusion' and the search for a 'form' to embody the mind's 'rude conceptions' that animate Hutchinson's lines. As with blank verse, the best writing in couplets won't just fulfil the demands of the form but will exploit and extend the opportunities it affords. The opening lines of John Wilmot, Earl of Rochester's 'Satire Against Reason and Mankind' (c. 1674) seem almost to attack the structure that houses them:

Were I (who to my cost already am
One of those strange, prodigious creatures, man)
A spirit free to choose, for my own share,
What case of flesh and blood I pleased to wear,
I'd be a dog, a monkey, or a bear,
Or anything but that vain animal
Who is so proud of being rational.

Rochester was an infamous libertine at the court of Charles II. He valued instinct and impulse over rationality, and once claimed that 'for five years together he was continually Drunk' during his early twenties.[61] That transgressive energy and distrust of the abstract carries over into his poem, which deploys its heroic (i.e. iambic pentameter) couplets only to begin by surging iconoclastically over their bounds. Almost before the first foot is out of the way, Rochester is launching into a parenthesis, lamenting his containment within the group he is taking as his target: 'man'. The sentence only gets back on track at the start of the third line, as Rochester mockingly speculates what 'case of flesh and blood' he would adopt if he had the choice to be whatever he wanted – a dilemma matched in the struggle with form going on in the lines themselves. All the while, the rhymes that knit the verse together are close to bursting at the seams. 'Am' and 'man' is an awkward mis-hit (as though Rochester cannot bear to throw his lot in with the rest of humanity); 'share', 'wear', and 'bear' disrupt the couplet pattern with a triplet before it has even been established; 'animal' and 'rational' are again a suggestively imperfect match.

Like those in blank verse, poems in couplets are able to make changes in focus, emphasis, or approach through switches between paragraphs. After his initial iconoclastic burst, Rochester opens a new paragraph which starts to set out its case against human 'reason' in a more systematic way, and the couplets become more regular:

> The senses are too gross,[26] and he'll contrive
> A sixth, to contradict the other five,
> And before certain instinct, will prefer
> Reason, which fifty times for one does err;
> Reason, an *ignis fatuus*[27] in the mind,
> Which, leaving light of nature, sense, behind,
> Pathless and dangerous wand'ring ways it takes
> Through error's fenny bogs and thorny brakes;
> Whilst the misguided follower climbs with pain
> Mountains of whimseys, heaped in his own brain;
> Stumbling from thought to thought, falls headlong down
> Into doubt's boundless sea where, like to drown,
> Books bear him up awhile, and make him try
> To swim with bladders of philosophy;
> In hopes still to o'ertake th' escaping light;
> The vapour dances in his dazzling sight
> Till, spent, it leaves him to eternal night.

Here is a single sentence concertinaed out across seven couplets and a closing triplet. Couplets often enable such elongated sentences, working as building blocks of sense that can be piled up into larger structures. And we might notice that to preserve coherence throughout this accumulation, Rochester curtails the disregard for boundaries and regularity that animates his opening salvo. The end of every second line, closing each couplet, is marked off by a comma or semicolon. The metre, too, upholds this more regular progress: moments of deviation tend to come at the start of lines, at moments where Rochester inverts a foot at the same time as he is talking about the intellectual activity leading man astray, or the tangles into which it is leading him: '**Reas**on', '**Path**less'. In the first instance, one of the most lurching enjambments within the paragraph, the voice is coaxed into a sceptical emphasis on 'Reason', and the word is held up for scrutiny by

[26] imprecise [27] a will o' the wisp

its rhyme-like repetition in the same place at the start of the succeeding line; a similar technique of enjambment is repeated to different effect later in the passage when Rochester speaks of those who 'try | To swim with bladders of philosophy', where the effort to keep oneself afloat is felt in the transition across the line ending. A more elaborate rhythmic effect ripples through the lines '**Stumb**ling | from **thought** | to **thought**, | falls **head** | long **down** / In**to** | doubt's **bound** | less **sea** | where, **like** | to **drown**', where the enjambment within the couplet and the difficulty of following the iambic pulse through 'In**to** | doubts **bound**less **sea**' (the unaccented syllable of the second iamb, 'doubt', is more heavily stressed than the accented one of the first syllable, 'to') enacts the waywardness it describes. The sentence culminates in a triplet composed of two lightly stressed pentameters which quicken the pace (the prose rhythm would be 'In **hopes** still to o'er**take** th' es**cap**ing **light**; / The **vap**our **danc**es in his **dazz**ling **sight**', skipping over the metrical stresses in the middle of each line), before the momentum of the final line is slowed by the final caesura, its rhyme tracing the dimming of the supposed 'light' of reason into moral and intellectual 'night'.

Is the Poem Composed in Stanzas?

Blank verse and rhymed couplets both enable lengthy arguments, descriptions, or narratives to be built up: the formal pattern repeated every one or two lines breeds familiarity; there is no need to meet a new and unexpected requirement at every turn. When rhyming and metrical patterns become more elaborate, they become harder to ignore, more prominently part of a poem's immediate effect. The result, usually, is a verse form less obviously suited to a continuous development of thought and feeling; intricacies of design come to the fore; argument advances in discrete units. A poet may create metrical and rhyming patterns which play out over any number of lines – there is no need in principle for a poem to follow any repeated order – though repetition makes patterns easier to perceive and provides something regular for the poem to play variations against. Longer poems might be divided into sections or numbered parts which can help to structure our reading and offer resting places, like chapters of a novel (and in reading a longer or even mid-length poem it is always worth asking how these sections constitute a self-contained unit within the whole). There are so many feasible combinations of metre and rhyme scheme that it is difficult to generalise about any one impact or effect. The question to ask is always how the demands and possibilities created by a particular stanza form, in combination with a poem's concerns, allow a poem to achieve unique expressive shape. How does the medium match the matter? Arthur Symons's 'White Heliotrope' (1895) shows the workings of one among innumerable possible combinations:

The feverish room and that white bed,
  The tumbled skirts upon a chair,
  The novel flung half-open, where
Hat, hair-pins, puffs, and paints are spread;

The mirror that has sucked your face
  Into its secret deep of deeps,
  And there mysteriously keeps
Forgotten memories of grace;

And you half dressed and half awake,
  Your slant eyes strangely watching me,
  And I, who watch you drowsily,
With eyes that, having slept not, ache;

This (need one dread? nay, dare one hope?)
  Will rise, a ghost of memory, if
  Ever again my handkerchief
Is scented with White Heliotrope.

The discrete units into which Symons arranges the lines of his poem are known as *stanzas*. We call three-line stanzas tercets, four-line stanzas quatrains, five-line stanzas quintains, six-line stanzas sestets, and so on. The rhyming and metrical pattern within those stanzas may vary indefinitely. Particular stanza forms might also carry associations, depending upon how they have been used before. Symons is here using a fairly rare stanza form – *abba* quatrains for iambic tetrameter – which had famously been deployed by Alfred Tennyson earlier in the nineteenth century in his poem *In Memoriam* (1850). *In Memoriam* is a sombre poem in memory of Tennyson's friend Arthur Hallam, so it is provocative of Symons to put it to sexier effect in describing a remembered love affair.

Symons drapes a single sentence across the poem's four stanzas, resisting the impulse inherent in the *abba* structure towards self-enclosure at the end of this stanza (this rhyme pattern is sometimes called *envelope* rhyme). Yet within each unit the syntax achieves its own unique movement. The first stanza lists the contents of the room: the *abba* pattern is submerged beneath the bricolage of bedroom paraphernalia strewn across the surface (a disorder nicely caught in the enjambment into the cluttered final line). In the second stanza, the shape comes more into focus: the lines speak of a mirror that, in the past, has shown the reflection of a lover's face, and their 'mirrored' *abba* shape reflects that, drawing us into its 'deep of deeps' in its central couplet. A mirrored shape is at work in the third stanza, too, though it is differently achieved. The image of the two lovers watching each other is paralleled in the structure of Symons's syntax across the middle of the stanza: we see the 'eyes' of the girl watching the poet, who watches her with eyes that – held achingly open for the delayed *b* rhyme – 'ache'. The whole poem trembles between past and present as it dwells upon a memory that may be triggered again in the future, and the rhymes of the last stanza are in tune with this poise. Hallam, who Tennyson's *In Memoriam* had mourned, once remarked that, thanks to its manner of conducting our gaze forward and backward, 'rhyme has been said to contain in itself a constant appeal to Memory and Hope',[62] and Symons's lines are a good example of that. The *a* rhyme of Symons's closing stanza falls explicitly on 'hope', which waits in anticipation for the 'Heliotrope' that will bring the memory into flower; meanwhile the central rhyme sees 'if' catching with more incidental force against 'handkerchief' – the rhyme operating like the coincidence that it imagines.

The whole movement of the poem's *abba* stanzas involves rhymes coming together and then pulling apart: Symons finds a form that enacts the process of separation and yearned-for renewal at the poem's heart. Not all poems in *abba* quatrains will manifest this feeling; it is not an inherent property of the stanza. Rather it is a matter of how the formal structure operates in combination with the concerns of the poem, enabling the poet to realise one of its manifold possibilities. The marriage of form and argument in each poem will be unique.

Poetry in stanzas often involves the voice repeating itself, sometimes by returning to the same metrical or rhyming shape, sometimes by returning to the same line or phrase at regular intervals. This latter device is known as a *refrain*. Imaginatively handled, the very persistence of a refrain can carry expressive point; it asks us to think about the different ways in which the repeated line inhabits a poem's evolving circumstances. William Dunbar's 'Lament for the Makaris' (1508), for instance, an elegy for a succession of fellow poets, returns at the end of each stanza to the Latin phrase '*Timor mortis conturbat me*' ('the fear of death disturbs me'). The remorselessness of the refrain carries a reminder of the inescapability of death itself; however, the situation of the poem changes, the fear remains. In other instances, the refrain may remain constant, but its tone may change. The anonymous medieval lyric 'Alison' ('Bytweene Mersh and Averil') tells of a lover's infatuation with a girl whom he regards as 'the "semlokest [i. e. fairest] of alle thinge"'. The poem begins in joy but grows increasingly fraught and desperate as its stanzas progress, so it is with increasing irony that its chirpy refrain strikes up at the close of each stanza (the poem is in an alien-looking Middle English, but read it phonetically and you'll get a feel for its rhythms):

An hendy hap ichabbe yhent![28]
Ichot[29] from hevene it is me sent;
From alle wymmen mi love is lent
Ant lyht on[30] Alysoun.

This sounds buoyant, but on the back of the increasingly despairing portrait the poem paints of what it is to be in love, the buoyancy comes to seem a little crazed. Other poets might seek to introduce variation into the refrain itself. William Barnes's 'My Orchard in Linden Lea' (1859) is a celebration in Dorset dialect of the pleasures of rural retirement: each stanza winds round to a subtly altered refrain:

An' there vor me the apple tree
Do lean down low in Linden Lea.

Wi' fruit vor me, the apple tree
Do lean down low in Linden Lea.

To where, vor me, the apple tree
Do lean down low in Linden Lea.

Barnes introduces an extra mark of punctuation into the penultimate line each time round, slowing the poem down and allowing it to settle in to the rhythms of its environment.

A poet does not have to repeat the same metre and rhyme scheme in each stanza. Charlotte Mew often writes lyrics in stanzas which grow and morph out of an original order, finding new shapes and movements responsive to shifting feelings and apprehensions of experience:

A quoi bon dire[31]

Seventeen years ago you said
Something that sounded like Good-bye:
And everybody thinks you are dead
But I.

So I as I grow stiff and cold
To this and that say Good-bye too;
And everybody sees that I am old
But you.

[28] I have received good fortune [29] I know [30] alights on [31] What good is there in saying

And one fine morning in a sunny lane
Some boy and girl will meet and kiss and swear
That nobody can love their way again
While over there
You will have smiled, I shall have tossed your hair.

If we ask how this poem (1916) apprehends so movingly the sense that a love affair is at once unique and something that replays itself across history, one answer has to be that it is to do with the pattern of repetition and variation across its stanzas. The first two stanzas tell a riddling story. One possibility is to interpret the first stanza's 'you said / Something that sounded like Good-bye' as a euphemism for death, and to read the thought offered in the second stanza that 'everybody sees that I am old / But you' as extending a curious form of consolation – at least the lover hasn't had to live to see the speaker ageing. Alternatively, 'everyone thinks that you are dead' might be read as implying a withdrawal from the public world into a relationship, and the observation in the second stanza as indicating a lover's intensity of focus on their beloved. Either way, the intimacy of the love affair is mirrored in the nearly matched shape of the stanzas. Both are rhymed *abab*. In the first, three lines of iambic pentameter are followed by a single-foot iambic line; in the second, the pattern is the same, apart from a pentameter third line, where the first stanza, omitting a 'that' which would have allowed it, too, to fall into a neat pentameter, offers something far less metrically clear-cut; the curt rhythm of the dimeter final lines, 'But I' and 'But you', shear the lovers off into their own world of private awareness.

The first two stanzas move from past to present; the third moves into the future and speculates about a couple who will feel that their love is similarly unique. In doing so it shifts to a pattern which remembers, but varies, that of the first two stanzas: five lines, rhymed *ababb*, all iambic pentameters apart from a penultimate dimeter. The opening out of the lines from one foot to five across the final stanza break corresponds with a surprising brightening of feeling in a lyric that might have seemed to be heading towards a downcast conclusion. Future experiences of love might replicate ours in rough outline, the poem seems to say, but will never be exactly the same. Yet this is as much a case for celebration as for lament: it is proof of each love affair's individuality. As it inhabits the evolving form, the writing apprehends the simultaneous truthfulness and irony of the lovers' confidence 'That nobody can love their way again'.

Is the Poem in Free Verse?

The influential critic F. R. Leavis wrote in 1932 that 'All that we can fairly ask of the poet is that he shall show himself to have been fully alive in our time. The evidence will be in the very texture of his poetry'.[63] The remark contains an important truth about the formal 'texture' of all poetry: rhymes, rhythms, movements, and structures are not just decoration, but rather the very substance of a poet's response to experience. Leavis felt that his 'time' was one marked by a particularly strong sense of fracture and dislocation, and by an increasing awareness of psychological complexity to which the inherited structures of metre and rhyme, exhausted by familiarity, had become incapable of responding. The irregularity of Mew's poem can be understood as part of a larger effort at the start of the twentieth century to find forms and 'textures' responsive to the rapidly shifting, disorderly nature of modern experience. Poets increasingly sought to discover unique, often fragmentary, shapes of expression by deviating entirely from metrical or formal norms. The logical extension of this pursuit of irregularity is a verse which eschews regular pattern altogether: what is known as *free verse*. Free verse doesn't mean the absence of form, but rather the pursuit of a form whose shape and movement is not predetermined and is free to follow closely the contours of thought, feeling, and experience rather than the stipulations of any metrical or rhyming pattern. It finds a rhythm and a pattern of its own.

Verse can be irregular without being 'free'. Here are some lines from the start of T. E. Brown's 'Dartmoor: Sunset at Chagford' (1900):

Is it ironical, a fool enigma,
This sunset show?
The purple stigma,
Black mountain cut upon a saffron glow–
Is it a mammoth joke,
A riddle put for me to guess,
Which having duly honoured, I may smoke,
And go to bed,
And snore,
Having a soothing consciousness
Of something red?
Or is it more?
Ah, is it, is it more?

The presence of rhyme and metre mean that it would not be accurate to call this verse 'free', but it nevertheless approaches the distinctive 'texture'

Leavis had in mind: the patterns of lineation and rhyme move unpredictably, in sympathy with the wavering attitudes of the poet as he tries to determine the significance of the sunset. The impulse to dismiss the beauty as a trivial 'riddle' sees the lines dwindle to a monometer ('And snore'); the yearning suspicion that the sight might communicate something 'more' (the presence of God, say) sees the lines expand, accompanied by the reiterative energy of the rhyming couplet, at the end of the paragraph.

For a more authentically free verse, uncoupled from rhyme and metre, we might compare Walt Whitman's description of the waves in 'After the Sea-Ship' (1855):

Waves of the ocean bubbling and gurgling, blithely prying,
Waves, undulating waves, liquid, uneven, emulous waves,
Toward that whirling current, laughing and buoyant, with curves,
Where the great vessel sailing and tacking displaced the surface,
Larger and smaller waves in the spread of the ocean yearnfully flowing,
The wake of the sea-ship after she passes, flashing and frolicsome under the sun,
A motley procession with many a fleck of foam and many fragments,
Following the stately and rapid ship, in the wake following.

These lines have a rhythm, which we cannot help but pick up as we read them aloud. And they are flecked with fragments of metrical regularity as they catch the motion of the waters ('**li**quid, un | **ev**en, | **em**ulous | **waves**'; '**flash**ing and | **fro**licsome | **un**der the | **sun**'). But their rhythm is not underpinned by any consistent metrical scheme: for all the incantatory buoyancy, we cannot sustain a regular pulse in reading the lines, nor is the number of beats along each line consistent. Each line has its own self-generated rhythm, appropriate, perhaps, to the sense that the poem might function as an image for the democratic ship of state, in which the distinctive identity of each citizen harmonises into the whole. Yet the lines achieve energy and coherence from the way they intermittently approach a more regular pulse. The effect would seem a good instance of what one of the poets Leavis had in mind, T. S. Eliot, said of free verse: 'The ghost of some simple metre should lurk behind the arras in even the "freest" verse; to advance menacingly as we doze, and withdraw as we rouse'[64] (the opening lines of Eliot's 'The Love Song of J. Alfred Prufrock' (1915), teasing us with the jauntiness of a conventional 'Love Song', before meandering around a hazily apprehensible iambic pentameter, would be another example).

Styles of free verse are as various as the poets who write it. D. H. Lawrence's 'Elemental' (1929) follows a more wildly irregular course than Whitman:

Why don't people leave off being lovable
or thinking they are lovable, or wanting to be lovable,
and be a bit elemental instead?

Since man is made up of the elements
fire, and rain, and air, and live loam
and none of these is lovable
but elemental,
man is lop-sided on the side of the angels.

I wish men would get back their balance among the elements
and be a bit more fiery, as incapable of telling lies
as fire is.

I wish they'd be true to their own variation, as water is,
which goes through all stages of steam and stream and ice
without losing its head.

I am sick of lovable people,
somehow they are a lie.

The impact is blunt, even bad-mannered: there is no effort to fade in and out of metrical regularity, as in Whitman's lines. Instead, true to its theme, the poem eschews any attempt to ingratiate itself with an audience or conform to a pre-existing formal pattern, finding a rhythm 'true to its own variation'. 'It is the hidden *emotional* pattern that makes poetry, not the obvious form', Lawrence once wrote, and his poem allows the force of argument to surface above the discipline of form.[65] The question that is always worth raising about this sort of formal freedom, though, is how, when the absence of regular pattern is the whole point, does a poem distinguish itself from being simply chopped-up prose? We can identify some principles at work: the poem moves from question to justification, to expression of desire, to assertion. Each sentence forms its own stanza. Ideas are worked out and given space to resonate. Lineation directs emphasis. Of the poem's sixteen lines, six end with the words 'element' or 'elemental' or 'loveable': not quite rhymes, but words with enough aural similarity to clang discordantly against one another in a way that feels like the inverse of rhyme (hear also how 'lie', 'lies', 'ice', and 'is' jar and jostle). As it cycles between these line endings, we can hear the poem shuttling between the two poles of its argument (humans are too ingratiating; they should be tougher). The poem's length and shaping loosely calls to mind the form of a sonnet. The form may be standing a long way behind the arras, but Lawrence's arrangement serves as a kind of rough sketch of the Shakespearean pattern: it is as though this were the draft – or elemental structure – of some ideas later to be tidied up and knocked into shape. The last two lines exist in parallel with a closing couplet: but instead of offering up a witty aperçu or graceful about-turn, they drive home Lawrence's distaste without ceremony.

Free verse is capable of dexterity as well as brashness. Alice Oswald's long poem *Dart* (2002) shows how free verse can operate as a principle of larger poetic structures. The poem traces the river Dart in Devon from source to mouth, and finds a form that can give voice to the river and the different lives it sustains along the course of its development. The poem takes its formal orientation from the very contours of the river itself. In the following passage the poem is moving through the river in its upper course, and encounters a walker:

> What I love is one foot in front of another. South-south-west and down the contours. I go slipping between Black Ridge and White Horse Hill into a bowl of the moor where echoes can't get out
>
> listen,
> a
> lark
> spinning
> around
> one
> note
> splitting
> and
> mending
> it
>
> and I find you in the reeds, a trickle coming out of a bank, a foal of a river
>
> one step-width water
> of linked stones
> trills in the stones
> glides in the trills
> eels in the glides
> in each eel a fingerwidth of sea

The impact is physical as well as intellectual. The writing affects us as much through its movement as through what is said. It seems to map the progress along the river, from the prose which enacts the 'one foot in front of another' progress of the walker, to the sudden shot of lyricism that sends a sentence spinning one word at a time over the line breaks like the note that the lark 'splits and mends', back to another trickle of prose as the walker's monologue tries to start up again, before the poem gets diverted back to the course of the channel once more, picking up momentum like the verse itself as it finds a form in which words cascade from one short line to the next. Here a metre of sorts establishes itself, at least as the lines '**trills** in | the **stones** / **glides** in | the **trills** / **eels** in | the **glides**' sway between trochee and iamb. The shape lives up to the demand made by the American poet William Carlos Williams, which offers a touchstone for thinking about all poets' dealings with form: 'It isn't what he *says* that counts as a work of art, it's what he makes, with such intensity of perception that it lives with an intrinsic movement of its own to verify its authenticity.'[66]

Who Is Speaking?

'All voices should be read as the river's mutterings', Oswald says in a headnote to *Dart*; a later line asks 'whose voice is this who's speaking in my larynx' (Oswald's sparse punctuation leaves it unclear whether that is two questions or one). To speak of a poem as having a 'voice' is to acknowledge that poetry thrills and consoles us because it creates a sense of human presence. Every poem presents itself as a record of someone (or something) speaking – telling stories, reflecting on experience, describing the world, expressing feeling, contemplating an issue, arguing. And just as what we enjoy in the company of friends is not just what they say but their distinctive way of saying things, the habits and timbre of the voice in which their character resides, the same is true of poetry. As Glyn Maxwell says: 'the form and tone and pitch of any poem should coherently express the presence of a human creature'.[67]

The usual recommendation is not to equate this 'human creature' with the poet. This is sensible advice on the whole, since even in a lyric poem, the voice on the page is never simply a transcription of a writer's speaking voice or a mouthpiece for their attitudes, experiences, or judgements. A poem imagines a voice in an imagined situation. And as we observed when thinking about the question of what a poem is 'about', that fact offers the poet the opportunity to create a gap between themselves and the voice of the poem. We should not assume that a poet entirely endorses what a poem says; a poem may be 'about' itself; it might invite us to look sceptically as well as admiringly at its argument. At the close of the second stanza of 'September 1, 1939' (1939), W. H. Auden presents us with a speaker sitting in a New York bar on the eve of World War II, asserting that while 'Accurate scholarship' can unearth in all their nuances the causes of Hitler's ascent to power, the real reasons can be pinned down in terms of pithy common sense: evil will be answered with evil.[68] One reading of the lines is that they are a 'low point' in the poem because, as Ian

Samson says, they indulge in 'the simplifying logic of the child' and exonerate atrocities.[69] But this is to suppose that a poet always advocates the perspectives a poem voices. Even when written in the first person, a poem allows the poet to put their thoughts and feelings at a distance and generates the potential for ironic self-awareness about their limitations. Auden does not say, 'here is the truth of the matter, and you must see things this way', as he might if he were giving a speech; he says, 'here is one way I can imagine myself putting it: what are the insights and flaws of this perspective?' Even as he 'indulges' in this 'simplifying logic', Auden's neat rhythms and pat rhymes suggest he knows that folk wisdom may be glib as well as penetrating. In the preceding lines, he even acknowledges that the moral code he is falling back on is one learned by schoolchildren, with all that suggests about its naivety as well as its innocence and clear-sightedness. The lines are as much about the temptations as the truthfulness of the perspective they adopt. Yeats's reflection that we make poetry 'out of the quarrel with ourselves' (see page 33) is pertinent here. The relationship between the poet and the voice of a poem, in the richest and subtlest poetry, is often shifting and provisional. A poem can imagine a voice in order to question as well as endorse it.

A poet, Yeats also said, 'is never the bundle of accidence and incoherence that sits down to breakfast; he has been reborn as an idea, something intended, complete'.[70] Everyday identities are refashioned in verse; a poet's biographical identity and personality are separate from those they assume in a work of art. Still, there are degrees of distance between the coffee-splattered 'bundle of accidence and incoherence' and the poetic identity that it creates, and the personalities that a poet imagined may speak with varying degrees of distinctiveness. At one end of the spectrum, a poet might bring the voice of the poem into close contact with their own personality. The idiosyncratic punctuation and fractured phrasing of Emily Dickinson's poems, for example, reflect an effort to find a language true to the unique rhythms of her feelings and perceptions:

They shut me up in Prose –
As when a little Girl
They put me in the Closet –
Because they liked me 'still' –

Still! Could themself have peeped –
And seen my Brain – go round –
They might as wise have lodged a Bird
For Treason – in the Pound –

Himself has but to will
And easy as a Star
Look down upon Captivity –
And laugh – No more have I –

Here is a fairly common theme – the struggle of an individual consciousness against external constraint. But the success of Dickinson's handling of this theme – and her success in the face of that constraint – depends upon her ability to create a voice that gives the situation a personal edge. The poem (1862) works by convincing us of the uniqueness of its voice. To start with, it is odd, from a technical perspective, to think of being 'shut up' in prose rather than verse, given the laws – of rhyme, rhythm, metre, etc. – that govern the latter. But Dickinson finds her own voice against the grain of constraint. The poem is testimony to the liberating power of form. The process starts to happen in the break between the first and second stanzas, and in the repetition that turns the oppressor's word 'still' sardonically back upon them. Notice how differently the lines ask us to intone the word: the first time plain, emotionless, coloured by the despondency of conforming to the demands made by the social world, the second incredulous, exasperated, full of protest. From here, a more individual rhythm and idiom takes hold, as Dickinson's dashes and deviations from common phrasing allow us to 'peep' into the quirky intensity with which her 'Brain – go[es] round'. There is the word 'themself', which we have to read as meaning something like 'they themselves'. Its effect is twofold. First, it further anonymises this faceless 'They' who have been trying to shut Dickinson up; second, it asserts the peculiarity of Dickinson's own voice as it rises up against them. Or listen to the effect of the idiosyncratic dashes with which Dickinson starts spacing her stanzas. What is the difference between 'And seen my brain go round' and 'And seen my Brain – go round –'? One is smooth, orderly; the other is abrupt, angular, capturing the movements of a febrile inner life.

Notice, too, how Dickinson's words seem to wriggle free from the confines of the rhyme scheme, breaking out of the *abcb* pattern of the first stanza (though even there the *b* rhyme of 'Girl' and 'still' only keeps a fragile hold, and the *a* and *c* rhymes, 'Prose' and 'Closet' have a wobbly visual, if not aural, resemblance), and seemingly abandoning any pattern by the last. The syntax in the last stanza is peculiar. The apparently fragmentary sentence with which the poem ends, 'No more have I –', is a good instance of the power of ambiguity that we talked about above. It hovers between triumph and exhaustion: it might say that Dickinson herself has no more difficulty than a 'Bird' does in 'Look[ing] down upon Captivity' through simple force of 'will', or it might be read as saying something like 'I've no more left – my spirit is crushed'. The uncertainty is caught in the uneasy harmony of 'captivity' and 'I' in the poem's final rhyme position: a less-than-full rhyme which pulls into focus the poem's central concern with the struggle between independence and constraint and leaves it unresolved. Even if the final line is read as an admission of defeat, the very idiosyncrasy of its movement represents a victory for Dickinson's effort to impress her personality on her style.

We relish, in Dickinson's poem, the sense of individual personality. That is not to say that we have to read the poem as a piece of autobiography, but it is to say that it is part of the poem's achievement to create the impression of an individual character. The writing shows life from a unique perspective and dramatises the struggle to impress that perspective upon the texture of the poem's language. Alternatively, a poet might project a voice out from themselves: either to take on the voice of another individual or just to adopt a more impersonal accent, attempting to speak of universal concerns in a manner free from personal idiosyncrasies. Here are two stanzas from Thomas Nash's 'A Litany in Time of Plague', a song written over two and a half centuries earlier than Dickinson's poem, and originally included in his play *Summer's Last Will and Testament* (1592):

Beauty is but a flower
Which wrinkles will devour;
Brightness falls from the air;
Queens have died young and fair;
Dust hath closed Helen's[32] eye.
I am sick, I must die.
Lord, have mercy on us!

Strength stoops unto the grave,
Worms feed on Hector[33] brave;
Swords may not fight with fate,
Earth still holds ope her gate.
'Come, come!' the bells do cry.
I am sick, I must die.
Lord, have mercy on us!

The poem brings to life another conventional theme – the brevity of human life – and does so, like Dickinson's poem, from a first-person perspective. But that perspective is granted far less particularity and serves far more as a conduit for an awareness common to all. That is not to say that the voice lacks expressive character: the trimeter rhythms, repeatedly allowing the falling cadence of an inverted opening foot to pass into an

[32] the most beautiful woman in ancient Greece [33] a Trojan prince and warrior

iambic upswing, so that no steady rhythm establishes itself before each line fades, give the voice compelling, saddened movement. But to ask, 'who is speaking?' in a poem such as this is to reveal the way in which the writing places emphasis not on the expression of a particular individual's experience or sensibility but rather on the plainspoken expression of general, tragic truths. The voice is no less sincere in what it says than Dickinson's poem, but it is less concerned to seem the authentic voice of an individual. The expression consists of lucid statements, delivered line by line, in common idioms. The imagery distils a vision of life with restrained pathos. Indeed, the word 'I' doesn't appear in each stanza until the refrain. When it does appear, it gives urgency to the poem's expressions of suffering by grounding them in a localised perspective, but it also reminds us of the individual's existence within a broader human community of suffering: within a line of the word's appearance, the poem is speaking not of 'I' but of 'us'.

Does the Poem Dramatise a Voice?

The difference between Nash's and Dickinson's approaches is not just between the accents in which their poems speak but also between the nature of the experience they record. We might frame it in terms of the distinction Robert Browning, writing in the middle of the nineteenth century, made between 'subjective' and 'objective' poets. The writing of the 'subjective' poet, says Browning, is 'an abstraction of his personality', 'the very radiance and aroma' of which is infused into the verse and the vision it presents; the 'objective' poet, meanwhile, writes 'with an immediate reference, in every case, to the common eye and apprehension of his fellow men'.[71] Dickinson is inward, idiosyncratic, personal, offering us truth to individual experience; Nash is plain, austere, appealing for validity to a common apprehension of the world. In thinking about the voice of a poem, that is, we are not only thinking about the character it presents, but the perspective afforded by that character.

Browning himself was master of a genre, the *dramatic monologue*, which calls on both 'subjective' and 'objective' faculties. In a dramatic monologue, the poet adopts the voice and perspective of a fictionalised character in an imaginary situation, usually speaking to an implied audience (though sometimes we might also find them soliloquising). The genre simultaneously exhibits an ability to match language to personal character, and the capacity to cast the imagination out into a voice beyond the self. The effect is as though a speech has been wrenched from a play, though in this instance all characterisation and information necessary to understand the speech is contained within the poem itself. It is a reminder of how much character is not just communicated by but embodied in a voice. One of Browning's masterpieces in the mode is 'Andrea Del Sarto' (1855), a poem spoken in the voice of an early sixteenth-century Florentine painter, as he addresses his wife, Lucrezia. The lines below come from the beginning of the poem, which begins with del Sarto agreeing to do some work for one of Lucrezia's friends and wishing for an evening's peace with his wife:

> But do not let us quarrel any more,
> No, my Lucrezia; bear with me for once:
> Sit down and all shall happen as you wish.
> You turn your face, but does it bring your heart?
> I'll work then for your friend's friend, never fear,
> Treat his own subject after his own way,
> Fix his own time, accept too his own price,
> And shut the money into this small hand
> When next it takes mine. Will it? tenderly?
> Oh, I'll content him,—but to-morrow, Love!
> I often am much wearier than you think,
> This evening more than usual, and it seems
> As if—forgive now—should you let me sit
> Here by the window with your hand in mine
> And look a half-hour forth on Fiesole,
> Both of one mind, as married people use,
> Quietly, quietly the evening through,
> I might get up to-morrow to my work
> Cheerful and fresh as ever. Let us try.

A good deal of the art of a dramatic monologue depends upon the way it manages to create the impression of somebody in conversation, and that impression depends on the way Browning represents the vocal tics, habits, and hesitations that one would usually purge from a poem. The art depends, too, on a creative realisation of the fact that writing can leave open multiple possibilities of voicing and intonation. As Eric Griffiths observes, these lines are 'magnificently dramatic; they open themselves to a variety of interpretations in performance, and so show a many-angled realization of what they record'.[72]

Let's sketch out some of the principal ways in which the impression of spoken character takes hold. First, there is the broader shape and situation of the poem: there's no sense here of a thought or feeling being worked through with a recognisable beginning, middle, and end. Instead, we're thrust right into the middle of a conversation, and have to scrabble together all the information necessary to flesh out an understanding of the scene as we go:

> But do not let us quarrel any more,
> No, my Lucrezia; bear with me for once:

To begin a poem with the word 'But' is to imply that its opening words rebound against something that has been said prior to the poem's start. Immediately a situation (a couple arguing) and the attitude of a listener (impatience, for whatever reason, with the speaker) are implied. Then there is the question of how we are to imagine these lines being spoken. Does that 'No' round aggressively on Lucrezia: 'No . . . bear with *me* for once . . . '? Or is it more tender and assuaging: 'No, let's not quarrel, trust me . . . '? Or is it businesslike and confident: 'No, let's get on with things . . . '? Those vocal habits – the interjections, hesitations, and exclamations, which would not usually appear in a lyric poem in the first person, but which in dramatic monologues become a crucial part of granting the voice a living presence – often carry flexible possibilities of interpretation.

There is a similar ambiguity a few lines later:

> I'll work then for your friend's friend, never fear,
> Treat his own subject after his own way,
> Fix his own time, accept too his own price,
> And shut the money into this small hand
> When next it takes mine.

How are we supposed to hear 'never fear'? Does it mean 'I'll work for your friend's friend, rest assured . . . '? Or does it mean 'I'll work for him, I won't worry about what motivations might lie behind it, I'll treat the subject how he wants it treated . . . '? Again, what might seem an inconsequential colloquialism creates ambiguity about the precise significance of the lines.

Another aspect central to the drama of the poem is the silence of its addressee, or interlocutor. How are we to envisage Lucrezia responding to del Sarto's questions?

> You turn your face, but does it bring your heart?

> Will it? Tenderly?

The poem asks us to imagine the eloquence of Lucrezia's silence: does she smile? Ignore the question? Hesitate? What might each possibility mean for del Sarto? Just as Browning imagines himself into his persona, we are invited to imagine ourselves into the position of the interlocutor or addressee.

A third aspect of the lines' artistry is what we might call their 'movement' – the way in which the language and the syntax operate to convey the expressive sweep and cadence of speech. This is part of what the poem shows us: that a person's character is embodied in the way they speak as much as in what they say. Consider the progress of the last two sentences in the passage quoted, as del Sarto tentatively entertains the possibility of a peaceful evening. The lines convey a sense of weariness and sadness without directly expressing those emotions. They demonstrate the ways in which feelings conduct and are captured in the performance of the speaking voice. What creates the impression is, first, the little nervous colloquial touch – 'forgive now' – with which the speaker broaches the possibility of spending some quiet time together (again, the character's speech indicates something of his addressee's response); then there is the slow, dragging progress of the passage through 'quietly, quietly', dwelling on the possibility of peace, and the modesty of what the lines finally come round to ask for. This long slow movement then plays off against a far shorter appeal: 'Let us try'. Again, the phrase raises questions of where emphasis might fall. If the heavier stress falls on the 'Let', the sentence shows del Sarto tenderly imploring his lover; if 'try' is emphasised, it gives a feeling that he doesn't hold out much hope for the possibility. The passage, then, is exemplary of dramatic monologue, in that it is a supreme instance of poetry asking us to listen to the way people speak and to think about what that particular way of speaking might convey. It shows us how much of our character and our relationship with others is carried on the voice – and how crucial voice is as a human and therefore poetic instrument.

Robert Langbaum observed in a famous account of the genre that, by putting us in the position of listener, the dramatic monologue invites both sympathy and judgement: sympathy, in that we sit up close to a character, gaining privileged insight into their thoughts and behaviour; judgement, in that the poet stands at an acknowledged distance from the voice of the poem, and since the behaviour a dramatic monologue presents is often morally complex.[73] The conflict between the two impulses is at its most acute and unnerving when a monologue affords proximity to a speaker whose behaviour is flawed or malicious. The poems of Ai Ogawa take the violence the form can do to our sensibilities to an extreme. Ai's 'The Kid' (1978) is written in the voice of a teenager who murders his parents and sister. The poem starts in a mundane setting, in which a boy is called by his father to help with some work on his car. The boy describes how he stands with a metal bar in his hand

> beside him, waiting, but he doesn't look up
> and I squeeze the rod, raise it, his skull splits open.
> Mother runs towards us. I stand still,
> Get her across the spine as she bends over him.

There is nothing of the rich conversational timbre of Browning's monologue here. The voice is depersonalised, brutally efficient: how rapidly the sentence passes from the description of the raising of the rod to the splitting of the skull, as though the deed were done before there was time to describe it being brought down; how cold, in context, is 'Get her'. The phrasing is less an insight into the nuances of the boy's character than a window on the awfulness of what he has committed. The kid then shoots his sister. The poem records one event after another in unflinching succession. At its close, the speaker's voice takes on a new force of character, as his sense of himself changes:

> Yeah. I'm Jack, Hogarth's son.
> I'm nimble, I'm quick.
>
> [. . .]
>
> I'm fourteen. I'm a wind from nowhere.
> I can break your heart.

The boy, like the poet, is playing a role: he sees himself as a sort of all-action hero, and there is perhaps a political point: the kid's behaviour has been shaped by the violence of the idols of film and popular culture. But is this enough to make us feel sympathy? The cockiness of the accent and the unsettling directness with which it speaks to us make that difficult. Ai presents no interlocutor, as in Browning's lines; instead, the voice speaks tauntingly out to us, the reader. The awfulness of the last line is that, contrary to the self-inflated heroic posturing that proceeds it, it is true: evil can break our heart, and what for us is bereavement is for the boy a boast.

Who Does the Poem Address?

'The Kid' is so troubling because it usurps the usual situation of the dramatic monologue to put us in the position of interlocutor. Expecting to observe a conversation, we become part of it. It is not always easy to decide whom a poem is addressing. The audience the voice of a poem imagines itself addressing will likely be different to the readership envisaged by the poet. In Browning's dramatic monologue, del Sarto addresses his wife; but she is a fictional figure, and it is only true on one level to say that she is the poem's intended audience: Browning is also writing with his nineteenth-century readership, and surely posterity, in mind. Other poems imagine a voice which doesn't seem to address anyone at all. The Victorian thinker John Stuart Mill said that lyric poetry exists in the condition of something being 'overheard', as though a poem was a way of letting us listen in on the poet's private reflections.[74] Yet such poems are still written to be read. One of the moving and generous things about all art is that it can never know all the audiences it cheers and consoles. We stand in relation to it as John Keats does to the mysterious figure of Moneta, the goddess of memory, when he gazes up at her eyes in *The Fall of Hyperion* (1819):

> they saw me not,
> But in blank splendour beam'd like the mild moon,
> Who comforts those she sees not, who knows not
> What eyes are upward cast.

Christopher Ricks writes beautifully, 'The consolation Keats here imagines, he at the same time provides; he comforts those he sees not, and this is of the essence of art'.[75]

Granted that all poetry behaves with serene blankness to the majority of its audience, to ask who the voice of a poem imagines itself addressing, even if it yields no clear answer, will always shed light on the situation a poem creates, the tact with which it fits itself to that situation, and the kind of utterance it makes. Who do we imagine is being addressed as we read the following short 'Monody' (1891) by Herman Melville?

> To have known him, to have loved him
> After loneness long;
> And then to be estranged in life,
> And neither in the wrong;
> And now for death to set his seal—
> Ease me, a little ease, my song!
>
> By wintry hills his hermit-mound
> The sheeted snow-drifts drape,
> And houseless there the snow-bird flits
> Beneath the fir-trees' crape:
> Glazed now with ice the cloistral vine
> That hid the shyest grape.

There is little sense that the poem is being spoken *to* anyone. It mutters its feelings to itself, and that sense of self-enclosure is the source of much of the poem's pathos: we feel that the voice could find no ear to which it is suited; it is essentially lonely. There is no sense of the speaker appealing for pity or advertising their grief; even the identity of the person being grieved for is kept secret (it was probably written for the novelist Nathaniel Hawthorne). The relationship is simply between the poet and his art; it is to his 'song' that Melville calls for 'ease'. Compare the impact with that of an earlier lyric of loss, Robert Herrick's 'Upon a Child that Died' (1648):

> Here she lies, a pretty bud,
> Lately made of flesh and blood,
> Who as soon fell fast asleep
> As her little eyes did peep.
> Give her strewings, but not stir
> The earth that lightly covers her.

Herrick's poem doesn't give any indication of being spoken to anyone specific, either: there is an appeal to a reader – 'Give her strewings' – but it is targeted at anyone who might be imagined to pass by. And yet, partly because of that awareness of at least the potential for an audience, the voice seems different, more public. Where Melville's poem seems to say to us, 'here is a speaker, pondering their feelings to themselves', Herrick's poem imagines putting a public face on its grief. The sadness of the poem is less personal, more a recognition of a shared human poignancy in the facts of loss. Herrick is concerned to address others, Melville to express himself.

Sometimes a poem will present itself as being addressed explicitly to someone or something – perhaps in tribute, appeal, query, mockery, or affection. A poem might even address its reader, offering direction about how it wants to be taken. Ben Jonson's epigram 'To the Reader' (1616) is an example:

> Pray thee, take care, that tak'st my book in hand
> To read it well: that is, to understand.

Every reader is both warned and welcomed by the poem; and to 'understand' the warning is to have fulfilled its demands. More commonly our position as reader will be that of bystander, and our response governed by how resourcefully the poem imagines the responsibilities and possibilities involved in addressing any particular object or individual. In Joanna Baillie's 'A Mother to her Waking Infant' (1790), we are invited to contemplate the ways in which a mother might relate to her child, and the ways in which speech might conduct that relationship:

> Perhaps when time shall add a few
> Short years to thee, thou'lt love me too;
> And after that, through life's long way
> Become my sure and cheering stay:
> Wilt care for me and be my hold,
> When I am weak and old.
>
> Thou'lt listen to my lengthened tale,
> And pity me when I am frail —
> But see, the sweepy spinning fly
> Upon the window takes thine eye.
> Go to thy little senseless play —
> Thou dost not heed my lay.

We are not far here from the dramatic monologue. One difference might be that the writing is concerned less with the revelation of a particular character than the demands made by any mother's effort to express her love for her child. And the relationship depends upon the fact that the child, as interlocutor, cannot reciprocate or even 'heed' what the poet is saying; words bounce off them. The success of the poem depends upon the way in which it discovers the potential for comedy as well as poignancy in being faced with the desire to communicate one's cares and anxieties to someone who can't even recognise, let alone return, one's affections. The lines are so attractive for the humour and sensitivity with which they realise the difficulties of bridging the gap between experience and infancy and the grace with which they realise that their reflections, as they tend towards self-pity, are not being listened to.

At an even more specific level, some poems address a named individual. Many of the love poems of the seventeenth-century poet Katherine Philips are addressed to Mary Awbrey, who often appears in the title of a poem under the initials 'M. A.', a shorthand which lends the expressions of affection a simultaneously private and public quality. What can we learn of Awbrey's character, and Philips's relationship to her, from the way in which she is addressed? There is a lovely interplay of formality and passion at the start of 'To Mrs Mary Awbrey at Parting' (1664), where accents of dry investigation yield to intense expressions of feeling:

> I have examin'd, and do find,
> Of all that favour me,

There's none I grieve to leave behind
  But only, only thee.
To part with thee I needs must dye,
Could parting separate thee and I.

It is a surprise to arrive at the fourth line, where what seems to be a slightly pompous piece of self-reflection is revealed to be a tender address to a loved one. The stanza tours the different registers and postures that intimacy with someone gives you the freedom to adopt. It moves from mock-scientific seriousness, to simple affection, to an eyebrow-raising elaboration and exaggeration: 'I'd die if we had to part – but that's impossible, because even if we part physically, we won't spiritually', the final couplet says. Philips's intimacy with Awbrey enables her to develop and extend her ideas with an irony that both revels in mutual affection and curtails sentimentality:

Our chang'd and mingled soules are grown
  To such acquaintance now,
That if each would resume their owne,
  Alas! we know not how.
We have each other so ingrost,
That each is in the union lost.

The solution to the fear of separation, with which the poem begins, has in itself become a source of worry: what if our souls are so intermingled that we've dissolved our individual identities? This is a genuine concern about any relationship, and yet such a sense of intimacy is the very condition that enables the speaker to address these anxieties to her lover. Asking who the poem addresses is crucial to understanding the way in which it matches its voice to its situation.

What Is the Poem's Tone?

The stanzas from Philips's poem are so beguiling because it is not easy to disentangle the feelings behind them. They seem to express impassioned commitment, but they also appear – how seriously it is hard to tell – troubled by the loss of selfhood implicit in romantic relationships. There is more uncertainty about how to take Philips's sentiments at the end of the poem, as she contemplates the eternal duration of the women's feeling for one another in a stanza that seems both tender and playful:

A dew shall dwell upon our tomb
  Of such a quality,

That fighting armies, thither come,
  Shall reconcilèd be.
Wee'l ask no epitaph, but say
Orinda and Rosania.

The statement that the women's love will have the power to reconcile warring armies is on the one hand testimony to the poem's strength of feeling; but on the other it stretches credibility in a way that is surely partly ironic (the suspicion is encouraged by the knowingly forced final rhyme: one has to say, 'Rosan-I-A', as the Beach Boys in 'Surfin' USA' sing 'Californ-I-A'). Even then, such playfulness may testify to and augment the feeling rather than undermine it: the expression of love is felt all the more securely for the knowledge that you can engage in such extravagance with someone who understands you.

To contemplate the attitude with which a line is spoken is to think about the poem's *tone*. Tone is a diffuse, slippery concept. It can reside in a poem's choice of language, its use of form, its approach to its subject. And it signals a series of mutually echoing qualities, as the following definition by J. A. Cuddon indicates: 'tone is the reflection of a writer's attitude (especially towards his readers), manner, mood and moral outlook in his work; even perhaps the way his personality pervades the work'.[76] To think about tone is to think about everything from how any given lines are tailored to their situation and audience, to the character of their speaker, to the whole outlook on experience which they embody. And yet, or perhaps because of, the way it pervades every aspect of a poem, to feel that one has attuned oneself to a poem's tone is to feel that one has got to the core of its perspective on the world. It is often a poet's characteristic tone – whether their view of life and manner of expressing it is tough-minded, compassionate, serene, exuberant, or whatever – that best describes what draws us to them. Tone distinguishes a poem; it describes its temperament, the way it bears up to experience. It says, 'take things – look at things – in this spirit'.

A comparison will help to bring the point out. Here are two stanzas on the way time slips through our fingers. First, from Praed's 'Good-Night to the Season' (1827):

Good-night to the Season!—another
  Will come, with its trifles and toys,
And hurry away, like its brother,
  In sunshine, and odour, and noise.
Will it come with a rose or a briar?
  Will it come with a blessing or curse?
Will its bonnets be lower or higher?

Will its morals be better or worse?
Will it find me grown thinner or fatter,
Or fonder of wrong or of right,
Or married, or buried?—no matter:
Good-night to the Season—good-night!

Second, from Byron's *Don Juan* (1822):

'Where is the World?' cries Young[34] 'at eighty? Where
The World in which a man was born?' Alas!
Where is the world of eight years past? 'Twas there –
I look for it – 'tis gone – a Globe of Glass!
Cracked, shivered, vanished, scarcely gazed on, ere
A silent change dissolves the glittering mass;
Statesmen, Chiefs, Orators, Queens, Patriots, Kings –
And Dandies, all are gone on the Wind's wings.

Both stanzas are about the rapid passing of time. Both square up to that rapidity with a bemused wonderment. Both deploy a stanza form which in its whirling rhymes catches the dizzying energy of time's passing. To regard the tone of either as anguished or sombre would evidently be to misjudge it. But their tone and temperament are not identical. For Praed, the passage of time is a matter of the pleasing transience of temporary fashions. His flurry of questions seems to suggest that nothing matters. Everything is reduced to the same level of triviality. The future may bring marriage or death. What will be will be. The tone has the breezy unconcern of the social world which the poem describes. And the writing seems to delight in as much as criticise that culture's trivialising impulse. The tone of Byron's lines, by contrast, suggests a deeper and richer response to experience. The picture of the world as a 'Globe of Glass' finds beauty, as well as a superficial thrill, in its transience; and, in combination with the searching rhymes, which seem constantly to want to hold experience still only to find it slipping through their fingers, finds pathos as well as pleasure in its ephemerality. 'I knew that nought was lasting, but now even / Change grows too changeable, without being new', Byron says in wearied, even hurt, accents a few stanzas later. It is true that Byron's stanza ends on a joke (the movement into the final line upsets the anticipated hierarchy), but it goes through a fuller range of responses to experience to get there.

Often, tone is difficult to pin down because it is ambiguous or evolves through a poem. Consider this inconstant poem on constancy by the seventeenth-century courtier John Suckling (1659):

[34] Edward Young, eighteenth-century poet

The Constant Lover

Out upon it! I have loved
Three whole days together;
And am like to love three more,
If it prove fair weather.

Time shall moult away his wings
Ere he shall discover
In the whole wide world again
Such a constant lover.

But the spite on't is, no praise
Is due at all to me:
Love with me had made no stay,
Had it any been but she.

Had it any been but she,
And that very very face
There had been at least ere this
A dozen dozen in her place.

Is the poem light-hearted or serious? It begins jokily enough: 'oh, what admiration I deserve', says the speaker, with a disillusioned, if carefree, estimation of male constancy, 'I've managed to stay true to the same woman for three whole days'. But the levity darkens as the poem develops. The change starts as the rhythms start to stumble over the underlying metre and the syntax delivers its meaning less straightforwardly in the third stanza: 'Love with me had made no stay, / Had it any been but she.' That is, 'I wouldn't have loved anyone even as long as this, had it been anyone but her I was thinking about'. When the poem repeats the line at the start of its final stanza, it is with the air of a poet only now pausing to register the seriousness of his feelings – as though his affection for the woman was just lodging in his mind, taking him by surprise. And yet, even as the poem seems to be transforming from a light-hearted exercise in masculine bravado into a genuine expression of love, surprises lie in store. The ending tries to make light of the poet's newfound depth of commitment: 'If it was any other woman, there'd have been a "dozen dozen" others that I'd have slept with by now' might be a rough paraphrase. But the remark comes over as much as a realisation of the hollowness of the code by which the poet has lived as an exuberant illustration of his rakishness. What starts as a caddish boastfulness turns into a piece of regretful self-reflection. And what might at first seem a throwaway exercise in love poetry emerges as the vehicle for a series of colliding attitudes towards experience, wavering between amusement, dismay, and genuine affection.

Tone is often carried on the speaking voice. We know whether someone's words are angry or distressed or sarcastic or whatever by the manner in which they are delivered. But the printed page generally offers no clues as to how a particular line is to be spoken. This can be a problem when we are trying to write to someone, as anyone who has tried to imbue a text message or a letter with sarcasm or compassion will know. But such uncertainties can create possibilities as well as problems for poets. Consider Derek Walcott's 'Sea Canes' (1971), which you can listen to the poet reading aloud, alongside a text of the poem, on the Poetry Archive website: https://poetryarchive.org/poem/sea-canes/. The first sentence of the poem ('Half my friends are dead')[77] might be spoken in any number of moods: despair, anger, bewilderment, anguish, acceptance. Walcott delivers it with a flat matter-of-factness, which epitomises the poem's toughened resolve in the face of loss. The reading is effective and affecting, but it is one of only a range of possibilities latent on the printed page. Likewise, the words imagined as being spoken by the earth in response, promising to make the poet new friends, hold out a range of possible intonations. Are we to think of the earth answering in sorrow or regret for its actions? Or is it impassive in its assumption that new friends can replace old? The potential dynamics of the conversation are pliable. In the wake of these uncertainties, by contrast, the resilient fury of the next sentence, in which the poet demands his old friends are returned with all their original imperfections, is unmistakeable: there is a far more limited range of feeling with which it could be read. Partly this is a matter of Walcott's description of the response as a 'cry', but the tone is manifest, too, in the emphatic 'No' with which the lines begin and the obduracy of the rhythm created by the recurrent commas. Walcott's voicing brings out this force thrillingly, lending the initial 'No' something like an edge of impatience. The range of possible intonations narrows as the poem works to clarify its feelings. But Walcott also realises the importance of tonal ambiguity in the appeal a poem makes to our imagination. So, when he addresses earth later in the poem, crying out ('O earth') that the earth has taken more friends than he has left to love, the lines on the page again hover between potential intonations. The expression may be simply despondent, it may be reproachful, but it leaves open the possibility, too, of a saddened sympathy with the earth, as if consoling one who knows they have gone too far. Walcott's reading renders the lines with a gently hurt quality, a softening of the poem's toughness in the face of grief. But this is just one of a range of potential readings; the multiplicities of tone left open on the printed page are crucial to the poem's representation of the search for the right attitude with which to regard its awareness of loss.

Contemplating tone in poetry, it is always worth being aware of the potential for irony – the possibility that a poet doesn't entirely endorse, or is conscious of the limitations of, what he or she says. Irony is by its nature hard to detect – poems don't carry signs advertising that they are being ironic – but one can attune oneself to it through experience and judgement. Phillis Wheatley, 'On Being Brought from Africa to America' (1773), seems, on the face of it, grateful:

> 'Twas mercy brought me from my pagan land,
> Taught my benighted soul to understand
> That there's a God, that there's a Savior too:
> Once I redemption neither sought nor knew.
> Some view our sable race with scornful eye,
> 'Their color is a diabolic dye.'
> Remember, Christians, Negros, black as Cain,
> May be refined, and join th' angelic train.

The sharpness of the poem depends on the subtlety of its tone. Wheatley was taken in slavery from her home in West Africa at the age of eight and was in later life freed. Her poem presents itself as a genuine expression of thanksgiving to a land of Christian 'mercy': 'for all the suffering involved, thank God that I've been granted the opportunity for spiritual enlightenment and redemption'. But it is a very elastic definition of 'mercy' that includes transporting someone from their native land and forcing them into slavery, and the gratitude of the opening lines is shadowed, without being eclipsed, by a bitter counter-voice which suggests that such treatment wasn't 'merciful' at all. The irony of the final lines is even defter, and more pointed. What they say is of course true, but the accent of deference is finely sardonic: their polite injunction to 'Remember' works against an awareness that it is the members of a supposedly 'angelic' slave-owning society who have proven themselves murderous and in need of refinement.

Wheatley's irony is coolly controlled; Jonathan Swift's in his 'Verses on the Death of Dr Swift' (1739) is wilder. The 'Verses' initially seem surprisingly buoyant in their contemplation of the aftermath of the poet's own death:

> Why do we grieve that Friends should dye?
> No Loss more easy to supply.
> One Year is past; a different Scene;

No further mention of the Dean;[35]
Who now, alas, no more is mist,
Than if he never did exist.
Where's now this Fav'rite of Apollo?
Departed; and his Works must follow:
Must undergo the common Fate;
His Kind of Wit is out of Date.

You'd expect the tone to be pained, or appalled, but Swift seems to contemplate the wake of his own demise with surprising chirpiness. The briskness of the rhythms, the blasé indifference of the questions, the blithe confidence of the statements: all support the shrugging implication that the death of friends is no big deal – you can just get new ones, you'll soon forget about the departed. But the very fact that the blitheness is so surprising should put us on guard. To read the lines at face value is to ignore the 'vein of satire', to take a phrase from later in the poem, that runs through them. It is not that the responses the lines describe won't happen exactly – Swift has no sentimental misconceptions about people's loyalties (for irony to take hold, there needs to be truth on both sides of the equation). But the lines are far less at peace with the scenario than they make out. Swift is naturally appalled at the prospect of being so quickly forgotten, and the serenity on the surface is in proportion to the disdain and despair that wells up beneath. Swift's 'Kind of Wit is out of Date', a future speaker is imagined saying in the final line, and the statement is wreathed in an irony with which its speaker is necessarily unaware, since the very utterance proves the enduring accuracy of Swift's vision.

How Does the Poem Convey Feeling?

Tone is a matter of a poem's control and expression of feeling. Poetry has long been felt to be intimate with the human heart. 'Feeling, love in particular, is the great moving power and spring of verse', said Gerard Manley Hopkins, suggesting how the movements of rhythm in particular might be thought to embody and tussle with emotional impulse.[78] We expect a poet to have special sensitivity to matters of the heart and a special ability to give voice to them. The poems for which we care most are always likely to be those that affect us most deeply. 'In the last resort,' said the critic Jonathan Wordsworth, 'literary criticism is personal: one has to fall back on "This moves me; this doesn't."'[79]

What is it that moves us in a poem? It is not enough for a poem simply to take a moving event as its subject. What matters, as Roger Scruton says, is

[35] Swift was Dean of St Patrick's Cathedral, Dublin

not just a poem's technical accomplishment, but its 'sensitivity to the experience conveyed' – the wisdom and humanity that flows through its language, and the care and intelligence with which it judges its response.[80] Poetry is not just the expression of feeling, but an education in what and how to feel.

William McGonagall's 'The Tay Bridge Disaster' (1880) is a notorious instance of a poem which turns painful circumstances into farce. In 1879, seventy-five people died when a bridge collapsed beneath a train in Scotland. These are the final lines of McGonagall's response:

> It must have been an awful sight,
> To witness in the dusky moonlight,
> While the Storm Fiend did laugh, and angry did bray,
> Along the Railway Bridge of the Silv'ry Tay,
> Oh! ill-fated Bridge of the Silv'ry Tay,
> I must now conclude my lay
> By telling the world fearlessly without the least dismay,
> That your central girders would not have given way,
> At least many sensible men do say,
> Had they been supported on each side with buttresses,
> At least many sensible men confesses,
> For the stronger we our houses do build,
> The less chance we have of being killed.

'Anything, however small, may make a poem; nothing, however large, is guaranteed to', Edward Thomas once said.[81] McGonagall's lines show that it is not a poem's subject but its treatment of it that matters. They fail because they are so preoccupied with proclaiming their own importance. Their focus is on persuading us to feel the 'awfulness' of the scene and the grandeur of their own response; by Yeats's definition they are 'rhetoric', not 'poetry'. They take no care to work out an appropriate response and find the words for it. Their carelessness is apparent in the casual wastefulness of the opening speculation ('it must have been . . . '), the over-inflated exclamations, melodramatic talk of 'Storm Fiends', the pretentiousness of speaking of a poem as a 'lay', and in the mismatch between the grandly inverted phrasing ('do say . . . do build' etc.) and the banality of the culminating lines. It is not that the poem isn't moving, exactly, but that it has judged its response so poorly that it moves us to laughter rather than tears.

McGonagall's poem is sentimental: it advertises rather than scrutinises its emotions. Much of the most affecting poetry comes from an effort to control and not display feeling. Only in setting ourselves in opposition to our feelings, not abandoning ourselves to them, can we discover their true nature and force. Where McGonagall bombastically performs his emotions, the following anonymous Elizabethan lyric (1603) is affecting precisely for the effort it makes to soothe its own anguish:

Weep you no more, sad fountains;
What need you flow so fast?
Look how the snowy mountains
Heaven's sun doth gently waste.
But my sun's heavenly eyes
View not your weeping,
That now lie sleeping
Softly, now softly lies
Sleeping.

Sleep is a reconciling,
A rest that peace begets.
Doth not the sun rise smiling
When fair at even he sets?
Rest you then, rest, sad eyes,
Melt not in weeping
While she lies sleeping
Softly, now softly lies
Sleeping.

There are two plausible scenarios: either the speaker cheers themselves up from some unspecified sorrow while their beloved lies sleeping, or (more likely) the speaker is trying to assuage their grief for the death of their beloved. In either case, the stanzas transmute sadness into beauty. What stays in our head after reading the poem is the hauntingly enfolded syntax with which each stanza ends: 'she lies sleeping / Softly, now softly lies / Sleeping.' Depending on how we interpret the poem's situation, the lines' patterned movement communicates the poet's contemplation of the beauty of their sleeping beloved or their effort to persuade themselves that her death is really a 'sleep' – an effort, the repetition of the stanzas implies, which has to be constantly kept up; but the delicacy of the patterning also shows us how art can redeem sorrow in the very process of communicating it. Attending to the subtleties of a poem such as this, we learn what it means to be graceful and robust in the face of feeling; we are not swept up in it, but rather granted a clearer sense of its quality.

Poetry is a vehicle as much for the contemplation as the expression of feeling. It requires intelligence, whose function T. S. Eliot once defined as 'the discernment of exactly what, and how much, we feel in any given situation'.[82] In Henry King's 'An Exequy To his Matchlesse never to be forgotten Friend' (1657), a poem upon the death of King's wife, it is not the painful circumstances that move us but rather the poem's portrayal of King's effort to define and give shape to his grief. There will come a time, King resolves at the end of the poem, when 'I shall at last sitt downe by Thee', and:

> The thought of this bids mee goe on
> And wait my dissolution
> With Hope and Comfort. Deare! (forgive
> The Crime) I am content to live
> Divided, with but half a Heart,
> Till wee shall Meet and Never part.

Perhaps the most surprising phrase in these lines is 'I am content'. 'Contentment' is not the first emotion we expect in a poem about the loss of one's wife. But the word is well judged: it doesn't express anything so vibrant as joy, or happiness, but rather a state of resigned acquiescence. King is working out 'exactly what, and how much', he feels. What the lines convey is not so much King's grief as his struggle to come to terms with that grief. That struggle is at work in the very fabric of the verse. As the first sentence is enjambed over the end of its couplet, the voice is made to pause for breath, as though awaiting its own 'dissolution' in the white space at the end of the line or gathering strength to express the 'hope' of which it will go on to speak. The expression of contentment to 'live / Divided', where the phrase hangs so limply over the line ending, makes felt what a heartbroken existence King faces. The poetry shows us how despair might be assuaged in art, but it also shows us, as the voice strains against the constraint and support of the couplet form, how hard-won that redemption is. We are moved by the poem's pain and sadness; but we are also moved by its resilience in the face of that sadness, and the fragile beauty that King wins out of it. Perhaps the most affecting moment in the lines is the intimate tonal drop as King turns to address his wife and pleads forgiveness for his resolution to try to live through his grief: 'Deare! (forgive / The Crime)'. Here the confliction of the two impulses driving the poem – the need to grieve and the need to find consolation – is most poignantly in tension. The effort to discipline grief wobbles, and in the accents of intimate address which emerge we can hear what Keats called 'the true voice of feeling'.[83]

The order of the adjectives in Keats's phrase is important: Keats is not claiming that poetry should be 'the voice of true feeling', as though it were always an outlet for biographical expression, but rather that it should find the words in which feeling finds its most truthful representation. Often, as we are beginning to see, the process involves restraint as much as the indulgence of emotion; feeling proves its strength by breaking through the poetry's effort to control it. Lady Mary Wortley Montagu's 'A Hymn to the Moon' (1758) shows how the most affecting poetry is often that into which personal feelings and circumstances only obliquely intrude:

Thou silver deity of secret night,
  Direct my footsteps through the woodland shade;
Thou conscious witness of unknown delight,
  The Lover's guardian, and the Muse's aid!

By thy pale beams I solitary rove,
  To thee my tender grief confide;
Serenely sweet you gild the silent grove,
  My friend, my goddess, and my guide.

E'en thee, fair queen, from thy amazing height,
  The charms of young Endymion drew;
Veil'd with the mantle of concealing night;
  With all thy greatness and thy coldness too.

The depth of feeling isn't immediately obvious. The first stanza conveys quiet gratitude for the moon's company and hushed wonder; the dominant emotion seems to be 'delight', related to the moon's ability to foster love and poetic inspiration. Then, in the second stanza, the expression becomes shadowed with a sense of the poet's isolation; but the moon tempers the poet's 'solitariness' and 'tender grief', and the outlook, for all the intimations of sadness, remains one of 'serene' 'sweetness'. We might expect the third stanza to elaborate upon the poet's pain, but instead the poem deflects attention to the moon herself, through an allusion to the myth of her affection for the youth Endymion: 'even you have been deflected from your "amazing height" by love', the lines say, and they end with a wondering reflection that someone so 'great' and 'cold' could be so distracted. The unspoken implication is that the poet sees their own predicament in the moon's dethronement, and the sense of an oblique and troubled sympathy that even the steeliest human beings can be waylaid by feeling colours the final line in particular. Montagu closes the poem on a pentameter rather than the tetrameter that we expect given the alternating pattern established from the second stanza. The extra foot allows room for the slightly prosaic awkwardness of the syntax, a descent into a plainer utterance as the 'true voice of feeling' breaks obliquely through the rather rhetorical gentleness of the rest of the poem.

Poetry dealing with the tragic spectrum of emotions will always touch most deeply on the human situation. But poetry would lack colour if it couldn't move us to smiles and laughter as well as tears. Indeed, it is very often humour that serves as the corrective to sentimentality and as the guarantor of 'true feeling'. This fragment by Thomas Lovell Beddoes (1823) delights in provoking an ironical laughter that corrodes false feeling:

> Ay, ay: *good man, kind father, best of friends—*
> These are the words that grow, like grass and nettles,
> Out of dead men, and speckled hatreds hide,
> Like toads, among them.

It is easy to lie about feeling, observes Beddoes (or, since he was a playwright, one of his characters), raising a grim smile. But the awareness means that when tenderness does arrive in Beddoes's poetry, as in the following 'Song' (1824), we can believe in it:

> How many times do I love thee, dear?
>   Tell me how many thoughts there be
>   In the atmosphere
>   Of a new-fall'n year,
> Whose white and sable hours appear
>   The latest flake of Eternity:—
> So many times do I love thee, dear.
>
> How many times do I love again?
>   Tell me how many beads there are
>   In a silver chain
>   Of evening rain,
> Unravelled from the tumbling main,
>   And threading the eye of a yellow star:—
> So many times do I love again.

The feeling is lucid and universal: 'I love you'. In the elegant contraction and expansion of his stanzas, Beddoes finds a form whose distinctiveness and precision give it 'true voice'.

How Does the Poem Handle Images?

Beddoes's song expresses feeling through images: the visionary delicacy with which he conceives of a 'new-fall'n year' as a 'latest flake of Eternity' and envisions the uncountable 'beads' of rain threading the starlight is in itself testimony to the quality of the affection. The way the image of the 'new-fall'n year' clouds its evocation of fresh possibilities with intimations of a demise (as though the 'fall' were not an arrival but a death) lends an unexplained sadness to the poet's expression of wonder at the depth of his passion. Beddoes's other lines wield a grotesque power grounded in what they ask us to visualise: words not just responding to 'dead men' but 'growing out' of them; hatreds, given a gruesomely concrete existence as 'toads' that squat amid the words we speak. Both passages reveal an unusually colourful imagination.

Imagery is poetry's means of appealing to the imagination and to the senses. It gives concrete shape to abstract feelings or ideas. It grants utterance strength, speed, and vibrancy. Rather than stating something to be the case, it shows it to be. Mary Robinson, in her poem 'January, 1795' (1795), could simply have stated that the world is full of injustice and hypocrisy; instead, she demonstrates it through a barrage of images:

Pavement slipp'ry, people sneezing,
Lords in ermine, beggars freezing;
Titled gluttons dainties carving,
Genius in a garret starving.

Lofty mansions, warm and spacious;
Courtiers cringing and voracious;
Misers scarce the wretched heeding;
Gallant soldiers fighting, bleeding.

Wives who laugh at passive spouses;
Theatres, and meeting-houses;
Balls, where simp'ring misses languish;
Hospitals, and groans of anguish.

The lines do not tell us what to think but allow the contrasting pictures they set before our eyes to speak for themselves. They work on our senses before our intellects.

Shira Wolosky describes imagery as 'the fireworks of poetry'.[84] It brings colour and character to a poem. Hart Crane's 'Voyages I' (1926), a lyric about childhood, and the potential unravelling of its innocence, begins with an image of children at play:

Above the fresh ruffles of the surf
Bright striped urchins flay each other with sand.[85]

We are made to feel the liveliness of the children, their brilliant energy and the loveliness of their environment; but in their behaviour, too, which remains for now a matter of 'Gaily digging and scattering', we glimpse the potential for a crueller, more primitive interaction, hinted at by the surprising violence of the verb 'flay'. At the end of Elizabeth Bishop's 'Sandpiper' (1965) we are shown a beach through the dazzlingly particularising eye of the wading bird:

> The millions of grains are black, white, tan, and gray,
> mixed with quartz grains, rose and amethyst.[86]

The familiar world is made unfamiliar by the intense patience with which the lines look. We see the world in new terms. 'With what eyes these poets see nature!' the Romantic critic William Hazlitt reflected, when Wordsworth pointed out to him the sight of the sun setting on a yellow bank: 'and ever after, when I saw the sun-set stream upon the objects facing it, [I] conceived I had made a discovery, or thanked Mr Wordsworth for having made one for me!'[87]

Imagery unites the faculties of observation and imagination. Like poetry itself, it can both recalibrate and expand our vision of the world. The imagery of some poems promises to document the world for us, to reveal the truth of what things are really like. Stephen Spender's 'An Elementary School Classroom in a Slum' (1933) is an effort to clarify our apprehension of the poverty of 1930s Britain, much like Robinson's poem turns its eye on the London of the 1790s. And like Robinson's poem, it brings awareness far more powerfully for the way in which, rather than preaching, it uses imagery to plunge us into the world of the classroom, where we find:

> The tall girl with her weighed-down head. The paper-
> seeming boy with rat's eyes. The stunted, unlucky heir
> Of twisted bones, reciting a father's gnarled disease,
> His lesson from his desk. At back of the dim class
> One unnoted, sweet and young: his eyes live in a dream
> Of squirrel's game, in the tree room, other than this.

The portraits get progressively worse, less recognisably human: a girl with her head weighed down (with unhappiness or disability?); a boy so thin he seems to be made out of paper; a child so poor all that he has to inherit is the 'twisted bones' of rickets. The imagery gives Spender's writing a journalistic quality, as it sharpens our sense of a world with which it is presumed we are unfamiliar. But then, at the end of the list, and the back of the class, a ray of hope: a boy, 'sweet and young', whose 'eyes live in a dream', and seem to be inhabiting their own world of imagery, a world 'other than this'. Here, suddenly, is imagery as a product of imagination not observation, creating new realities rather than revealing things as they are.

The ability to conjure visions has long been felt to be at the heart of poetic inspiration. It 'cannot be learnt from others and is a sign of inborn power', said Aristotle in his *Poetics*.[88] The speaker of the anonymous seventeenth-century ballad 'Tom o' Bedlam's Song' (c. 1615), a figure of the divinely inspired poet, makes a similar claim for his visionary insight:

I know more than Apollo
For oft when he lies sleeping
I see the stars at bloody wars
In the wounded welkin[36] weeping.

These lines make their point with a double literal and symbolic force. Apollo is the god of the sun, and on one level Tom 'knows more' than him because his madness causes him to stay awake all night: he sees what goes on while Apollo is sleeping. But Apollo is also the god of poetry, and Tom connects his insomnia with a visionary power that extends beyond Apollo's, too. 'Awake at night', he says, 'I see the stars warring with one another in the bloody and tearful sky.' He becomes aware of the tragedy and conflict at the heart of experience with a depth even beyond what the god of poetry achieves. The movement of stars across the night sky and the falling of comets and meteors are represented as military conflicts and signs of the sky crying, or bleeding. Observation and imagination fuse, as the poet reconfigures a common sight into an image which opens an aperture onto the tragic machinations felt to lie at the heart of existence – an effect made all the more dazzling thanks to the constellation of *w*'s that turn the image into an aural as well as visual phenomenon.

The final stanza of 'Tom o' Bedlam's Song' is a triumphant exclamation of the power of imagery to carry the poet beyond the realities of this world and his painful incarceration in a madhouse:

With an host of furious fancies,
Whereof I am commander,
With a burning spear and a horse of air
To the wilderness I wander.
By a knight of ghosts and shadows
I summoned am to tourney
Ten leagues beyond the wide world's end:
Methinks it is no journey.

The claims made for the power of the imagination here blend with questions of tone. Is Tom mad or inspired? Deluded or self-aware? Irony

[36] sky

and heroism hang in the balance around the claim that he will conquer his circumstances with an army conjured from the air. It might seem an absurd and unrealistic boast, but the 'fury' with which Tom commits to his imaginings suggests the power of the mind to give substance to what is insubstantial. The intimation that the knight's invitation to the poet is a call to meet his death then gives the final quatrain a more tragic tint, but one whose intensities are brilliantly shrugged off in the final line. Imagination, it is suggested, may involve delusion, but those who know that they live by delusions are not deluded.

As a means of 'showing' rather than 'telling', imagery often blurs as well as heightens suggestiveness, allowing authors to present more complicated and ambiguous attitudes than a poetry of statement. Andrew Marvell's 'Horatian Ode upon Cromwell's Return from Ireland' (1650) has at its heart a portrait of the execution of Charles I. The poem was written at a time of political turmoil, shortly after the English Civil War which had resulted in the overthrowing of the monarchy and the ascent to power of Oliver Cromwell as Lord Protector. The Ode narrates and reflects on these events. Expressing sympathy with Charles would be politically dangerous; celebrating his death would be callous. The poem has to negotiate a tricky predicament, so instead of announcing what he thinks or feels, Marvell paints a picture:

> He nothing common did, or mean,
> Upon that memorable scene;
>   But with his keener eye
>   The axe's edge did try.
>
> Nor call'd the gods with vulgar spite
> To vindicate his helpless right;
>   But bowed his comely head
>   Down, as upon a bed.

It might seem an admiring portrait. Charles's bravery is reflected in the tightening of the rhythms as he eyes up the axe's edge; his dignity is caught in the graceful way the enjambment brings emphasis onto 'Down', as though the poetry moved in sympathy with his own movements. He does not appeal for divine intervention, despite the violation of the kingship that is a divine 'right'. And yet the writing flickers with suggestions that the silence itself is all for show. In the word 'bowed', there is an intimation of Charles's penchant for performance (Marvell has described him as a 'tragic actor' in the stanza preceding these two), and the writing is so powerful because it is able to keep an amused eye on the actorly side of Charles's behaviour in this 'memorable scene', his fondness for ceremony to the very death, without blurring the focus of the sympathetic eye it keeps on the genuine tragedy.

Does the Poem Use Figurative Language?

The final line quoted from Marvell's poem works in two contradictory ways: by comparing the manner in which Charles laid his head upon the block to someone putting their head onto a pillow, it heightens our feeling for his bravery and calm dignity; but the comparison also has the opposite effect of reminding us that the place he lay his head was terribly *un*like a bed.

Poets often use imagery *figuratively* like this. Poetry, as Shelley said, is 'vitally metaphorical'.[89] It invites us to see life in altered terms; it shows us one thing in terms of another. 'Whatever the sun may be', said D. H. Lawrence, 'it is certainly not a ball of flaming gas',[90] implying the need for language which describes what things mean, not just what they are. When Robert Burns says 'My Luve is like a Red, Red rose' ('A Red, Red Rose' (1793)) he doesn't mean that his darling is made of petals, but that she provokes in him a similar exhilaration to a beautiful flower. We can distinguish two types of figurative device: *simile* and *metaphor*. In short, simile makes an explicit comparison, whilst in metaphor the comparison is implicit. Simile involves words such as *like* and *as*, while metaphor by contrast says that something *is* something else. When Amy Lowell, in her prose poem 'Spring Day' (1916), writes 'I am a piece of the town, a bit of blown dust, thrust along with the crowd', she is using a metaphor to describe the thrill of being swallowed up in the life of a city. She is not literally 'a bit of blown dust', but the image describes how she momentarily sees herself (behind the comparison, perhaps, is the awareness that human beings are on another level 'dust', 'blown' together through the cosmos). When at the end of the poem Lowell looks back at the city lights and describes them as being 'like a garden stirring and blowing for the Spring' she is using a simile. The image surprises because an urban nightfall is, on the face of it, utterly unlike a garden in spring.

Such comparisons work best when, like the example from Marvell, they find points of contrast as well as similarity, distance as well as harmony; a metaphor needs to convince us of its truth as well as surprise us with its vitality. To say, for instance, that a fence is like a wooden wall doesn't allow us to see the world in any new or unexpected way. At the other end of the spectrum, to compare a fence to a blueberry would leave one wondering what the points of similarity could possibly be. Of course, a sense of predictability or outrageousness might be something that a poet might seek to create, but in most instances familiarity and surprise will be held in poise.

We can dissect figurative language into three parts: *tenor*, *vehicle*, and *ground*. The tenor is the thing being described, the vehicle is the thing to which it is being compared, and the ground is the reason or reasons for the comparison. Mary Wroth begins a 'Song' (1621) with the metaphor 'Love a child is ever crying': 'Love' is the tenor and the crying child the vehicle; Wroth is inviting us to consider the ways in which the one is like the other. The opening line, leaving the ground of the comparison in abeyance, has us guessing about the exact relation: perhaps images of Cupid come into our mind, though Cupid is generally depicted as being cheeky and cheerful, which hardly fits with the neediness implied by 'crying'. In the next lines, the poem goes on to clarify the comparison:

> Please him, and he straight is flying,
> Give him he the more is craving
> Never satisfied with having.

Love is like a child because it is never 'satisfied'. The more you feed it, the more it will demand. The metaphor is enriched by certain ambiguities in the comparison. First, it is unclear whether 'Love' means 'the emotion which one experiences' – in which case the lines encourage us to think about how we feel when we are in love – or 'the demands a lover makes on you when you are in love' – in which case it is one's lover who is being compared to a needy child. Secondly, there are different ways in which a child might be needy. A baby cries endlessly for the attention of the same person, their mother – and if we think of the comparison in those terms then we can see the lines as an expression of how wearying love becomes. But a toddler might 'fly' from person to person seeking gratification – and with that thought in mind the lines entertain a contrasting complaint about love's inconstancy.

As much as figurative language has a power to illuminate, it can also suggest that concepts or objects are resistant to comprehension. George Herbert's sonnet 'Prayer' (1633) consists of a cascade of metaphors which imagine what prayer is, but the effect is to dazzle as much as clarify, and to communicate a sense of prayer's mysterious resistance to understanding:

> The soul in paraphrase, heart in pilgrimage,
> The Christian plummet sounding heav'n and earth;
> Engine[37] against th' Almighty, sinner's tow'r,
> Reversed thunder . . .

[37] machine/weapon

And the comparisons go on. The torrent of comparisons suggests a phenomenon that can't be defined from any single perspective, something being held up to multiple different angles of inspection. In the final phrase of the poem, imagery falls away, and prayer is described plainly as 'Something understood'. There is a suggestive ambiguity here, though. Prayer is 'Something understood', by God, in the sense that it is a message received; from a human perspective, however, the phrase flirts with paradox: the poem has devoted its energies to making prayer understandable, but it remains, vaguely, 'Something', rather than anything clearly defined – a phenomenon that is finally mysterious.

Herbert's poem shows how in thinking about metaphor we should attend not just to the comparisons a poet makes, but to how those comparisons are handled. Sometimes figurative language is smuggled into a poem. Samuel Johnson's 'On the Death of Dr Robert Levet' (1783) opens with a line, 'Condemned to Hope's delusive mine', which offers a bleak summary of the human condition without making it explicit that it is offering up a metaphor. Unpack the phrasing, and we can see two metaphors folded into one another: we human creatures are like criminals condemned to work in a mine in search of hope, and hope itself is like an illusory mineral, which you can toil for but never find. The succinctness is impressive, but it also sneaks the metaphor past us: not all human life is a matter of condemnation, and not all hope is illusory, but Johnson's moroseness wins our assent before we've had time to realise how the language is working on us. Along similar lines, Hazlitt admired Shakespeare not just for his writing's metaphoric power, but for the swiftness with which he moves between metaphors. 'His language is hieroglyphical. It translates thoughts into visible images. It abounds in sudden transitions and elliptical expressions'.[91] Hazlitt's observation about 'sudden transitions' cuts to the quick of Shakespeare's verbal power. Single images are rarely held before our eyes for long in Shakespeare's poetry. It can often feel difficult to keep up. When, at the start of *The Tempest* (c. 1611), Prospero recounts his brother Antonio's treachery which has led to his exile to an island, he describes him as a man who:

having both the key
Of officer and office, set all hearts i'th' state
To what tune pleased his ear, that now he was
The ivy which had hid my princely trunk
And sucked my verdure out on't.

'Thou attend'st not!' Prospero goes on to admonish his daughter Miranda; we might feel that Shakespeare has one eye on his own audience. In a little over four close-packed lines, we see Antonio as possessor of a 'key' that is both real (to the offices of state) and metaphorical (to other officer's hearts), the setter of the musical 'key' in which political events will be played, and as a vine of ivy that lives parasitically on Prospero's virtues. Thoughts are 'translated into visible images' with a mix of flamboyance and acuity. Metaphors whirl out of one another with a spontaneity that mimics the clandestine machinations of Antonio's rise.

Other poets may choose to extend a single comparison through a whole poem. The tactic often enables extravagant or surprising comparisons. In William Empson's 'Camping Out' (1940) the poet looks down at the toothpaste bubbles made as his lover cleans her teeth into a lake, and compares the white specks on the dark water to 'a straddled sky of stars'.[92] Empson imagines the impression made as the bubbles spread apart as resembling what the stars would look like as you hurtled towards them through space, and the image becomes a metaphor for the exhilaration of a romantic relationship. Valentine Ackland's 'The eyes of body' (1933) treats seduction in terms of a military conquest in which the imagination 'orders out a hand' which 'cleaves between your thighs / Clean, as a ray-directed airplane flies'.[93] The hand, first envisaged as a kind of spy-plane sent from the command-centre of the mind, mutates into a destructive, 'cleaving' weapon, and we are made to feel the tension between – and perhaps proximity of – erotic attraction and conflict. Extended metaphors demand agility from both reader and writer as they invite us to track the points of contact and distance between the image and what it is being used to describe. Often, part of the pleasure involves an awareness of the ways in which a comparison does not completely hold. Henry Vaughan's 'The Shower' (1655) uses the movement of moisture through the water-cycle as a metaphor for the poet's spiritual desiccation:

1.

'Twas so; I saw thy birth. That drowsy lake
  From her faint bosom breath'd thee, the disease
  Of her sick waters and infectious ease.
      But now at even,
      Too gross for heaven,
Thou fall'st in tears, and weep'st for thy mistake.

2.

Ah! it is so with me: oft have I press'd
  Heaven with a lazy breath; but fruitless this

Pierc'd not; love only can with quick access
Unlock the way,
When all else stray,
The smoke and exhalations of the breast.

3.

Yet, if as thou dost melt, and with thy train
Of drops make soft the Earth, my eyes could weep
O'er my hard heart, that's bound up and asleep;
Perhaps at last,
Some such showers past,
My God would give a sunshine after rain.

The first stanza develops, with a winning insouciance (''Twas so . . . '), a metaphor of a rain shower as the product of the exhalation of a stagnant lake which, ascending to heaven, discovers itself too 'gross' to be admitted (i.e. too heavy or coarse, but with a suggestion of moral impurity, too) and so falls as its own tears. In the second stanza, with an intensification of the poem's emotional charge ('Ah!'), that metaphor is applied to the poet's own situation: it becomes an image for the poet's own idle and fruitless attempts to enter heaven (his half-hearted prayers but also, the image of his 'lazy breath' might suggest, his habit of writing poems). Then, in the final stanza, the relationship between the tenor and vehicle becomes more precarious. 'If – just as rain softens the ground – I can weep tears of regret which stir my heart, then perhaps God will grant sunshine in the wake of such rain', the poem hopes. But it is a hope, not an assurance. For all the logical inevitability suggested by the poem's numbered stanzas, the syntax – piling a 'perhaps' upon an 'if' – shadows the poem's optimism about the validity of the comparison with doubt.

Does the Poem Tell a Story?

Another way of thinking of 'The Shower' is as a little versified story – it is an autobiographical tale with a beginning, a middle, and a hoped-for end. We might instinctively associate stories more with novels and plays than with poems. But poems were telling stories long before the novel established itself: the epics of the ancient world, such as Homer's *Iliad* and *Odyssey*, were written in verse. And while prose has one obvious advantage for the purpose of storytelling, in that its freedom from fixed rules or regular patterns gives it flexibility to the flow of events, the idiosyncrasies of character, and the particularities of setting and situation, the opposite side of that observation is that the patterns and structures of verse provide a framework to shape the sequence of a narrative and drive action forward. Verse shapes our experience of time. The penultimate stanza of Book I of Spenser's *The Faerie Queene* (1590) ends by playing a trick on the reader, as the knight who is the poem's main protagonist, turns to find the Lady he is travelling with (who unknown to him is in fact a malicious witch in disguise) 'dead with Feare' as the result of a story they have just been told. There is then a stanza break, in which we ourselves absorb this unexpected turn, before the final stanza strikes up: 'Her seeming dead he found with feigned Feare . . . ' The witch had just been playing dead in order to distract the knight from a story which might have revealed the trick she is playing on him, and Spenser's narrative manages to entangle us in her deception, too. That sort of narrative effect is unique to verse. It is an example of the way the patterns of versification can entangle themselves with the unfolding of a poem's events. The point can be observed most boldly in ballad, the genre of poetry in which the narrative frame is at its starkest. Ballads are the product of oral culture. The process of being passed from generation to generation by word of mouth whittles their stories down to their essentials. 'Sir Patrick Spens', a poem probably of medieval origin, tells the tale of a sailor who has been chosen by the king to go on a treacherous sea voyage. In the poem's fourth stanza, we are presented with the image of Sir Patrick receiving the news:

> The first line that Sir Patrick red,
> A loud lauch lauched he;
> The next line that Sir Patrick red,
> A teir blinded his ee.[38]

Here are two narrative events: Sir Patrick laughs, and then he cries. Patrick's state of mind passes from scornful incredulity that someone could ask him to go to sea in such conditions to saddened acceptance of his fate. Action conveys feeling with minimal fuss. A narrator in a novel, or even a less sparse genre of poetry, might be tempted to burrow further into Sir Patrick's consciousness, but, for the ballad, there is no need; the very swiftness with which we move from one half of the stanza to the other conveys with brilliant economy Patrick's resolve and resilience and his unwillingness – wise or otherwise – to dwell on his emotions.

Appreciating ballads often involves getting a feeling for the gaps left by all those aspects of narrative – setting, motivation, a narrator's perspective – which have been stripped away: analysis and reflection yield to a naked

[38] eye

presentation of events. One question which can be asked usefully of any narrative, but particularly of ballad, is: 'what has been left out?' In the ballad 'Matty Groves', we are left to handle by ourselves the multiple criss-crossing reactions provoked by the details of the plot. The poem begins with 'little' Matty Groves being seduced in church by Lord Darnell's wife, while Lord Darnell is away (the epithet used to describe Matty is an instance of how in such a sparse linguistic landscape the tiniest detail can colour one's responses). A servant overhears their conversation and rushes to tell his master. The servant's loyalty is surely admirable, and Lord Darnell has been wronged; but we can't help but feel anxiety for little Matty in his precarious situation. Once the servant has gone on his way, we hear nothing of his conversation with Lord Darnell, nor of Matty's escapades with his wife; the poem offers only the barest outline of events:

Little Matty Groves, he lay down
And took a little sleep
When he awoke, Lord Darnell
Was standing at his feet

Time has been compressed. The ballad moves swiftly between stanzas which repackage the continuous flow of experience into a series of intense, sometimes obliquely related, flashes; this is not a form that affords time to stop and reflect. In the conflict that follows, Lord Darnell challenges Matty to a duel, letting him use his best sword and have the first strike:

So Matty struck the very first blow
And he hurt Lord Darnell sore
Lord Darnell struck the very next blow
And Matty struck no more

And then Lord Darnell he took his wife
And he sat her on his knee
Saying, 'Who do you like the best of us
Matty Groves or me?'

And then up spoke his own dear wife
Never heard to speak so free
'I'd rather a kiss from dead Matty's lips
Than you or your finery'

'And . . . And . . . And': one thing follows hot on the heels of another, the narrative is terse, laconic; but each event changes our attitude to the character in question. Sympathies ricochet. Lord Darnell is honourable and fair, and his power is conveyed through the swift inevitability with which he wins the fight: 'Matty struck no more'. But from another perspective, that line rings with an understated sadness about Matty's fate. In Lord Darnell's conversation with his wife, sympathies are further muddied: the answer he receives to his question is painful; but that his wife has never before spoken 'so free' gives a subversive gloss to her own behaviour, painting it as a kick against his domineering nature and 'finery'. The upshot is that Darnell kills his wife, too, and calls for 'a grave [. . .] To put these lovers in' (a gesture that respects their feelings), but he specifies that his wife should be buried on top 'For she was of noble kin', suggesting he has not learnt his lesson about the importance of feeling above 'finery'. In poetry of this kind, we are given no guidance or central moral perspective: the poem presents us with the bare bones of the story, and the questions, feelings, and implications that emerge are allowed to rattle in the gaps between them.

Ballad depends on bold, exciting action. But storytelling is seldom purely a matter of delivering a plot. We need to consider the aspects of human behaviour and relations that the plot raises and illustrates. The verbal pressure and intensity of verse enables it to shift emphasis from a sequence of events onto the psychology and emotional impact surrounding them. Wordsworth, who named one of his collections *Lyrical Ballads*, implying the emotional significance with which he invested his narratives, realised these possibilities with particular humanity. He explained that he wrote narrative poems in which the 'feeling . . . developed gives importance to the action and situation, and not the action and situation to the feeling'.[94] That is, while the actions that take place in his poems might seem inconsequential, their significance for the people to whom they are happening is profound. 'The Sailor's Mother' (1807), a poem from one of Wordsworth's later collections, illustrates the point. In it, the poet recalls encountering an old woman carrying a bird cage. Where time in the ballad moves relentlessly forward, Wordsworth's poem takes place when the woman's journey has stopped: significance floods into a single moment. The poet asks the woman where she is going, and she tells her story:

'I had a Son, who many a day
Sailed on the seas; but he is dead;
In Denmark he was cast away;
And I have travelled far as Hull, to see
What clothes he might have left, or other property.'

The son left the bird behind before his final voyage, the woman says, and she 'trails' it with her because 'he took so much delight in it'. And there the poem ends, without the poet adding any further comment. There is no great spectacle here. The important events are not external but take place in the inner lives of the poem's characters. The story does not depend on the occurrences of the sailor's life and death, which if devastating, are unremarkable, but on the feelings to which they give rise. The woman's slightly odd behaviour speaks of human peculiarity, commitment, grief, tenderness, and hope. And Wordsworth, telling the story of the woman telling her story, knows that poetry lies in those feelings as much as the events that provoke them.

Narrative poems tell stories, but they also suggest and explore the implications of those stories. They invite us to ask: 'why is this story being told? What is the poet, or narrator, trying to show us through it?' Sometimes, a poem will offer clues. Chaucer's *Pardoner's Tale* (c. 1400), for instance, takes the form of an *exemplum:* a story that delivers a moral lesson – in this case one summed up by the Pardoner's mantra, *Radix malorum est cupiditas* ('greed is the root of evil'). But Chaucer deploys a complex narrative framework which frustrates the possibility of arriving at any easy answer about the poem's purpose and motivations. The poem is one of a sequence of stories told by the pilgrims in the *Canterbury Tales*: it is part of a longer story about people telling stories. So, really, we have two stories, each with diverging purposes: the Pardoner's tale and Chaucer's tale about the Pardoner telling his tale. To add further complication, the purposes of the story for the Pardoner – who holds his hands up immediately to seeking to deceive listeners with his 'false japes' – and for the assorted pilgrims who form his audience, also diverge. The host, who directs the *Canterbury Tales*, initially asks the Pardoner to 'Telle us som myrthe or japes'. The rest of the pilgrims object, demanding instead that the Pardoner 'Telle us som moral thyng, that we may leere / Som wit' – they want a tale which will offer them moral instruction, rather than just frivolous entertainment (a pardoner is someone licensed to sell people pardons for their sins). The Pardoner then promises that he will tell them 'som honest thyng' – a promise which, though it echoes the pilgrims' phrasing, is not exactly the same as what they demand, not least because of the variety of ways in which we might interpret the word 'honest': in its Middle English guise, the word incorporated meanings ranging from 'decent' to 'profitable' (and what 'profits' the unscrupulous Pardoner might be different to what profits the other pilgrims). From its beginnings, then, Chaucer's story shows itself to contain a headier blend of 'myrthe', morality, and mischief than any straightforwardly 'moral thyng' might give us cause to expect. The notion that this – or any – story can be reduced to a single, simple purpose, is called into question.

The attraction of the *Pardoner's Tale* revolves as much around the character of the Pardoner as of the tale he tells; or rather, its interest depends upon the intersection of the two. Chaucer reminds us that any moral perspective a poem has to offer is tangled up in the morality of the teller. And the poem explores the gap between the morality of the Pardoner and his narrative with ironic force. For though the Pardoner eventually tells a tale that warns of the effects of greed, he fulfils his promise of 'honesty' with disarming candour:

> Of avarice and of swich cursednesse
> Is al my prechyng, for to make hem free
> To yeven hir pens, and namely unto me.

'All my preaching is about avarice and suchlike sins; and I do it to make people free, free to give their money away, that is – and specifically to me!' The Pardoner is honest, but only about his own dishonesty. He goes on to tell a tale which illustrates the benefits of giving one's money away. But the morality of that tale is not one that he himself adheres to, since the result of his efforts to get people to empty their pockets (however spiritually purifying for them that may be) is to fill his own. And yet the situation is further complicated, since the Pardoner's greed and hypocrisy is offset by the force and frankness of his personality. It is hard not to enjoy the chutzpah and flamboyance he displays in the passage above: if we pause at the end of the second line, then we read the aim of the Pardoner's 'preaching' as being to make his listeners 'free', which seems an admirable enough purpose, presumably liberating them from the burden of sinfulness; it is only when following the syntax on that we discover that he wants to make them 'free / To yeven hir pens', i.e. to give their money away – 'and namely unto me', as he adds with a flourish of self-delight. Chaucer fleshes out the character of his narrator in order to pose questions about the moral effects of storytelling: if someone tells a moral tale to immoral ends, how does that leave things balanced? The Pardoner's money-grabbing hypocrisy suggests that he hasn't learnt the lesson of his own tale, or doesn't see it as one worth learning; and Chaucer's depiction of his behaviour bears out the truth of his message about greed being the root of all evil, nevertheless. Stories seldom have a single point.

How Does the Poem Depict Character?

John Dryden described Chaucer as 'the Father of English Poetry' and admired how, in the *Canterbury Tales*, 'All his Pilgrims are severally distinguished from each other; and not only in their Inclinations, but in their very Phisiognomies and Persons.'[95] Dryden's remarks draw attention to another pleasure of storytelling: the representation of character. All poetry is concerned with character, to the degree that it involves the creation of a voice. But character is a particularly prominent feature of narrative poetry. The average poem is shorter than the average novel or play, and the formal properties of verse create different expressive possibilities than those of prose. There is usually not the scope, in a poem, for the minute portrayal of day-to-day activities and conversations that are often means of characterisation in a novel, nor is there usually space to present up-close the entwined development of multiple personalities. Poems are well-suited, though, to presenting snapshots of behaviour that distil character. They can show us, to take a line from W. B. Yeats's 'The Circus Animals' Desertion' (1939), 'Character isolated by a deed'. A single moment might be all we are given to judge the nature of a poem's protagonists:

> The cock crows and you
> Wake up with a start:
> But you spent the night
> In your own bed, husband.

This is a poem from the *Gāthāsaptaśatī*, a collection supposedly compiled by a South Asian king, Hāla, in the second century AD and here translated from the Prākrit language by Arvind Krishna Mehrotra (1991). We learn, in its four short lines, about a husband, comically panicked by his own infidelity, and clumsily exposing it, and a wife, either hurt or seething – or perhaps even amused – by what his startled awakening reveals. The characters are to some extent stock figures – they are not individualised in their 'Phisiognomies and Persons' – but the situation in which they find themselves is given distinctive life. And in fact, the poem's brilliance is in its brevity. The single event is the fulcrum of a whole love story and a window on the personalities it involves, but we are left to imagine the circumstances leading up to this moment of crisis, and its consequences.

Verse is also a potent medium for description. It can give succinctness and precision to a poet's effort to pin down an individual's characteristics. One of Dryden's most piercing 'Phisiognomies' is the portrait of the priest

Zimri in *Absalom and Achitophel* (1681). The poem retells an Old Testament story of a plot against King Absalom, and Zimri is one of the plotters. Dryden describes him as a man so riddled with conflicting personalities that he lacks any identity:

> A man so various, that he seemed to be
> Not one, but all mankind's epitome.
> Stiff in opinions, always in the wrong,
> Was everything by starts, and nothing long;
> But, in the course of one revolving moon,
> Was chemist, fiddler, statesman, and buffoon:
> Then all for women, painting, rhyming, drinking,
> Besides ten thousand freaks[39] that died in thinking.

The lines tell us about Zimri rather than showing him in action. The action lies in the lines themselves, which dramatise a mind in the process of judging character and, in expressing that judgement, testing out the tensile, malleable possibilities of a sentence in verse. As Dryden's syntax twists and turns, he builds both a vision of an individual and a general understanding of human inconsistency. The lines leave us as much with the impression of Dryden's authority as a judge of character as with the impression of Zimri's character itself. And they show, too, the importance of thinking not just about the personality of the characters in a poem but the nature of a poet's attitude towards them. Dryden's account of Zimri balances its satire with a measure of sympathetic good humour, and his discretion in this regard negotiates real-life as well as artistic pressures. *Absalom and Achitophel* retells its biblical narrative as an allegory for a contemporary plot against King Charles II. Zimri stands for the figure of George Villiers, Duke of Buckingham, who had been one of the plotters against the king; but the narrative affords Dryden the chance to pursue a personal vendetta here, too, since Buckingham had written a play ridiculing Dryden's skill as a dramatist. Dryden later commented that the potency of the portrait as satire depended on its lack of malice: 'If I had railed, I might have suffered for it justly', but 'I applied myself to the representing of Blind-sides, and little Extravagancies: To which, the wittier a man is, he is generally the more obnoxious . . . the Jest went round, and he was laught at in his turn who began the Frolick.' 'There is still a vast distance between the slovenly butchering of a man, and the fineness of a stroke that separates the head from the body, and leaves it standing in its place', he reflected.[96]

Dryden describes character from the outside, and we are invited to contemplate the art and judgement of the artist as well as the nature of

[39] whims

the character depicted. But, as we saw when considering dramatic monologue, poetry is also adept at imagining character from within. In Arthur Hugh Clough's *Amours de Voyage* (1858), interest in narrative incident gives way almost entirely to explorations of character and feeling. The poem imagines the lives of a group of English tourists in Italy during a moment of political turmoil in mid-nineteenth-century Rome. Allowing the flow of large events to fade into the background, the poem thrusts attention onto the less heroic hesitations, predicaments, and failures of individuals as history intersects with their private lives; the poetry is interested less in the grand sweep of events than the foibles and passions of the humans that they pass by and through. The poem is constructed as a series of letters. Letters by their very nature are ancillary to action and event (or are different sorts of events to those that usually form the basis of narratives), and the story of the travellers' escapades and interactions consequently becomes a kind of anti-narrative, while the political turmoil and violence plays out in the background. The lead protagonist, Claude, dithers about his affections for Mary Trevellyn, the daughter of a well-to-do family of fellow travellers. The story ends, in a manner that you might suppose is true to life, not in fulfilment and resolution, but in missed opportunity and disappointment. The narrative mode and texture are caught nicely in a sequence of letters in which Claude attempts to deny his feelings for Mary:

> I am in love, meantime, you think; no doubt you would think so.
> I am in love, you say; with those letters, of course, you would say so.
> I am in love, you declare. I think not so . . .

Everyone knows that the surest sign that someone is in love is that they deny it, and what sticks in the mind is less Claude's refutations than the four words to which he insistently returns: 'I am in love'. Sure enough, by the end of the letter, Claude has risen in spite of himself to a lyrical eulogy to Mary's lyrical way of speaking:

> . . . though she talk, it is music; her fingers desert not the keys; 'tis
> Song, though you hear in the song the articulate vocables sounded,
> Syllabled singly and sweetly the words of melodious meaning.
>   I am in love, you say; I do not think so, exactly.

The lines show how vital a role poetry's rhythms and syntax can play in the delineation of character and feeling. Read the above passages aloud, and we hear brittle self-deception crumbling in the face of delighted rapture, against which the return to a mode of pernickety protest in the last line holds out forlornly. The stanza's capacity to move from an accent of strained denial into the cascading baroque rhythms in which Claude contemplates Mary's gracefulness reveal a form suited to a kind of narrative whose emphases are very different to the action-driven storytelling shaped by the terse units of the ballad. And a whole personality is caught in the depiction of Claude's response to the charge that he is in love with the words: 'I do not think so, exactly.'

The effect of Clough's poem depends on the fact that the answers to Claude's letters aren't presented, so that we are faced with comic juxtapositions as his attitudes unfold. The next letter sees Claude meditating on the two 'different kinds [. . .] of human attraction' – 'One which simply disturbs, unsettles, and makes you uneasy, / And another that poises, retains, and fixes and holds you' – before declaring 'I do not wish to be moved', which is not the same thing, exactly, as saying that you are not moved. In the next, he is hoping that love might arrive spontaneously, without consideration or intervention ('Let love be its own inspiration!'). One further letter later he is confessing behaviour which flatly contradicts his denials: 'She goes – therefore I go; she moves, – I move, not to lose her.' The structure and shape of the narrative reveals Claude's very English passivity in the face of feeling. At last Claude falls into the role of rejected suitor: 'She doesn't like me, Eustace; I think she never will like me'; and it is hard not to reflect that if he continues dithering in this vein then he is probably right.

When Was the Poem Written?

Clough's friend Matthew Arnold was ambivalent about what he called Clough's 'excessively, needlessly rough' hexameters; he felt that Clough's six-feet lines didn't manage to carry over into English the 'plainness and directness' achieved by Homer's use of the form in *The Iliad*.[97] But in *Amours de Voyage* that 'roughness' – the refusal, presumably, to stick to the regular iambic alternations of the metre – is just what gives the poetry its suppleness, its ability to move between the chatty and the lyrical, and what weaves a wavering sense of direction into the fabric of the whole work. The irregularity of Clough's hexameters shows that his characters' lives fall short of heroic ideals; it is part of what makes *Amours de Voyage* a nineteenth-century poem.

Throughout the book I have provided, wherever possible, the dates of publication of the poems that I have quoted. How can this information prove useful? The answer is that it gives us a clue to the various biographical, social, political, historical, intellectual, and aesthetic contexts that might have informed a poem's composition and within which it acquires significance; it lets us know a poem's place in literary history and the history of its culture and society at large. 'To judge rightly of an author' as Samuel Johnson argued, 'we must transport ourselves to his time, and examine what were the wants of his contemporaries, and what were his means of supplying them. That which is easy at one time was difficult at another.'[98] A poem's form, genre, language, and subject matter will all be conditioned by the 'wants' and circumstances of its age; the poems that last will be those which 'supply' those wants and meet those circumstances most resourcefully, but which find a way, too, of anticipating (perhaps defining) the wants and fashions of future ages.

Some poems bear witness to historical events so directly that we need to know something of their context in order to make any sense of them. The reader who doesn't know that the title of Auden's 'September 1, 1939' indicates the date of the Nazi invasion of Poland is going to miss a good chunk of the poem's significance; likewise Marvell's 'Horatian Ode upon Cromwell's Return from Ireland' imagines a readership familiar with the events in the aftermath of the English Civil War. As long as we are reading the poem in a good edition (see page 205), we can expect crucial contextual information such as this to be indicated in an editor's explanatory notes.

More frequently, knowledge of a poem's contexts is a matter of amplifying rather than unlocking its significance. Here is T. E. Hulme's 'Above the Dock' (1912):

> Above the quiet dock in mid night,
> Tangled in the tall mast's corded height,
> Hangs the moon. What seemed so far away
> Is but a child's balloon, forgotten after play.

It is possible to appreciate the clarity of Hulme's images, the polished concentration of his form, and the economy of the poem's contrast between dreamy nightscape and urban landscape without knowing when or where it was written. We might, even without knowing anything about the circumstances of its composition, detect in the poem's central contrast a concern with the uneasy coexistence of commerce with the Romantic ideals embodied in the moon (though the contrast is intensified when we know that the 'docks' in question are those in London at the height of Empire). But if we read the poem in light of Hulme's lecture 'Romanticism and Classicism' (1911–12), in which Hulme presses the case for the beauty of 'small, dry things', and declares the aim of art to be 'accurate, precise and definite description', the nature and force of the poem's qualities and the complexity of its apprehension of the relationship between commercial and poetic concerns come into sharper focus. The sensory precision of the poem, its sense that the moon and all it suggests of man's longing and transcendence must in reality be 'Tangled' in a world of economic pursuit, and its final belittling of a symbol in which earlier poets had invested such significance, are all of a piece with Hulme's preference in that lecture for the manner and temperament of classical, as opposed to Romantic, art. The poem is at war with the taste for 'vagueness' and the accompanying suggestion of boundlessness Hulme saw as characteristic of the poetry which had dominated the previous century: it is a product of 'the classical poet [who] never forgets this finiteness, this limit of man'. And Hulme's essay enables us to reach a more refined understanding of the attitude the poem dramatises towards the entanglement of 'poetical' and ordinary, commercial existence. The Romantic, says, Hulme, is always 'gloomy': 'there is always the bitter contrast between what you think you ought to be able to do and what man actually can'.[99] But the poem shows us, without lamenting, this contrast. Reading the poem in the context of Hulme's lecture enables us to understand more fully its clear-eyed vision of the world.

The transactions between a poem and the world from which it emerges are two-way. Reading often involves allowing a poem and its historical circumstances to shine mutually illuminating light upon one another. A contextual note to Aemilia Lanyer's 'The Description of Cookeham' (1611), for instance, might inform us that Cookeham was a country residence of Lanyer's patron, Margaret Clifford, Countess of Cumberland, and that the poem describes Lanyer's stay at the property, where she was probably working as a tutor for Clifford's daughter, during a period when Clifford was engaged in a legal battle with her estranged husband over the ownership of the family estates. That information helps us to make sense of the poem and what it has to show us: we can expect from it an account not only of life at a Jacobean country manor but a life lived amid an exclusively and unusually female society. In this light, we might detect a social as well as aesthetic impetus behind Lanyer's description of a landscape in which even the trees 'Embraced each other, seeming to be glad'. And yet a curious event Lanyer narrates towards the end of the poem suggests ructions beneath the apparently idyllic surface. As Clifford was preparing to leave the estate, and consequently to cut ties with Lanyer, she went and kissed a favourite tree. Immediately, Lanyer stole the kiss from the tree, 'Scorning a senseless creature should possess / So rare a favour':

> Though it oft had given me much content,
> Yet this wrong I never could repent;
> But of the happiest made it most forlorn,
> To show that nothing's free from Fortune's scorn,
> While all the rest with this most beauteous tree
> Made their sad comfort sorrow's harmony.

To comprehend the lines, we might need to go back to the world outside the poem and place them in the context of their times: Clifford grants to the tree a 'favour' that was reserved for social equals. Consequently, in Lanyer's odd behaviour there is an intimation of submerged resentment at the social hierarchies that remain within this pastoral retreat, and at Clifford's perceived slighting of her. At the end of the poem, the undercurrent of tension persists as Lanyer reminds Clifford of her poetry's power over her reputation: beneath the apparent generosity of her observation 'When I am dead thy name in this may live' is a pointed reminder of the debts which Clifford owes and a warning that, since poetry is one of the ways in which future generations will come to understand the past, the poet has a power over the ways in which individuals 'live' for posterity. Here, then, is a small example of how reading involves an ongoing negotiation between attention to the poem and knowledge of the world in which it was written. Knowledge of the poem's social and historical circumstances helps us to understand the poem: we see the poem more clearly for understanding the conditions Lanyer's writing negotiates. Yet the poem also shines a light on those conditions. Evidently, the events that Lanyer's poem narrates do not have the universal significance of a civil or global war. But even if we care nothing for the events in which the poem takes root, understanding them helps us to apprehend not just what the poem is about but what it shows us. Lanyer depicts a landscape cultivated by women, against a male-dominated world. But she shows, too, that such idylls can never be perfect, and seldom last. The episode at the poem's close gives expression to the complex mix of sadness, resentment, nostalgia, and futility that comes at the close of any unequal relationship. Lanyer shows how in rejection we might balance self-pity and petulance with compassion and self-deprecation. We're back to the thought that a poem's surface concerns are not the only thing that it is 'about'.

'A great Poem', said Shelley, 'is a fountain forever overflowing with waters of wisdom and delight; and after one person and one age has exhausted all of its divine effluence which their peculiar relations enable them to share, another and yet another succeeds, and new relations are ever developed'.[100] While reading a poem involves understanding it within its original contexts, it also involves asking how it discovers in its apprehension of its own time a significance that endures for others. Art outlives the conditions in which it originated; it raises permanent questions. 'What would Adam make of women today?' asks Anne Finch's 'Adam Pos'd' (1709). Reading the poem three centuries on, we can enjoy the poem from a double perspective. We can imagine how the 'wisdom and delight' afforded by the poem's contemplation of the question might have reverberated with an early eighteenth-century audience, and we can think about how the poem speaks to current concerns:

> Could our First Father, at his toilsome Plough,
> Thorns in his Path, and Labour on his Brow,
> Cloath'd only in a rude, unpolish'd Skin,
> Could he a vain Fantastick Nymph have seen,
> In all her Airs, in all her antick Graces,
> Her various Fashions, and more various Faces;
> How had it pos'd that skill, which late assign'd
> Just Appellations to Each several Kind!
> A right Idea of the Sight to frame;
> T'have guessed from what New Element she came;
> T'have hit the wav'ring Form, or giv'n this Thing a Name.

To understand the poem's original question, we need knowledge of the relationship between men and women in early eighteenth-century England. If we pin down the particular 'Fashions' and 'antick Graces' the poem has in mind – the 'unguarded follies' and aristocratic self-importance of the early eighteenth-century drawing room which Alexander Pope satirises in *The Rape of the Lock* (1714), a poem provoked by two families who fell out over the snipping off of a lock of a young woman's hair – we might feel justified in regarding it as a question which Finch poses with some satiric bite. Knowledge of Finch's life might also give some indication of where her sympathies lie: having been banished from London for her political allegiances, Finch lived on an estate in Kent, and at the heart of the poem is not only a collision of the masculine and the feminine, but a crossing of rural and urban sensibilities: Finch presents Adam toiling hard, in contrast to a frivolous luxury which renders him astonished. Information about the poem's contexts deepens our understanding of its original significance. And yet, the poem also outlives those contexts. To a twenty-first-century reader, it might prove differently valuable. While we might relish the poem's satire against vacuity and vanity, and enjoy, even if we are less inclined to nod along with, the restrained bite of Finch's portrayal of gender relations, we are likely to be grateful, too, that the poem poses a question, rather than imposes an answer: Finch merely states that, had Adam, fresh from the Garden of Eden and the business of assigning names to the animals, been faced with one of these 'vain Fantastick Nymphs', he would have been at a loss for words as to how to characterise her. The poem leaves space to read the encounter it imagines as an illustration of female iconoclasm as well as upper-class frivolity.

Good poems find new significances as they discover 'new relations' with new audiences in new contexts, just as a good olive oil might be made to accompany a few hunks of ciabatta but prove surprisingly delicious poured over a scoop of vanilla ice cream. We should ask not only 'what does a poem mean?' but 'what different things has it meant for different readerships?' When Gertrude Bell translated the poems of the medieval Persian poet Hafez in 1897, she explained that she was motivated to do so on the grounds that the poems illuminate the spiritual and intellectual life both of Hafez's time and of her own. She found in them the encapsulation of a Sufi philosophy from which her own age could draw nourishment:

> Though heaven and earth before me God unroll,
> Back to thy village still my spirit flies.
> And, Hafiz, at the door of Kismet[40] lies
> No just complaint – a mind like water clear,
> A song that swells and dies upon the ear,
> These are enough for thee!

The longing to settle in one's home village, satisfaction with serenity of mind, and accommodation to the passage of time: the ideals are an expression of Hafez's fourteenth-century Shiraz; yet for Bell, the lines map out the 'provinces of thought that we of later age were destined to inhabit'.[101]

Other translators have found Hafez's poems valuable for their form and idiom as much as for their spiritual content or 'philosophy'. Hafez wrote in a form known as the *ghazal*, one of the conventions of which is that it must at some point contain the poet's name, so that the poems often turn on a moment of self-address, which, as in the above lines, sees the poet's behaviour or character with sudden clarity from the outside. For Dick Davis, translating the poems in 2012, it is precisely the force and fascination of the poetry's formal patterns that gives them enduring life. The vitality of

[40] fate

Hafez, says Davis, resides not in his ideas but in the verve with which he negotiates them, the way he 'slips and swerves from possibility to possibility',[102] as in the plaited questionings of 'I see no love in anyone':

> This town was full of lovers once,
> Of kindness and benevolence,
>
> And when did kindness end? What brought
> The sweetness of our town to naught?
> The ball of generosity
> Lies on the field for all to see –
>
> No rider comes to strike it; where
> Is everyone who should be there?
> Silence, Hafez, since no one knows
> The secret ways that heaven goes.
>
> Who is it that you're asking how
> The heavens are revolving now?

Many poems express dissatisfaction with a world gone wrong; and the timelessness of the disillusion is part of what makes the poem endure. But the poem expresses a disillusion that might speak to any age in the idiom of a particular time and place. Davis's translation captures and makes available to us the vitality and self-ironising sophistication of Hafez's voice. The poem's spiralling questions about the draining away of virtue from the world delight in the transition from honest perplexity to an ending which in itself perplexes: the final lines either put the poem to bed by suggesting the need to trust in divine providence or open a chasm beneath it with the intimation that there is no one to trust in at all. And so, a century on from Bell's translations, Hafez's poems prove Shelley's point: in Davis's hands the poems establish 'new relations' with an early twenty-first-century Western society whose understanding of Islamic culture is narrowed by media portrayals. What shines from Davis's translation is less the expression of a particular belief than the poem's tapestry of moral certitude with self-doubt.

Knowing when a poem was written can also help us to understand its place in a poet's own career. The differences between the following poems by W. B. Yeats can be explained by the fact that they were written forty years apart:

He Hears the Cry of the Sedge

> I wander by the edge
> Of this desolate lake

Where wind cries in the sedge:
Until the axle break
That keeps the stars in their round,
And hands hurl in the deep
The banners of East and West,
And the girdle of light is unbound,
Your breast will not lie by the breast
Of your beloved in sleep.

The Spur

You think it horrible that lust and rage
Should dance attendance upon my old age;
They were not such a plague when I was young;
What else have I to spur me into song?

Full appreciation of the poems is difficult without a sense of the literary climate that fostered them and of which they are a manifestation. The knowledge provides another way of answering the question we asked near the start of the book: 'what kind of poem is this?' The first of these lyrics, from the collection *The Wind Among the Reeds* (1899), was written when Yeats was in his thirties. The pained beauty it derives from its sense of the opposition between self and nature and its image of a soul fated to separation from a loved one epitomises the fascination with 'life at its most intense moment' and 'sensuous loveliness [. . .] separated from all the general purposes of life' Yeats felt to be characteristic of the 1890s poets he would later label as the 'Tragic Generation' (we might compare the Dowson poem on page 48 for something similar in spirit).[103] Were Yeats to have written this poem at the end of his career in the 1930s, however, it would seem anachronistic, an outdated exercise in an old style. The second poem, from Yeats's penultimate volume *New Poems* (1938) manifests a totally different assumption of how poetry should speak. Compared to the lush anguish of the earlier lyric, the writing here seems sparse, we might even say unpoetic. It would have jarred among Yeats's 1890s collections. But in the wake of the modernist movement of the early twentieth century and a shift in attitudes characterised, for example, by Hulme's advocacy of a 'dry, hard, classical verse', over a weary Romanticism which is always 'moaning or whining about something or other', the clipped, aggressive manner in which it turns on its reader makes sense.[104] As the poem of a young man, its anger would seem confected; as the poem of an old man, it seems righteously appalled that the old be treated any differently to the young.

How Does the Poem Balance the Old and the New?

'You cannot value [a poet] alone' said T. S. Eliot: 'You must set him, for contrast and comparison, among the dead.'[105] The works of past writers provide a standard against which to measure and orientate present achievement, but a poet will understandably want to do more than just replicate them – just as Clough does something new with Homer's form, and just as Yeats leaves behind his past self. One of the tasks of a great poet, as Wordsworth said, is that of '*creating* the taste by which he is to be enjoyed'.[106]

There is no point in a poem simply repeating what already exists. At the same time, a completely original poem would be unrecognisable as a poem at all. A successful poem will marry familiarity with strangeness. The balance a poet finds between tradition and originality will be a matter of temperament. 'All we can do is to write on the old themes in the old styles, but try to do a little better than those who went before us', said Thomas Hardy, and he wrote great poetry out of this glum principle.[107] 'Talk to me of originality and I will turn on you with rage', snapped Yeats: 'Ancient salt is best packing'.[108] Behind both attitudes is a belief that tradition, in terms of technique, outlook, subject matter, provides a stabilising force, a soil that grounds the flimsiness of personal whim. Traditions develop because they embody the most important and enduring aspects of human experience. On the other side of the question, few poets have written so thrillingly of our hankering for newness as Gerard Manley Hopkins, who in an 1864 letter expressed impatience with poets who find a way of writing and then just rest on their laurels: 'In a fine piece of inspiration every beauty takes you as it were by surprise . . . every fresh beauty could not in any way be predicted or accounted for by what one has already read.'[109] That is, the best poetry will always defy our expectations.

How do we establish the expectations against which to measure a poem's debt to or deviation from the past? How do we set a poet among the dead? The best long-term answer is through extensive reading. The more poems we read, the more we see how each poem situates itself alongside those that exist already, discovering new things and developing old ones. Poems will often indicate the traditions they grow out of and the genres to which they belong. Toru Dutt in her 'Sonnet – Baugmaree' (1882) adapts a form usually associated with male praise of women, the Petrarchan sonnet, and a mode associated with idealised images of nationhood, the pastoral, to celebrate the inspiration she found in the garden of her family home in the suburbs of Kolkata. The poem lulls us into an expectation of something conventional in its opening line, which stirs up memories of John of Gaunt's vision of England as an 'other Eden' 'set in a silver sea' in Shakespeare's *Richard II* (1597), before exploding into a realm of colour beyond English pastoral greenery: 'A sea of foliage girds our garden round, / But not a sea of dull unvaried green'. The vibrancy of Dutt's pastoral world is epitomised by the seemul trees at its heart: 'oe'r the quiet pools the seemuls lean, / Red – red, and startling like a trumpet's sound'. Dutt's simile has its own startling force, thanks to the way it encourages us to *hear* a colour, and the lines show how originality might be combined with simplicity, as they revolve upon the adjective so that the word is held before our eyes, as though the intensity of colour were too strong for a single utterance to express. The poem ends with Dutt looking on the beauty of her home environment 'in amaze': the sense of homely familiarity usually associated with pastoral is transformed into a state of wonderment, and she has to buckle the ordinary grammar of the language ('amaze', not 'amazement') in order to express the depth of her feeling.

Other poems might signal expectations through their subject matter rather than their form. The title of Denise Levertov's 'Caedmon' (1987), for instance, directs us via its title back to the fountainhead of English poetry, a hymn dating from the end of the seventh century. The hymn is recorded in Bede's *History of the English Church and People* (c. 731), where it is framed with the story that it was composed by an illiterate cowherd, Caedmon, who was one night divinely inspired to sing in praise of 'the beginning of created things':

> the work of the Glory-Father,   when he of wonders every one,
> eternal Lord,   in the beginning established.

Levertov's title, then, evokes a whole chain of creation narratives: Caedmon sings of God's creation of the universe, recounting the beginning of the Book of Genesis; Bede tells the story of the origins of English poetry in Caedmon's poem (to add a further layer, Levertov has a note to her poem saying that she first came across Bede's narrative in Richard Green's *History of the English People* (1855)). Levertov's poem extends this tradition. Just as Caedmon's poem grows out of Genesis by turning emphasis more directly towards praise for 'the Measurer's might' than the opening verses of the scripture do, so Levertov adds new colourings and inflections to Caedmon's story as she encounters it in Bede. She assumes Caedmon's voice, fleshing out his character to imagine him as an oafish figure who sneaks out of the room once talk turns to poetry, to find comfort among the 'body sounds' of the animals:

All others talked as if
talk were a dance.
Clodhopper I, with clumsy feet
would break the gliding ring.

These opening words, breaking two sentences across two lines each, pick up the alliterative patterns and two-part rhythms that characterise Caedmon's Old English verse. Levertov allows us to glimpse her poem's roots. But as the poem develops and starts to recount the moment of divine inspiration, it acquires a more fluent eloquence: repetitions accumulate through elongating lines, replacing the tentative balance of the opening with a gathering momentum and visionary brilliance. The world seemed aflame, Caedmon says, but:

nothing was burning.
nothing but I, as that hand of fire
touched my lips and scorched my tongue
and pulled my voice
into the ring of the dance.

The poem ends with Caedmon's voice taking its place in its community, and with Levertov, as she finds an original style and turns an old story into a new one, completing a circle with a thirteen-hundred-year-old poem, and finding her own place in a tradition. To keep the flame of a tradition burning, Levertov's images suggest, a poet must sacrifice their individuality to it.

Every poem engages in conversation with those that have gone before, entering 'the ring of the dance', in Levertov's phrase; and every poem reimagines what a poem can be. The process of reconnection and reimagining takes place across all the features we have been discussing in this book: we can always consider, within the framework of the questions we have been asking about form, language, and content, what a poem inherits from previous poems and what it does that is new. It is worth introducing a couple of more specific ways in which the question of originality can be brought into focus. First, the matter of *allusion*, the practice of calling someone else's words into play either covertly or through direct quotation. A lot of fuss is made when literature, films, and music are being discussed on radio or television over the 'references' a work contains, as though simply by 'referencing' other parts of a culture a work can acquire meaning. But while it can be illuminating to know of other works and achievements a poet has in mind – and wants to call into our mind – a poem is not just a museum of inert memories of other poems, nor is it sufficient for us as readers just to spot these echoes. Allusion is a matter of transformation as well as tribute. We need to ask why a poem is calling the words of another poem to mind and what it is doing with them. In 'Toads' (1955), Philip Larkin complains about his work commitments, wishing that he had the courage to cry '*Stuff your pension!*' before reflecting ruefully that 'that's the stuff / That dreams are made on'. 'We are such stuff as dreams are made on', says Prospero in Shakespeare's *The Tempest* (1610–11). Larkin punctures Prospero's poignant sense of human transience and glimmering apprehension of human possibility by dragging his image into the drab reality of daily routine and responsibility; a language of dreaming aspiration is transformed into world-weary insult: 'get stuffed'. Yet Larkin doesn't simply desecrate Shakespeare's words: the very fact of his remembering them shadows his lines with a sad reminder of a more elevated conception of human life. Allusion balances tradition and innovation, making something new out of the old. U. A. Fanthorpe, in 'BC:AD' (1982) writes of Christ's birth that 'This was the moment when nothing / Happened'. Her lines imagine the balance of continuity and change between past and present so potently because they give a new turn to a line from another poet, W. H. Auden, whose 'In Memory of W. B. Yeats' (1939) contains the line 'Poetry makes nothing happen'.[110] Fanthorpe's allusion makes something 'happen' with Auden's words, sharpening the ambiguity of the phrase against the edge of the line to present an old thought in a new way.

The effort to be original is an effort to avoid cliché. One value of good poetry is that it rids our minds of stale and imprecise observations. As Shelley says, poetry 'creates anew the universe, after it has been annihilated in our minds by the recurrence of impressions blunted by reiteration'.[111] It shows us the world in greater nuance and more vivid colour. It weans us off a life of easy slogans and the deadening effect of over-familiar rhythms and forms of expression. Poetry that predictably repeats the past – that is too bound by what Wordsworth called 'pre-established codes of decision'[112] – unthinkingly inherited notions of how things should be – deadens our apprehension of experience. If you look up the poems published in your local newspaper – or, increasingly, broadcast on social media – you'll see that the reason the majority of them are so banal is that they are written according to an ossified notion of what a poem is: artificially elevated language, sing-song rhymes and rhythms, false expressions of feeling, rather than words made expressive by feeling. And yet clichés persist because they contain truths, and engaging with cliché can be one way in which a poem shows us old things in new ways or gives familiar form to unfamiliar apprehensions. Donald Justice's sonnet 'Mrs Snow' (1987) reminisces about a former music teacher who, despite a fondness for kitsch, introduced him to art and looked indulgently on a waltz he once composed 'full of marvellous clichés'. The poem follows its account of this childhood initiation with a half-line, broken off from the rest of the poem: 'Ah, those were the days'. That is as sentimental a cliché as they come, but it is winningly and wittily deployed, earning its nostalgia by its acknowledgement that part of what it is longing for is the age when one could get away with writing clichés. Justice discovers new expressive force in his cliché through his ironic handling of it; at other times, it is the very lack of ironic self-awareness with which a cliché is deployed that brings it to life. Robert Burns's poems are full of such moments:

Or were I in the wildest waste,
Sae black and bare, sae black and bare,
The desert were a Paradise,
If thou wert there, if thou wert there . . .

It is as though the back-and-forth momentum of the stanza form has swayed the poem (1800) into its exaggerated expression of commitment. And yet the very exaggeration seems to cause the feeling to transcend cliché: the lines promise not just to protect a lover, but say that to suffer in their company would be a pleasure. We are startled, amid the predictable alternation of the rhythms, by a feeling which, to take a wonderfully hesitant phrase from Justice's sonnet, is 'Too innocent to be completely false / Perhaps'. The dialect authenticates the feeling by individualising the stock situation, and the lines are unsettlingly free of irony.

Poems can also give birth to clichés. Our first reaction to the following stanza from Tennyson's *In Memoriam* (1850) is likely to be surprise at discovering the source of a proverb:

I hold it true, whate'er befall;
    I feel it, when I sorrow most;
    'Tis better to have loved and lost
Than never to have loved at all.

To look closely at the lines is to realise that poetry's presentation of 'What oft was thought but ne'er so well expressed', in Alexander Pope's words ('An Essay on Criticism' (1711)), is a matter of its precision. Tennyson doesn't merely present us with the lines, which, even though he is minting them new, have the ring of a proverb: he winds them into a sentence which shows the desperation with which he clings to them. When we encounter what seems to be a cliché, we should treat it with patience, smile on it like Mrs Snow. It pays to remember T. S. Eliot's observation that 'to be original with the minimum of alteration is sometimes more distinguished than to be original with the maximum of alteration'.[113]

The most original poems often dramatise an awareness of how difficult it is to achieve originality. Samuel Beckett's last poem 'what is the word' (1989) takes us into the struggle to find something new to say:

> what is the word –
> see –
> glimpse –
> seem to glimpse –
> need to seem to glimpse –
> folly for to need to seem to glimpse –
> what –
> what is the word –
> and where –
> folly for to need to seem to glimpse what where –

It would be obvious, even to a reader new to poetry, that not all poems are written like this. If we try to read the lines in the way I have suggested, following their sense, and the construction of their sentences, we find that we cannot – the poem isn't written in anything we would ordinarily recognise as sentences. Lines advance and retreat, groping into the white space beyond them by outlining an ever-diminishing apprehension of what they might achieve – 'see – / glimpse – / seem to glimpse –' – before these forays towards articulation collapse as they realise the 'folly' of their own efforts. But does the writing record a failure to communicate? Or does it embody the discovery of a new mode of expression?

There will be some for whom such an endeavour is itself 'folly' – who want to reach for A. E. Housman's tart remark that 'originality is not nearly so good as goodness, even when it is good'.[114] And certainly we ought to be on our guard against cheap forms of newness: it is easy to do something that hasn't been done before, but the reason for that is that most of the time it isn't worth doing. Beckett's originality, however, was achieved at great cost: the poem was written when age and illness had damaged his powers of speech. And its voice is buttressed in a consciousness of tradition. The 'goodness' of Beckett's poem is at one with its continuity with what has gone before. 'In the beginning was the word', begins John's Gospel. Playing on these words, Beckett's poem seems to take us back not only before the process of its own composition, but to imagine going back to before the 'beginning' of the whole universe. The form of the writing is very new; but it takes us newly back into an old problem: how do we say anything new? What is the nature of art and creativity? 'Beckett's originality is of the highest kind: one aware that the word *original*, comprehensively comprehended, takes up within its history not only "existing now for the first time" but also "having existed from the first"', as Christopher Ricks has said.[115]

How Does the Poem End?

How can a poem such as Beckett's, which seems to be embroiled in an endless process of going nowhere – of struggling, even, to find a place to start – reach an end? Here is its final movement:

> glimpse –
> seem to glimpse –
> need to seem to glimpse –
> afaint afar away over there what –
> folly for to need to seem to glimpse afaint afar away over there what –
> what –
> what is the word –
>
> what is the word

The longest line in the poem – the one which stretches furthest but builds that achievement on a description of its diminishing sense of what expression might gain purchase on – collapses back to the shortest. The movement contains both comedy and tragedy; it tracks an absurd but heroic struggle. It delivers us to two final lines which bring the poem to a standstill. The lines cause the poem to end, appropriately, on a moment of repetition: both in that they take us back to the opening line of the poem and in that the last line replicates the penultimate one. The final line is set off by a stanza break, as though the poem were taking a breath before resolving that these were to be its final words. It is the only occasion in the poem other than the title itself in which the words appear without being followed by a dash that reaches out into the void. The last line creates a sense of rest and finality, then, and one which, for all it reiterates the poem's defeated puzzlement, might make us think that the poem has made a tiny breakthrough: if, all through the poem, we have been reading the phrase as a question, here the rhythms raise the possibility that we could hear it as a statement, too – one that, after the poem has repeatedly edged towards the question, 'what is the word?', comes to realise that the question itself is the whole point: '"what" is the most appropriate word with which to respond to the mysteries of creation.

'In all metrical compositions', said John Donne, 'the force of the whole piece, is for the most part left to the summing up; the whole frame of the Poem is a beating out of a piece of gold, but the last clause is as the impression of the stamp, and that is it that makes it current'.[116] Just as the beginning of a poem might pose a dilemma, or set up an issue to be resolved, so one can expect the ending of a poem to bring a degree of resolution, even if, as in Beckett's poem, it is only the resolution that nothing can be resolved. Donne's image reminds us that such resolution might be a matter of a poem's form as well as its argument. Beckett achieves that formal closure through his use of repetition. In poems following a more pre-determined formal structure, then the shape of the ending might be more definitive. In a Shakespearean sonnet, for instance, the closing couplet affords the opportunity to resolve the issues explored in the poem with a sharp turn of phrase. 'Who can stop time destroying beauty?' asks Sonnet 65 (1609):

> O, none, unless this miracle have might,
> That in black ink my love may still shine bright.

This is a satisfyingly crisp ending. But even here there is a certain restlessness about the poem's point of rest. 'O none', with its echoing nothingness, mounts the most negative of answers before the about-turn on the 'unless' directs things towards a more hopeful conclusion. We have said that poems often involve a 'miniature drama' of opposed perspectives, and an ending might seek to resolve them one way or another; but stamping too firm a closure upon a poem leaves it liable to the charge of making too clean a breast of the poem's conflicts and complexities to be convincing. One of Donne's own most finely judged endings deflects from taking too much pride in its own achievement. 'The Relic' (1633) reflects on a love affair in three intricate eleven-line stanzas, each of which closes with a seemingly resonant rhyming triplet, which the final stanza devotes to remembering the treasure of the poet's lover. The effect might be overly emphatic were it not for the deftness with which Donne handles the form:

> These miracles we did; but now alas,
> All measure, and all language, I should pass,
> Should I tell what a miracle she was.

The finale undercuts its own grandiosity in two ways. First by having as the final rhyme a word, 'was', whose shorter final *s* means that it doesn't wholly accord with the 'alas'/'pass' sound that precedes it. Secondly, by ensuring that the prose rhythms of the final line pull against the underlying metre so that as one reads the line aloud, thanks to the repetition of 'miracle', the emphasis falls not on the final word, 'was', but, generously and lovingly, on 'she': the poem closes in a gesture of failure that is an artistic triumph.

At the other end of the spectrum from Donne's notion of the ending as 'the impression of a stamp' is the kind of poem which does not so much end as stop. Kathleen Jamie closes 'The Shrew' (2015) with some lines that imagine a coincidence between the ending of her poem and the way she herself wants to die:

when my hour comes,
let me go like the shrew
right here on the path: spindthrift on her midget fur,
caught mid-thought, mid-dash

It is not that there is no formal resolution here, but that resolution comes more out of a sense of suspended animation than achieved closure. The poise and delicacy owe to a twine of internal rhyme. And careful ambiguity ('dash' as hurry, 'dash' as punctuation; 'go' as departure and new beginning) leaves the poem caught in the suspended animation the poet desires for herself. It is a more modern, open-ended effect, and it carries with it a different sense of how a poem exists: this is an ending fitted not to the artificial, finely wrought 'piece of gold' that Donne imagines, but one whose fragile poise belongs to the notion of art as a more provisional entity, open to the flow of experience, rather than standing against its current.

The contrast between Donne and Jamie shows how endings can bring about different degrees of resolution. Coming to the end of a poem as a reader, we are inclined to expect everything to fall into place: even if we've been left utterly baffled by the poem up to this point, the final line, we feel, or hope, will elucidate everything, like the moment of revelation in a detective story. Sometimes this is the case. A poem will reach a satisfying closure which causes everything – formally and in terms of argument – to make sense. Other poems are happy to leave us perplexed. In such cases, we should trust our judgement: our perplexity is just as liable to reveal something about the poem as it is our own incapacity as readers. A poem may want to show us that the difficulties it addresses are irresolvable. One of the reasons we go to poetry is to apprehend and deal with complexity, so we should be grateful, not appalled or panicked or self-critical, when we find it there.

We might remember at this stage that one of the best ways of tackling difficulty in poetry is to return to the question of what a poem is trying to achieve. And endings can be just as informative as beginnings in this respect. Endings leave us with a sense of a poem's dominant concerns – its 'ends' in another sense of the word. Here (in translation) is the Madagascan poet Jean-Joseph Rabearivelo's 'Une Autre' ('Another', 1934), the third in a sequence of poems on the dawn:

All the stars are melted together
in the crucible of time,

cooled in the sea
and turned into a block of faceted stone.
Dying lapidary,[41] the night,
putting all her heart
and all her grief into her millstones
which crumble, crumble,
like ashes in the wind,
cuts caringly the prism.

But it's a monument of light
which the artist has erected on her invisible tomb.

The poem is an aubade, a welcome to the dawn. It offers a visionary take on the genre, presenting day as a phenomenon constructed from the materials of night. For all the opening paragraph's gorgeous imagery, the poem saves its emotional and conceptual depths for the final pair of lines. They reveal that the poem's deepest concern is with art itself, and its effort, forlorn, perhaps, but luminous, to build a permanent monument in the face of time's progress. Yet even as they seem to offer a key to the poem's significance, these final lines unlock, too, the complexity of the poem's sense of its own achievement. Dawn, they suggest, is a 'monument of light' that obscures the night that fashioned it, just as, it is implied, a work of art might obliterate its artist. The image speaks beautifully and sadly of the sense that all that art illuminates is our own inconsequence. Yet the very radiance and memorability of the image calls that despair into question. The 'summing up', in Donne's phrase, generates ironies as well as certainties. While endings often promise to make sense of a poem, they often also show us the conflicting senses a poem might make.

Endings involve not only a consideration of how to stop, but where to stop. As we approach the end of a poem, it pays to keep in mind the question of how we would be tempted to round things off, if we were the author, and what the effect might be of stopping a poem sooner. The final verse paragraph of Samuel Taylor Coleridge's 'Frost at Midnight', as he published it in 1798, ran like this, with the poet sitting in his cottage sending blessings to his son asleep in a cot beside him:

Therefore all seasons shall be sweet to thee,
Whether the summer clothe the general earth
With greenness, or the redbreasts sit and sing
Betwixt the tufts of snow on the bare branch
Of mossy apple-tree, while all the thatch
Smokes in the sun-thaw; whether the eave-drops fall

[41] stone mason

Heard only in the trances of the blast,
Or if the secret ministry of cold
Shall hang them up in silent icicles,
Quietly shining to the quiet Moon;
Like those, my babe! which ere tomorrow's warmth
Have capped their sharp keen points with pendulous drops,
Will catch thine eye, and with their novelty
Suspend thy little soul; then make thee shout
And stretch and flutter from thy mother's arms
As thou would'st fly for a very eagerness.

When Coleridge published the poem in his *Poetical Works*, over thirty years later, he chose to cut the last six lines, ending on the vision of icicles 'Quietly shining to the quiet moon.' Coleridge's justification, scribbled in the margin of his 1798 version of the poem, was that the deleted lines 'destroy the rondo and return upon itself of the Poem. Poems of this kind of length [it is about eighty lines long] ought to lie coiled with its tail round its head.' What he had in mind was the way in its revised ending the poem closes by returning to its opening line, 'The frost performs its secret ministry' – achieving that formal neatness and sense of closure courted to varying degrees by Beckett, Shakespeare, Donne, Jamie, and Rabearivelo (among a handful of other small changes Coleridge made was to alter 'secret ministry of cold' to 'secret ministry of frost'). But the ending also shows Coleridge's feeling for the art of knowing when to shut up: how much more vividly the icicles hang in our mind's eye once the noise of the succeeding six lines is done away with; the ending now achieves the 'quietness' that it cherishes.

Notes

1. Louise Bogan, 'Juan's Song', *The Blue Estuaries: Poems, 1923–1968* (New York, NY: Farrar, Straus, and Giroux, 1996), 10.
2. Gerard Manley Hopkins, *The Collected Works of Gerard Manley Hopkins: Correspondence*, ed. R. K. R. Thornton and Catherine Phillips, 2 vols. (Oxford: Oxford University Press, 2013), i. 477.
3. William Empson, *Seven Types of Ambiguity* (1930), 3rd ed. (London: Penguin, 1961), 7.
4. Charles Olson, *Collected Prose*, ed. Donald Allan and Benjamin Friedlander (Berkeley: University of California Press, 1997), 240.
5. Francis T. Palgrave, preface to *The Golden Treasury: Selected from the Best Songs and Lyrical Poems in the English Language* (London, 1861), ix.
6. Dante, *Literary Criticism of Dante Alighieri*, ed. Robert S. Haller (Lincoln, NE: University of Nebraska Press, 1973), 99.

7. W. B. Yeats, 'A General Introduction for My Work' (1937), *The Major Works*, ed. Edward Larrissy (Oxford: Oxford University Press, 2001), 411.
8. F. W. Bateson, *English Poetry: A Critical Introduction* (London: Longman, 1950), 59.
9. John Keats, *The Complete Poems*, ed. John Barnard (Harmondsworth: Penguin, 1976), 519.
10. Arthur Symons, 'Ernest Dowson', *The Poems and Prose of Ernest Dowson* (London: John Lane, 1905), xxv.
11. See Garrett Stewart, 'Keats and Language', *The Cambridge Companion to Keats*, ed. Susan J. Wolfson (Cambridge: Cambridge University Press, 2001), 133–51.
12. William Wordsworth, 'Preface to *Lyrical Ballads*' (1800–02), *The Major Works*, ed. Stephen Gill (Cambridge: Cambridge University Press, 2008), 602. The phrase 'such as Angels weep' is quoted from Milton's *Paradise Lost*, a poem which embodies a more high-flown poetic idiom than Wordsworth advocates.
13. Rebecca Watts, 'The Studio', *The Times Literary Supplement*, 29 May 2020.
14. Rebecca Watts, 'After rain', *The Met Office Advises Caution* (Manchester: Carcanet, 2016), 51.
15. Carol Ann Duffy, *The Christmas Truce* (London: Picador, 2011).
16. Thomas Gray, *Correspondence of Thomas Gray*, ed. Paget Toynbee and Leonard Whible, 3 vols. (Oxford: Clarendon Press, 1935), 192.
17. Kathleen Jamie, 'Interview with Kathleen Jamie', by Lilias Fraser, *Scottish Studies Review* 2.1 (2001): 22.
18. Samuel Taylor Coleridge, *The Collected Works of Samuel Taylor Coleridge, Vol 12: Marginalia II: Camden to Hutton*, ed. George Whalley (London: Routledge and Kegan Paul, 1984), 220.
19. Michael Ondaatje, 'Driving with Dominic in the Southern Province We See Hints of the Circus', *Handwriting* (London: Jonathan Cape, 2011), 54.
20. Rosemary Tonks, *Bedouin of the London Evening: Collected Poems and Selected Prose* (Northumberland: Bloodaxe, 2016).
21. I draw here on a reading of Gurney's poem published in my *The Poetry of Clare, Hopkins, Thomas, and Gurney: Lyric Individualism* (Basingstoke: Palgrave Macmillan, 2020). 'After War' is quoted from *The Complete Poems*, ed. P. J. Kavanagh (Manchester: Carcanet, 2004), 145.
22. Empson, *Seven Types of Ambiguity*, 3.
23. Empson, *Seven Types of Ambiguity*, 147–9.
24. Empson, *Seven Types of Ambiguity*, 235.
25. T. S. Eliot, letter to *The Times Literary Supplement*, 27 September 1928.
26. Matthew Arnold, 'On Translating Homer', *The Complete Prose Works of Matthew Arnold*, ed. R. H. Super, 11 vols. (Ann Arbor: University of Michigan Press, 1960), i. 146.
27. William Wordsworth, *The Letters of William and Dorothy Wordsworth. The Early Years*, 2nd ed., ed. Ernest de Selincourt, rev. Chester L. Shaver (Oxford: Clarendon Press, 1967), 434.

28. Judith Wright, 'Egrets', *Collected Poems, 1942–1985* (London: HarperCollins, 2017), 168.
29. Elinor Wylie, 'Cold Blooded Creatures', *Selected Works of Elinor Wylie*, ed. Evelyn Helmick Hively (Kent, OH: Kent State University Press, 2005), 44.
30. Percy Bysshe Shelley, 'A Defence of Poetry', *The Major Works*, ed. Zachary Leader and Michael O'Neill (Oxford: Oxford University Press, 2008), 482.
31. John Betjeman, 'I. M. Walter Ramsden', *Collected Poems*, introd. Andrew Motion (London: John Murray, 2006), 166.
32. Timothy Steele, *All the Fun's in How You Say a Thing: An Exploration of Metre and Rhythm* (Athens, OH: Ohio University Press, 1999), 3.
33. Empson, *Seven Types of Ambiguity*, 28.
34. Alexander Pushkin, *Eugine Onegin*, tr. Charles Johnston (London: Penguin, 1979), 81.
35. The rhythmic complexity of Cowper's poem arises from an effort to marry a classical verse form known as the Sapphic ode with English metrical practice.
36. Langston Hughes, 'The Weary Blues', *Collected Poems of Langston Hughes*, ed. Arnold Rampersad and David Roessel (New York, NY: Vintage, 1995), 50.
37. James Smith, 'Wordsworth: A Preliminary Survey', in *Shakespearean and Other Essays* (Cambridge: Cambridge University Press, 1974), 298.
38. Bateson, *English Poetry*, 31.
39. Claude Rawson, introduction to *The Cambridge Companion to English Poets*, ed. Rawson (Cambridge: Cambridge University Press, 2011), 8.
40. Gerard Manley Hopkins, 'On the Origin of Beauty: A Platonic Dialogue' (1865), *The Collected Works of Gerard Manley Hopkins: Volume IV: Oxford Essays and Notes*, ed. Lesley Higgins (Oxford: Oxford University Press, 2006), 153.
41. Samuel Daniel, 'A Defense of Rhyme' (1603), *Selected Poems and A Defense of Rhyme*, ed. Geoffrey G. Hiller and Peter L. Groves (Asheville: University of North Carolina Press, 1998), 205.
42. Oscar Wilde, 'The Critic as Artist' (1891), *The Major Works*, ed. Isobel Murray (Oxford: Oxford University Press, 1989), 244.
43. John Dryden, 'Dedication to *The Rival Ladies*' (1664), *Of Dramatic Poesy and Other Critical Essays*, ed. George Watson, 2 vols. (London: Dent, 1962), i. 8.
44. Ralph Waldo Emerson, *The Journals and Miscellaneous Notebooks of Ralph Waldo Emerson: Volume VII, 1839–1842*, ed. A. W. Plumstead and Harrison Hayford (Cambridge: Harvard-Belknap, 1969), 219.
45. Oscar Wilde, 'The Critic as Artist', *Major Works*, 244–5.
46. Primo Levi, 'Rhyming on the Counterattack', *The Mirror Maker: Stories and Essays*, trans. Raymond Rosenthal (London: Minerva, 1990), 113.
47. Algernon Charles Swinburne, 'Matthew Arnold's New Poems', in *Essays and Studies*, 2nd ed. (London: Chatto and Windus, 1876), 162.
48. Lyrics by Jarvis Cocker. Quoted from 'The Fear', *This Is Hardcore*, Universal Island Records, 1998.

49. Gertrude Stein, 'Susie Asado', *Selected Writings of Gertrude Stein*, ed. Carl van Vechten (New York: Vintage, 1990), 547.
50. Gertrude Stein, *Look at Me Now and Here I Am: Writings and Lectures, 1911–1945*, ed. Patricia Meyerowitz (London: Peter Owen, 1967), 116.
51. Tom Paulin, *Thomas Hardy: The Poetry of Perception* (Basingstoke: Macmillan, 1975), 3.
52. Ruth Padel, *52 Ways of Looking at a Poem: Or, How Reading Modern Poetry Can Change Your Life* (London: Chatto and Windus, 2002), 13.
53. Reeves, *The Critical Sense*, 68–9.
54. Stephen Spender, *World Within World: The Autobiography of Stephen Spender* (Berkeley, CA: University of California Press, 1966), 313–14.
55. Don Paterson, *101 Sonnets: From Shakespeare to Heaney* (London: Faber and Faber, 2012), xxvii.
56. Stephanie Burt, *Don't Read Poetry: A Book About How to Read Poems* (New York: Basic Books, 2019), 104.
57. Edward Young, *Conjectures on Original Composition* (London, 1759), 60.
58. David Ferry, *Virgil: The Aeneid* (Chicago, IL: University of Chicago Press, 2017), xv–xvii.
59. Ferry, *The Aeneid*, xv.
60. William Wordsworth, *The Letters of Dorothy Wordsworth: Volume IV: The Later Years, Part One: 1821–1828* (Oxford: Clarendon Press, 1978), 547.
61. David Farley-Hills (ed.), *Rochester: The Critical Heritage* (London: Routledge and Kegan Paul, 1972), 50.
62. Arthur Hallam, 'The Influence of Italian upon English Literature' (1831), *The Writings of Arthur Henry Hallam*, ed. T. H. V. Motter, (New York: MLA, 1943), 222.
63. F. R. Leavis, *New Bearings in English Poetry* (London: Penguin, 1976), 24.
64. T. S. Eliot, 'Reflections on *Vers Libre*' (1917), in *To Criticize the Critic and Other Writings* (1965), new ed. (London: Faber, 1978), 187.
65. D. H. Lawrence, *The Letters of D. H. Lawrence, Volume II: June 1913–October 1916*, ed. George Zytaruk and James T. Boulton (Cambridge: Cambridge University Press, 1981), 104.
66. William Carlos Williams, 'Introduction to *The Wedge*' (1944), in *Selected Essays* (New York: Random House, 1954), 257.
67. Glyn Maxwell, *On Poetry* (London: Oberon, 2012), 29.
68. W. H. Auden, *The English Auden: Poems, Essays, and Dramatic Writings, 1927–1939*, ed. Edward Mendelson (London: Faber and Faber, 1986).
69. Ian Samson, *September 1, 1939: A Biography of a Poem* (London: Fourth Estate, 2019), 140–1.
70. W. B. Yeats, 'A General Introduction for My Work', *Major Works*, 379.
71. Robert Browning, 'Essay on Shelley' (1852), in *Selected Writings*, ed. Richard Cronin and Dorothy McMillan (Oxford: Oxford University Press, 2015), 159–61.
72. Eric Griffiths, *The Printed Voice of Victorian Poetry* (Oxford: Clarendon Press, 1989), 241.

73. Robert Langbaum, *The Poetry of Experience: The Dramatic Monologue in Modern Literary Tradition* (New York: Random House, 1957).
74. John Stuart Mill, 'What Is Poetry?', 'Thoughts on Poetry and its Varieties' (1833) in *Autobiography and Literary Essays*, ed. John M. Robson and Jack Stillinger (Toronto: University of Toronto Press, 1981), 348.
75. Christopher Ricks, *Keats and Embarrassment* (Oxford: Oxford University Press, 1974), 191.
76. J. A. Cuddon, *The Penguin Dictionary of Literary Terms and Literary Theory* (Harmondsworth: Penguin, 1999).
77. Derek Walcott, 'Sea Canes', *Selected Poems*, ed. Edward Baugh (London: Faber and Faber, 2007), 105.
78. Hopkins, *Correspondence*, i. 333–4.
79. Jonathan Wordsworth, *The Music of Humanity: A Critical Study of Wordsworth's 'Ruined Cottage'* (London: Nelson, 1969), 153.
80. Roger Scruton, *The Aesthetics of Music* (Oxford: Oxford University Press, 1997), 387.
81. Edward Thomas, *Maurice Maeterlinck* (London: Methuen, 1911), 28.
82. T. S. Eliot, 'Wordsworth and English Poetry', *Egoist*, 4 (1917), 118–19.
83. John Keats, letter to John Hamilton Reynolds, 21 September 1819, *The Letters of John Keats, Vol. 2: 1819–1821*, ed. Hyder Edward Rollins (Cambridge: Cambridge University Press, 1958), 167.
84. Shira Wolosky, *The Art of Poetry: How to Read a Poem* (Oxford: Oxford University Press, 2001), 29.
85. Hart Crane, 'Voyages I', *Complete Poems and Selected Letters*, ed. Langdon Hammer (New York: Library of America, 2006), 34.
86. Elizabeth Bishop, 'The Sandpiper', *Poems*, ed. Saskia Hamilton (London: Chatto and Windus, 2011), 131.
87. William Hazlitt, 'My First Acquaintance with Poets' (1823), in *Selected Essays*, ed. George Sampson (Cambridge: Cambridge University Press, 1917), 15.
88. Aristotle, *Poetics* quoted in F. L. Lucas, *Style: The Art of Writing Well* (1955), 3rd ed. (Petersfield: Harriman House, 2012), 169.
89. Percy Bysshe Shelley, 'A Defence of Poetry' (1821), in *The Major Works*, ed. Zachary Leader and Michael O'Neill (Oxford: Oxford University Press, 2003), 676.
90. D. H. Lawrence quoted in David Abercrombie, *Problems and Principles: Studies in the Teaching of English* (London: Longman, 1956), 15.
91. William Hazlitt, 'On Shakespeare and Milton', in *Lectures on the English Poets* (London, 1818), 107.
92. William Empson, *The Complete Poems*, ed. John Haffenden (London: Penguin, 2001), 29.
93. Valentine Ackland, 'The eyes of body', in *Journey from Winter: Selected Poems*, ed. Frances Bingham (Manchester: Fyfield-Carcanet, 2008), 43.
94. Wordsworth, 'Preface to *Lyrical Ballads*', 599.

95. John Dryden, 'Preface to *Fables Ancient and Modern*' (1700), in *The Works of John Dryden, Volume VII: Poems, 1697–1700*, ed. Vinton A. Dearing (Berkeley: University of California Press, 2000), 37.
96. John Dryden, 'A Discourse Concerning the Original and Progress of Satire' (1693), in *The Works of John Dryden, Volume* IV*: Poems 1693–1696*, ed. Vinton A. Dearing (Berkeley: University of California Press, 1974), 71.
97. Matthew Arnold, *On Translating Homer: Three Lectures Given at Oxford* (London: Longman, 1861), 79.
98. Johnson, 'Life of Dryden', *Lives of the Poets*, 167.
99. T. E. Hulme, 'Romanticism and Classicism' (c. 1911–12), *The Collected Writings of T. E. Hulme*, ed. Karen Csengeri (Oxford: Clarendon Press, 1994), 68, 62.
100. Shelley, 'A Defence of Poetry', *The Major Works*, 693.
101. Gertrude Bell, *Poems from the Divan of Hafez* (London: Heinemann, 1897), 63.
102. Dick Davis, *Faces of Love: Hafez and the Poets of Shiraz* (Harmondsworth: Penguin, 2012), xxxviii.
103. W. B. Yeats, *The Trembling of the Veil, Book IV: The Tragic Generation* (1922), in *Autobiographies*, ed. William H. O'Donnell and Douglas N. Archibald (New York: Scribner, 1999), 242.
104. Hulme, 'Romanticism and Classicism', 69, 66.
105. T. S. Eliot, 'Tradition and the Individual Talent', *The Sacred Wood: Essays on Poetry and Criticism* (London: Methuen, 1920), 28.
106. William Wordsworth, 'Essay, Supplementary to the Preface of *Poems*' (1815), *Major Works*, 658.
107. Thomas Hardy, quoted in Robert Graves, *Goodbye to All That* (1929) (Harmondsworth: Penguin, 2000), 377.
108. W. B. Yeats, 'A General Introduction for My Work', *Major Works*, 387.
109. Hopkins, *Correspondence*, i. 69.
110. W. H. Auden, 'In Memory of W. B. Yeats', in *The English Auden: Poems, Essays, and Dramatic Writings, 1927–1939*, ed. Edward Mendelson (London: Faber and Faber, 1977), 241.
111. Shelley, 'A Defence of Poetry', *Major Works*, 698.
112. Wordsworth, 'Advertisement to *Lyrical Ballads*', *Major Works*, 591.
113. T. S. Eliot, 'Poetry in the Eighteenth Century', *The Pelican Guide to English Literature, IV: From Dryden to Johnson*, ed. Boris Ford (Harmondsworth: Penguin, 1957), 272.
114. A. E. Housman, letter to Robert Bridges, 30th December 1918, *The Letters of A. E. Housman*, ed. Archie Burnett, 2 vols. (Oxford: Oxford University Press, 2007) i. 393–7.
115. Christopher Ricks, *Reviewery* (Harmondsworth: Penguin, 2003), 315.
116. John Donne, 'Sermon No. 1: Preached upon the Penitentiall Psalmes, April, May, or June, 1663,' in *The Sermons of John Donne*, ed. Evelyn M. Simpson and George R. Potter, 10 vols. (Berkeley: University of California Press, 1953), 6: 39–61, 41.

CHAPTER 2

Studying a Poet

Most readers will at some point wish to know and understand more than a scattering of individual poems. One option is to tailor our reading so that we become acquainted with the history of a particular genre or the characteristics of a particular period. Another is to develop a relationship with a particular poet. Becoming familiar with the work of a poet is one of the great pleasures of poetry: we get to know their characteristic voice, their way of viewing and presenting the world, the life they lived, their relationship with other poets and with the life of their times. This section arranges guidance about building up that understanding around two worked examples: Emily Brontë (1814–1848) and Srinivas Rayaprol (1925–1998).

Reading Emily Brontë

Imagine we want to find out about the work and career of Emily Brontë. If we're familiar with Brontë's name, it might be as the author of *Wuthering Heights*, the novel she published in 1847, which relates the tempestuous love affair between Catherine and Heathcliff. Perhaps we might have heard too of Brontë's sisters Charlotte and Anne, also novelists, and their life together in Haworth in the north of England, in the middle of the nineteenth century. We'll turn to that life in due course, but the best place to start with a new poet is with their poems. Often a tutor will assign some poems to read, but let's assume that we've been asked to find our own material, as part of a private research project, or just as a matter of personal interest. All poets have works in which, by common consent, they display their virtues more forcefully and memorably than others, or which stand out as being especially characteristic of their methods and concerns. And it makes sense to make these our point of departure: studying a poet doesn't necessarily mean reading everything they wrote; we want to sample something representative of them at their best. Develop a taste, and we'll become all the thirstier for the more obscure contents of a writer's cupboard. One way to find these works is by consulting an anthology. Three anthologies worth having to hand, commonly available in most libraries, are *The Norton Anthology of Poetry*, *The Oxford Book of English Verse*, and *The Penguin Book of English Verse*; for a more expansive selection, we might also consult some anthologies specific to the period in which Brontë wrote, such as *The New Oxford Book of Victorian Verse* and *The Penguin Book of Victorian Verse*. If we look up Brontë in the contents of the first three of these volumes, we'll find that they contain the following poems: 'Long neglect has worn away' (twice), 'Hope', 'Remembrance' (thrice), 'The Prisoner', 'The Visionary', 'No coward soul is mine', 'Stanzas' ('Often rebuked, yet always back returning') (twice), 'What winter floods what showers of spring', 'The night is darkening round me' (twice), 'All hushed and still within the house', 'I know not how it falls on me', 'Fall leaves fall die flowers away'. The range suggests that there is some disagreement about what constitutes Brontë's best work – room, eventually, for us to develop our own position – but there are some poems that recur, and it makes sense to begin with one of those.

Let's pick 'Remembrance' (1846). Our first task is just to absorb the poem as we would any other:

Cold in the earth—and the deep snow piled above thee,
Far, far, removed, cold in the dreary grave!
Have I forgot, my only Love, to love thee,
Severed at last by Time's all-severing wave?

Now, when alone, do my thoughts no longer hover
Over the mountains, on that northern shore,
Resting their wings where heath and fern-leaves cover
Thy noble heart forever, ever more?

Cold in the earth—and fifteen wild Decembers,
From those brown hills, have melted into spring:
Faithful, indeed, is the spirit that remembers
After such years of change and suffering!

Sweet Love of youth, forgive, if I forget thee,
While the world's tide is bearing me along;
Other desires and other hopes beset me,
Hopes which obscure, but cannot do thee wrong!

No later light has lightened up my heaven,
No second morn has ever shone for me;
All my life's bliss from thy dear life was given,
All my life's bliss is in the grave with thee.

But, when the days of golden dreams had perished,
And even Despair was powerless to destroy,
Then did I learn how existence could be cherished,
Strengthened, and fed without the aid of joy.

Then did I check the tears of useless passion—
Weaned my young soul from yearning after thine;
Sternly denied its burning wish to hasten
Down to that tomb already more than mine.

And, even yet, I dare not let it languish,
Dare not indulge in memory's rapturous pain;
Once drinking deep of that divinest anguish,
How could I seek the empty world again?

We can use some of the questions outlined in the first part of the book to begin to organise a response. In terms of genre, the poem is a lyric, but also an elegy, since it shows someone mourning the loss of a loved one. Those two genres help to outline the poem's concerns: love, loss, memory, the passage of time, and the difficulty of going on with life. Formally, the poem is in cross-rhymed (abab) quatrains, but unusually these are composed of iambic pentameter rather than tetrameter lines, which lends the voice a dragging, laboured quality (the effect is accentuated by the preponderance of hypermetric, eleven-syllable lines: Cecil Day Lewis described it as 'the *slowest* rhythm I know in English poetry, and the most sombre').[1] The poem seems obsessed by a single image – that of the dead lover 'Cold in the earth' with which the opening line startles us and whose memory the poem struggles to shake off. And tonally, the poem tracks a movement from anguish to the repression of painful feeling: it shows the poet getting on with her 'existence' (not her 'life' exactly) by quelling her emotions but leaves us with a question that hints at the enduring temptation of indulging in 'memory's rapturous pain'. Obviously, there is much more to be said. But the point of our initial notes is not to create a fine-grained account but rather a useful aid to memory: something that can help to build up contrasts and similarities across Brontë's work and provide a launch-pad for more in-depth attention should we return to the poem.

The next step is to repeat the process across some of the other poems in the anthologies, looking for ways in which they extend or expand the qualities and concerns we've observed in 'Remembrance'. Consider another of the poems that appears repeatedly in the anthologies, 'Long neglect has worn away' (1837), for instance, and we can start to pick out similarities and differences in its handling of form and feeling:

Long neglect has worn away
Half the sweet enchanting smile
Time has turned the bloom to gray
Mold and damp the face defile

But that lock of silky hair
Still beneath the picture twined
Tells what once those features were
Paints their image on the mind

Fair the hand that traced that line
"Dearest, ever deem me true"
Swiftly flew the fingers fine
When the pen that motto drew

Our task here is not just to read the poem but to read it against the observations we've made in reading 'Remembrance'. We should look for things the poems have in common, in order to build up a sense of Brontë's distinctive traits; we should look, too, for moments of difference: Gerard Manley Hopkins coined the term 'Parnassian' to describe the kind of poem in which a poet is all-too-predictably themselves, viewing and expressing things without the surprise that comes from 'inspiration'.[2] We might begin by noting the similarities in feeling and situation: both poems deal with love, loss, and grief; both contemplate time as an agent of separation from the source of one's grief, and wonder how to overcome that separation – in the previous case through memory, in this case through art. Both poems begin with an image around which memories congregate: in 'Remembrance' the image takes us into an outdoor world, where feeling seems wild, untameable; here the focus remains domestic. 'Remembrance' also moves further from its initial image into an account of the speaker's own feelings than this poem does. Indeed, one of the things that is subtly absent from 'Long neglect' is the word 'I', and the absence creates ambiguities around the poem's situation. Are we to read the poem as the utterance of a lover reflecting on the memories of their beloved? Or is the situation rather one of someone looking from a greater distance at someone else's relationship? Our interpretation of the situation bears upon our reading of the poem's tone, particularly in its final lines, whose observations about time's ability to reduce the promises we make to our loved ones to rubble will sound differently depending on whether or not we see them as being spoken from within or without the relationship in question. Finally, we might make an observation about the form. Like 'Remembrance', this poem is in cross-rhymed quatrains, but in this instance quatrains of catalectic trochaic tetrameter: the shorter lines seem suited to the poem's more shielded involvement in its own feelings. Again, it's worth making simple notes of what strike us as the poem's most salient features.

Merely from two poems, we can start to sketch some of Brontë's characteristics: her fondness for songlike forms; her interest in how we deal with loss, and the aftermath of feeling; her capacity to register intense feeling at the same time as struggling against it. These generalisations may turn out to be only partially accurate, but they constitute our developing understanding of the kind of poet Brontë is – the standpoints she tends to adopt, the forms and language she uses, her subjects and the way she treats them. They give us a platform for continued reading: a set of expectations which future poems may fulfil, or – hopefully – surprise. Imagine, now, that we've exhausted the poems in the anthologies and we've decided we want to know a wider range of Brontë's work. The next step is to go to a library or a bookshop and get hold of a good edition of Brontë's poems. With some poets, this might mean a *Selected Poems*, but since Brontë wrote a relatively small amount, there is scope for getting hold of a *Complete* volume. What constitutes a 'good' edition? Primarily, it means an edition which has been professionally edited so that we can be sure of the accuracy of the texts we are reading, and one which contains some scholarly apparatus: annotations to offer information about the poems, and perhaps an introduction. It means, above all, a print or professionally published electronic edition: the screen of a mobile phone will not give a poem space to breathe. Browsing the shelves, the Penguin edition of *The Complete Poems*, edited by Janet Gezari, seems best to fit the bill.

We can read the contents of that volume cover to cover; we can read them in tandem with works of criticism (see below), looking up poems which feature frequently in essays about Brontë's work; or we can begin with poems which, on account of their length, are less suitable for anthologies. However we choose to negotiate the material, the point will be to develop and refine the generalisations we made from the anthology poems. So we might ask how a poem such as 'Why ask to know the date – the clime?' (1846), which runs to 263 lines, develops possibilities not available to a short lyric. There isn't space here to offer a full answer to that question, but we should be able to see how a poem which tells a story in the first person of a soldier in a civil war capturing and torturing an opposition leader and his daughter, before pleading with the captive to send a letter of mercy upon receiving news of the capture of his own child, both shares the interest in turbulent and anguished feelings developed in the two poems we looked at above and shows how, in a different form, Brontë can explore them in varied and more extended directions. The ending of the poem, describing events once the captive leader has instructed his own forces to grant mercy and then died, provides a point of focus for contemplating how the poem expands our conception of Brontë's work:

His child
I found alive and tended well
But she was full of anguish wild
And hated me like we hate hell
And weary with her savage woe
One moonless night I let her go

The lines carry over the laconic, elliptical quality of the lyrics, which suggest circumstances and relations that elude further explanation, into a narrative mode. The interest in the bleakly intense passion is familiar, but the four-beat lines, alternating between cross-rhymes and couplets, deal swiftly with feelings and relations whose complexities Brontë's stanzas would characteristically investigate more fully. The difficulty of love remains a concern – but here it is a quasi-parental rather than romantic affection. The ending shows a similar interest to the lyrics in the possibilities of irresolution.

We can carry on the process of expanding our familiarity with a writer for as long as we want: we could even extend questions – about Brontë's representation of pain or landscape or evil – into *Wuthering Heights*, to ask how Brontë's poems afford opportunities to present her vision of the world differently to her prose. The important thing is to read purposefully: to be building up understanding, to be evolving a conception of what lies at the heart of a poet's achievement or of what most interests us about them. Students are often at a loss when invited to come up with an aspect of a poet that they would like to write about for an essay or dissertation. The problem can usually be solved by spending more time reading – with broad topics or questions in mind – before deciding on what to write about. Just as with reading an individual poem, in reading a poet, absorption in and description of what is there on the page are the precursor to interpretation: let yourself be guided by the material rather than straining to find within it what you hope to be there.

Reading about Emily Brontë

There is more to getting to know a poet than reading their poems. We want to know about the author's life and the times they worked in; we want to know how their work relates to that of other poets – their influences, their contemporaries, and those they have influenced; we want to engage with the critical debates surrounding their work. A good edition of the poems can provide a springboard for addressing all of these issues.

Gezari's edition contains a brief account of Brontë's life and a chronology of its important events. This knowledge can shed light on the concerns and subjects a poet writes about; it introduces us more fully to their vision and experience of the world. We learn that Brontë spent almost all of her life in Haworth, a 'small, isolated, hill village surrounded by moors', and that her only close friends were her three siblings. Even a shard of detail such as this illuminates the work. It supplies a context for its private, inward nature; it suggests a source for the dreariness of its atmosphere and imagery; it implies that the world which it emerges from and describes is one of intense, perhaps rather claustrophobic and repetitive isolation: it would be a surprise to find in Brontë's poems a bustling panorama of cosmopolitan activity. To discover the life in richer detail, though, we need to consult a biography. Gezari provides a guide to further reading which lists four items which sound like they might fit the bill: *Emily Brontë, Her Life and Work*, published by Muriel Spark and Derek Stanford in 1951; Winifred Gérin's *Emily Brontë: A Biography* (Oxford University Press, 1971); Edward Chitham's *A Life of Emily Brontë* (Blackwell, 1987); and Katherine Frank's *A Chainless Soul: A Life of Emily Brontë* (Ballantine Books, 1990). We won't want to read them all, unless we are writing a doctoral thesis. And it is a good idea, generally, to read the most recent, which will contain the most up-to-date knowledge and research. But it is worth, too, thinking about the intended readership: the slightly more sober title of Chitham's biography, and of the fact that it is published by an academic press imply a level of scholarly authority.

One of the stories told in Chitham's biography is of the difficulty Brontë had getting her poems published. It wasn't until 1850, over a year after her death, that any poems appeared under her own name (in an edition edited by her sister, Charlotte). In Emily's lifetime they were published along with poems by Charlotte and Anne under a male pseudonym in a collection called *Poems by Currer, Ellis, and Acton Bell* (1846) – only two copies of which sold in the book's first year (a beacon of consolation to aspiring poets everywhere). We might return to the poems to consider them in light of what these circumstances suggest about the limitations shaping the lives of women in the provinces of Victorian England. Could we, for instance, understand the poems' concern with the powers and limitations of the imagination as an effort to transcend and transform the constraints of the social world? Or does it, from another angle, constitute longing for even deeper retreat? The publication details also suggest the collaborative nature of Brontë's literary endeavour, which seems at odds with the often-idiosyncratic personal intensity of the writing. Another defining moment in Brontë's life was the receipt from her father of a box of toy soldiers, which in the later years of the sisters' childhood became the basis for a whole saga set in the imaginary world of Gondal. Many poems formed part of now lost narratives from this story, and awareness of this fact may change the degree to which we read them as uncomplicated expressions of personal feeling.

How else can we place the poems within the world in which a poet lived? One answer is to ask how their vision of the world refracts the social or political events of their era. 'Why ask to know the date – the clime?' suggests from its first line that the events and relations it records are timeless and universal: but there was barely a year of Brontë's life when the British weren't involved in a war in one of their colonies, and the poem's translation of its story of civil war into the realm of Gondal – which consisted of the imaginary North Pacific island of Gondal and the South Pacific island of Gaaldine, its subject realm – cannot but be informed and provoked by Brontë's awareness of those conflicts – whether we want to see it as a way of displacing attention or of refocusing it upon them. Another answer is to read the writers a poet themselves read: how do Brontë's poems develop the manner and concerns of Romantic poets such as Wordsworth and Shelley who wrote in the decades immediately preceding her? (A poet's letters or journals, or again a biography, can be valuable sources of information about their reading.) Or we might even be able to visit a writer's home and see how physical traces of their world survive in ours. In Howarth, we can visit the Brontë Parsonage Museum to imagine Brontë's life from the rooms in which she lived it, tread the streets and paths she would have trodden. The prospect might seem to take us a long way from the initial steps of leafing through an anthology, but it might allow us to read poems with which we have become familiar with fresh eyes.

Reading Criticism

I once asked a student who was struggling with their work how they typically prepared for a seminar. Their admirably honest answer was that they read the set material once, quickly, before searching for an explanation of the poem online and making notes from that. The student realised, even as they were responding to the question, why they weren't developing as a reader. Criticism of poetry does not give you 'the answers'. A poem is not a crossword puzzle, and, in any case, there is no joy to be had out of a puzzle if you don't work it out for yourself. The best advice regarding criticism is to ignore it until you have reached your own judgements about a poem or poet: what you like, what you dislike, what seems important, what leaves you puzzled and wanting somebody else's thoughts. Think of critical discussion as a debate for which you need to prepare your own opinions before entering. Even if we finally decide that a critic's judgement of a poem is truer than our own, we will gain far more from having worked out our own understanding and then challenged and developed it, rather than just having someone else's thoughts poured into our head.

Start with the poet, rather than a particular poem. Aim to get a general impression of how people have read and characterised a writer, within which you can situate your own readings. There are a number of volumes which offer points of departure: *The Cambridge History of English Poetry* and *The Cambridge Companion to English Poets* are always worth consulting – both contain essays on Brontë (by Michael O'Neill and by Dinah Birch); looking more narrowly within Brontë's period, *The Oxford Handbook of Victorian Poetry* also has an essay by Michael Wood; Michael Schmidt's *Lives of the Poets* never fails to whet the appetite and often manages to say in one sentence what would take other critics a whole book (of Brontë, Schmidt says, for instance, that there is an 'intense life in the verse' which 'strains the forms and breaks them into new configurations').[3] As you read these introductory pieces, assemble a sense of the main ways in which critics have attributed significance to the poet in question: a common thread running through the essays in the above collections, for instance, is, as Dinah Birch puts it, that the poems evoke 'a natural world whose austerity expresses and also tests the fortitude of the solitary speaker'.[4] We might then go back to the poems with this thought in mind, testing out the ways it is or isn't true of them. We should note down, too, any poems which are mentioned as being important which we have not yet read. And we should jot down any remarks which aid our understanding of the poems we have read.

As we start to build an understanding of a poet, we'll want to consult books as well as essays. We might find that there are studies which are repeatedly mentioned in the introductory material we've been reading so far, but the main source of guidance will be the bibliographies and reading lists attached to the end of them. The list of further reading in Gezari's edition contains a number of titles which suggest that they will get to grips with the central issues of Brontë's poetry: an essay by Cecil Day Lewis on

'The Poetry of Emily Brontë', a collection edited by Anne Smith called *The Art of Emily Brontë*. Begin with pieces whose titles suggest that they are going to offer observations which will interest any reader; titles which suggest a more specific thematic concern, such as Lawrence Lipking's *Abandoned Women and Poetic Tradition*, are the sort of thing we turn to on a second run through, as we start to narrow down our focus to the particular aspect of the poet's work that we are interested in. Don't be afraid to read selectively: if a monograph only contains a chapter or a couple of pages relevant to the poem or aspect of the work you are interested in, then focus your attention on that. I will say more about how to *use* criticism in the 'Writing About Poetry' section, but the crucial thing is to read with a sense of purpose and with your own evolving response to the poet in mind. As when reading a poem, you need to be active and to train yourself to ask questions: how does this fit with my understanding of this poem or poet? Does it cause me to change my mind, or consolidate my opinion?

Lastly, broaden your search. Expand your conception of what constitutes critical material and where you might find it. The excellent series of *Critical Heritage* books, for instance, offers histories of the responses to authors from the moment they were first published: we can see what Brontë's poems meant to her original audience and reviewers. Search out creative responses to the poems. Emily Dickinson had Brontë's 'No coward soul is mine' read at her funeral. We might get hold of a copy of Dickinson's poems and ask whether and how she seems to have learned from Brontë – in terms of form, imagery, vision. Charlotte Mew introduced a selection of Brontë's poems in 1904: how does her eye-catching characterisation of them as the record of a 'unique and in some senses appalling personality'[5] define Brontë's achievement and what might it suggest about Mew's work in the light of Brontë's example? There is even a set of recordings of Brontë poems made by the band The Unthanks: we could think about the way the music is shaped by and animates the implications of Brontë's writing. Reading one poet always leads you to another.

Reading a Contemporary Poet: Srinivas Rayaprol

Many books and essays have been written about Brontë's life and work. The question is how to negotiate them. But what if we want to study a poet about whom not much has been written? We'll close this section by considering that question in relation to the work of the Anglophone Indian poet Srinivas Rayaprol.

Rayaprol was born in 1925 in Secunderabad, India. As a young adult he studied in the United States, where he encountered the poets Yvor Winters and William Carlos Williams.[6] After America, Rayaprol returned to India, where he worked as a civil engineer. He published three books of verse: *Bones and Distances* (1968), *Married Love and Other Poems* (1972), and *Selected Poems* (1995). (The catalogue of a legal deposit library, which receives copies of every published book, or a poet's or publisher's website, if they have one, is a good source of a poet's publication history.) There is little critical or biographical material on Rayaprol that is easily accessible in English: an article by the poet Dom Moraes introduces him as the 'Poet whom no one discovered'; the edition of *Selected Poems and Prose* (2019) edited by Graziano Krätli and Vidyan Ravinthiran contains a preface and an afterword. We might also find it useful to consult studies of Indian poetry as a whole, which even if they don't contain any material on Rayaprol directly, will offer a sense of the traditions in which he worked and the writers who might have influenced him (who in turn might become the next poets we read): *A History of Indian Poetry in English*, edited by Rosinka Chaudhuri, would be a good place to start. We can use these pieces to orientate ourselves (it is almost impossible to find a poet about whom *nothing* has been written), but we will need to find our own way through the poems. What I'd like to show here is how – again – by asking the right questions (perhaps guided by snippets from those critical introductions that we can lay our hands on), we can develop an understanding by ourselves.

In his preface, Ravinthiran writes of the allure of what he calls Rayaprol's 'skew-whiff' English idiom: 'The poems evince, when they become unidiomatic or phrasally clenched, an Indian English distinctively his. He writes of an emotional disorder which his language to some extent reproduces, but with felicities that imply deliberation. This seems to be the big question: are the poems consciously (not haplessly) wonky?'[7] Here is a question we might use to direct our reading. It suggests the strange appeal and vitality of Rayaprol's *style*. Style – a poet's characteristic manner of thinking and expression – is central to the life of all poetry. The pleasure of getting to know a writer, as Al Alvarez says, is the pleasure of becoming familiar with 'a voice unlike any other voice you have ever heard' that is 'speaking directly to you . . . in its own distinctive way'.[8] And since, as we have observed all through this book, *how* a poem says something is inseparable from *what* it says, to think about style is to approach everything a poet has to show us. Rayaprol's style is freighted with many of his defining concerns. For a poet writing in English as their second language, style is the very nexus of the poems' explorations of national and literary identity; as Ravinthiran suggests, it is a matter of the poetry's ability to communicate the feelings that provoke it; and in its unpredictability and occasional disconnectedness it is the arena of the aesthetic dilemmas Rayaprol's work provokes. Approaching the poems armed (again) with a well-defined question – 'where can we find this "wonkiness" in Rayaprol's style and what should we make of it?' – will help us to enjoy them with more purpose and sensitivity.

If we don't have even a single critical remark from which to take off, then we might as an alternative find a point of origin in the poems themselves. On the back cover of the 2019 *Selected Poems*, the following lines are quoted, as though a touchstone for Rayaprol's appeal:

I speak of the lonely word
That will not reach beyond my tongue
Nor fulfil my frustrations.

The lines are about style: they talk about the difficulty of expression, even as they are themselves lucid and forthright. The poem from which they are taken, 'This Poem' (1995), orbits a concern with the 'frustration' of giving voice to the imagination of which Rayaprol writes in the preface to his 1995 *Selected Poems*: 'There they were, in the mind, the beautiful unbelievables, the fire and the flame burning within me. But the minute I put pen to paper, a million trite words would rush out. And so it would remain, a solitary word or a single line to convey the magnificence of my unwritten poem.'[9] The poem both thinks about and enacts this anxiety. We can read any 'wonkiness' in its style as a manifestation of its concern with its own expressive powers. It begins with the poet saying that he cannot speak of important matters such as 'women', 'God', 'love', or 'people', and, after the lines quoted above, passes into a contemplation of the everyday realities which interpose themselves between the imagination and the printed page:

There are things beyond this word.
I know –

That the grocer's bill and the rising
Prices occupy me most,
Concern my body with their ignominy
Break my will with their boundary
Reduce my rest and snatch the spoken thought
Before it can find the page.

'Life has been mostly a matter of living the days', says Rayaprol in his preface.[10] The business of getting through the day blocks inspiration. The style of the lines embodies the point. The syntax is dramatic, responsive, and self-performative. The words 'I know –' present themselves as the gateway to an epiphany to what lies 'beyond this word', as though the sentence were going to go on to list what these things are; but the lines take another turn, and mundane reality comes rushing in one phrase after another to illustrate the everyday necessities which lie 'beyond' poetic expression in another sense, so that the 'spoken thought' of something more profound can never find 'the page'. And yet even as these lines lament their inarticulacy, their 'spoken' energy finds its own expressive force.

The above paragraph shows how just by finding an angle of approach – a question, a set of lines – we can prise open a poet's work. We have started to get a sense of some of Rayaprol's concerns: the day-to-day nature of living, the illuminations and 'frustrations' of the imagination, the act of writing itself. We might even feel that we've discovered one of Rayaprol's animating tensions: that between the urge to give expression to the visionary power of inner experience and the clutter of life and language which gets in the way. We have perhaps strayed a little from defining the nature of Rayaprol's style, however. One way of refocusing might be to observe that the remark 'life has been mostly a matter of living the days' has another life at the start of one of Rayaprol's poems (1972):

Life Has Been

Mostly
a matter of living these days
Simply
a subject of the senses
surrounding this body
Really

Here the words are given a form and woven into a syntax which shows the peculiar fluidity with which Rayaprol writes. The first thing we might observe about the style is that, in this poem, it resists conventional punctuation: though the capitalisation and lineation offer clues, it isn't certain where the sentences begin and end, and as a consequence the thoughts melt into one another. Here is a non-standard way of using English, liberated from the discipline of punctuation. Rayaprol's manner gives the sense of a mind apprehending and composing ideas in the moment. Even the title seems less a label to fix a theme on the poem than a means of getting the ball rolling. And yet the sense that life has passed by which the words 'Life has been' intimate when taken in isolation strikes a keynote of the poem, too. And this, perhaps, suggests another aspect of Rayaprol's style: his interest in the way different arrangements of a sentence on the page can generate different emphases and intonations. The mournful implications ghosting the poem's title foreshadow the sadness with which the opening sentence returns at the poem's end, as Rayaprol reflects on:

a life
that has been
mostly a matter
of living the days.

Rayaprol's unpunctuated manner is liable to throw meanings up in the air; but here, as the sentence slumps down the steps of the lineation, is evidence of the 'deliberation' over minutiae that Ravinthiran urges us to attend to in Rayaprol's voice. 'Life' has become 'a' life, 'these days' have become, distantly, 'the days'. The phrase ends the poem by viewing a whole life in sad retrospection.

Again, a question about style has directed us to an apprehension of a poem's vision and emotional content. The leap is to be welcomed. When we don't have much critical material to guide us, we want to ask questions which open up rather than close down our sense of a poet's interests and significance. We can emerge from our consideration of 'Life Has Been' with a sense of Rayaprol as a poet alert to the way form brings different expressive inflections to language and keen to test out new postures of expression. But we also sense a poet who has an abiding concern with the passage of time and the waste of experience, and who has an emotional palate capable of expressing sadness as well as wonder and exhilaration. We might also step back and ask how the instability of Rayaprol's voice animates the deliberations of a hybrid Indian-American identity.

We could go through the work illustrating this way of accumulating a picture of a poet endlessly. The key is always to be building generalisations out of local observations. Let's just end by showing how we can keep our dialogue with a poet fresh by persistently reframing it. Do the aspects of Rayaprol's style and outlook that we have started to identify change over the course of his career? We can only begin to shape an answer to that question here. But the poems of the first collection, *Bones and Distances*, do seem to fizz with the unsettled, exploratory character of Rayaprol's English. What are we to make of the opening stanzas of 'A Letter for Mother' (1968)?

For heaven's sake, mother
how you've aged!
You could have been kinder.

Roots twist
and the rinse
of leaves under rain
has different smells;
white loads them
differently
and the sun sets
a new yellow.
Trees grow old too.

Couldn't you crust your kindness
in another way?

There is a disarming impetuousness here, a half-embarrassing, half-exhilarating disregard for decorum which both exemplifies and has an impact like Rayaprol's description in his preface of 'the actual birth of the poem' as being 'like the first spark of semen that shoots out, uncontrollable, at the climactic moment'.[11] The exasperation towards the mother for ageing unpleasantly is unsettling but it's also very funny. But a more subtle manner of disrupting the language is at work in the second stanza – and the transition from one to the other is characteristic of Rayaprol's style in itself. By twisting idioms, Rayaprol wrings new expressive life from familiar phrasing. Take the phrase 'the sun sets / a new yellow': that is at once an afterthought to the remarks about trees – the sun discovers a new brilliance as it ages and sets – but it is also a continuation of the argument about how gracefully the leaves themselves age: the sun, drying the leaves, 'sets' them a new beautiful autumnal colour. The two manners fuse in the third stanza, where the accusatory directness returns, but the notion of 'crusting' one's 'kindness' seems to retreat into a private idiom (what could the verb mean?). The exploratory energy of the style here, even if we might feel that it transcends boundaries, is a discovery of joy in language's ability to reframe the world typical of a poet who ends another poem in the same collection with the thought that there are 'windows to be opened, / every day in this world that I am' ('Here it is Spring Again'). In those lines, the jumbled syntax creates an ambiguity: Rayaprol means both 'every day that I am in this world' and 'every day that I inhabit this world of myself' – and his language brings that self, and its aperture on the world, to idiosyncratic life.

When we turn from this early vitality with a poem from later in Rayaprol's career, we discover a poet more secure in his idiom, but one whose ability to invest language with vibrant wonder has perhaps dimmed (1995):

On Approaching Fifty

I have come a way now
and the meanings of life
are clearer to me.

I have read a little
seen somewhat
tasted a bit

of everything. But
there is nothing I know
really

Full circle
I am back
at the beginning

but without the wonder
of being a child again.

Here are many of the concerns which are starting to become familiar: time's passage, the sadness of ageing, the difficulty of getting one's perceptions and emotions into words, the hapless feeling that there is nothing certain one can pin down about experience. The ironies of a life unfulfilled are filleted as the reflection on having 'seen somewhat / tasted a bit // of everything' progresses over the lineation and stanza break. What starts out as a modest survey of personal experience turns into a shrug of dissatisfaction at the limitations of what the world has to offer. And in the end, the poem does pin something down, expertly. As Rayaprol pivots from 'everything' to 'nothing', his ironies yield to the flat matter-of-factness of a sentence in which words and experience do find plain correlation, and in which the 'wonder' and exuberance communicated through the manner of the earlier poems gives way to sober clarity. Here are words that keep feeling intact.

Notes

1. Cecil Day Lewis, 'The Poetry of Emily Brontë', *Brontë Society Transactions* 13 (1965): 91.
2. Gerard Manley Hopkins, *The Collected Works of Gerard Manley Hopkins: Correspondence*, ed. R. K. R. Thornton and Catherine Phillips, 2 vols. (Oxford: Oxford University Press, 2013), i. 69.

3. Michael Schmidt, *Lives of the Poets* (London: Phoenix, 1998), 526.
4. Dinah Birch, 'Emily Brontë', *The Cambridge Companion to English Poets*, ed. Claude Rawson (Cambridge: Cambridge University Press, 2011), 412.
5. Charlotte Mew, 'The Poems of Emily Brontë' (1904), *Charlotte Mew: Collected Poems & Selected Prose*, ed. Val Warner (Manchester: Carcanet, 1997), 363.
6. For Rayaprol's correspondence with Williams, see *Why Should I Write a Poem Now: The Letters of Srinivas Rayaprol and William Carlos Williams, 1949–1958*, ed. Graziano Krätl (Albuquerque: University of New Mexico Press, 2018).
7. Vidyan Ravinthiran, preface to *Srinivas Rayaprol: Angular Desire: Selected Poems and Prose*, ed. Graziano Krätl and Vidyan Ravinthiran (Manchester: Carcanet, 2019), 6.
8. Al Alvarez, *The Writer's Voice* (London: Bloomsbury, 2005), 15.
9. Rayaprol, 'Preface to *Selected Poems*' (1995) in *Angular Desire*, 154–5.
10. Rayaprol, 'Preface to *Selected Poems*' (1995) in *Angular Desire*, 154.
11. Rayaprol, 'Preface to Selected Poems' (1995) in *Angular Desire*, 154.

CHAPTER 3

Writing about Poetry

The surest way to improve as a reader of poetry is to practise writing about poetry. Writing about a poem is the most reliable, pleasurable, and challenging way of working out what we think and feel about it. Just jotting down a few sentences to define our response to a poem will bring us closer to it. Writing a poem out by hand, sentence by sentence, is a surprisingly effective way of inhabiting the progress and texture of its argument; and simply paraphrasing a poem can aid understanding and bring its distinctiveness into relief. When there is the chance to write a formal essay, there are on the whole two kinds you might be invited to submit. The first is a commentary or 'close-reading' exercise, where you are asked to give an account of a single poem or passage. The second is a more argumentative essay, where you are required to build up a case out of your reading of several poems or poets. The following sections offer some thoughts about both genres.

Whose Voice Should You Use?

The first principle to hold on to is that in writing an essay you are not expected to become someone else. Your aim is to discover and communicate your own ideas. Many essays go awry because students feel there is a special, alien, 'academic' register that they need to adopt. Dismiss this suspicion. You are a human being responding to the creations of another human being. An essay is a chance for you to substantiate your personal response. You will need to communicate your ideas in a more formal and organised manner than you would in a message to friends, naturally. But this should be a matter of tailoring your voice accordingly, not adopting a whole new language. Think of yourself as putting on some slightly smarter clothes, not adopting a whole new personality.

Writing a good essay also involves giving thought to who you are writing for. The commonest and most easily addressed flaws in essays stem from a failure to imagine an audience. As a rule of thumb, imagine that you are writing for an informed, interested, and intelligent reader who is nevertheless unfamiliar with the poems under discussion. Your aim is to introduce them to these poems and to tell them what you think and feel about them. Your marker is sitting on the side-line, as it were, judging how successfully you do this. Too often students omit or skim over the first of these tasks, perhaps assuming that describing the material under discussion is too simple a matter to be bothered with, or that an understanding can be taken as read. But the main thing that your marker wants to see is that you can pay patient attention to a poem's details and communicate that attention in an orderly manner. An essay should contain all the materials needed in order for it to be understood. If you don't place the evidence in front of a reader in a lucid and organised form, how can they follow or judge the persuasiveness of the arguments that you build upon it?

How Do You Develop Ideas?

The starting point for a good essay is not abstract 'planning' but attentive reading. Planning involves organising your ideas: you need to have developed those ideas first. When I tried to answer the question 'How do you read?' at the start of this book, I suggested that the answer might fall into three stages: description, analysis, and interpretation; and a good essay will do all three, building from the first stage upwards. The basis for any persuasive argument about a poem is a thorough, precise, and accurate account of the words on the page. Beginning work on an essay by annotating a poem, or making notes on a separate sheet, ensures that your argument will grow out of a close engagement with the materials under discussion. Your ideas about a poem might change as you write and revisit its details, but the richer your engagement with the poem to begin with, the richer your final essay will be. Make note of whatever interests or puzzles you; don't feel that you have to work through every question that we considered above. As a recap, issues to make notes on could include:

1. What is the argument of the poem? What is it about?
2. What genre of poem is this? What expectations are associated with the genre?
3. What expectations are established by the title? At what point in the poem (if at all) does the significance of the title become clear?
4. How does the poem begin? What expectations does the opening establish and does the poem fulfil them?

5. Does the poem dramatise a conflict of different perspectives? Are there any moments in the poem where it seems to change direction, attitude, or feeling?
6. Whose voice(s) do we hear in the poem? What perspective(s) are they speaking from?
7. Is there an addressee? If so, can you tell who it is?
8. Does the poem portray or assume a specific scene or location?
9. Read the poem aloud: how does it sound?
10. What is the metre? Does the rhythm at any point vary from the underlying metrical pattern?
11. What is the rhyme scheme? What relations does it encourage us to see between the rhymed words?
12. What kind of language does the poem use? Look up any words you are unsure of in a dictionary.
13. Do you notice any allusions to other works?
14. How does the poem end? Has it met the expectations established at the outset? Does it resolve the issues at hand, or does it leave loose ends?
15. Does the poem react appropriately and imaginatively to its situation? Does it move you?

Annotate with the aim of producing an organised list of observations rather than a jumbled heap. The aim is to describe the poem, but also to arrive at an understanding of what it is about and a view of its significance. This view might evolve as you write your essay, but to 'improve opinion into knowledge' in Johnson's phrase (see page 8) you need to have an opinion to begin with.

What Are You Trying to Achieve?

One key to writing a good essay is having a sense of purpose. In any assessed piece of writing, that purpose is on one level straightforward: to get a good mark. And one of the surest ways to achieve that mark is to write with a firm sense of what it is that you want your essay to say and do. Students of literature are often troubled – and even put off literary study – by the feeling that the criteria for success are murky and unreliable and can't be objectively applied. If there is no set notion of what makes a good essay, no right or wrong answers in matters of interpretation, then how do you know how to do well?

The first point to make is that the qualities that make for a successful essay aren't as murky as all that. While there is no definitively 'right' answer in writing a literary essay, there are good and bad answers, and there are principles by which we determine how persuasive and engaging an argument is. The main features of a good essay will be laid out in the marking criteria, which your examiners will make available, but they shouldn't come as a surprise: the more eloquent, imaginative, ambitious, wide-ranging, and focused your writing is, the better. A good essay will clarify, not confuse complex issues. It will integrate the three different strands which we have suggested are involved in reading: its foundations will be in a precise and accurate description of the words on the page; it will analyse the effects of those words, and how they are created; and it will interpret their significance. Just as in writing literary criticism you are passing reasoned judgement on a literary work, so your marker will use the principles applied by the mark scheme to pass a reasoned judgement on your work.

The question or task you are set will also have a bearing on what it is you write: just as poems are governed by the conventions of a particular genre, so the kind of essay you are writing will determine the kind of thing you should aim to accomplish. In a commentary or close-reading essay, your primary objective is to give a clear and accurate account of the poem in question. But a commentary is more than just a description of a poem. It requires you to arrange local details and observations in support of a particular case or line of argument: your individual observations need to amount to something. This argument need not be too complex; in many ways the simpler the better: think of it as a starting position which you can use the details of the poem to extend, challenge, elaborate, and qualify. (A friend suggests that an essay ought to be like a river, starting with something small – an anecdote, observation, or quotation – and allowing the thought to wind downstream as more evidence flows into the course of its argument, before it finally opens out into a conclusion having taken the reader somewhere new, and shown them (at the seaside) something they couldn't have seen at the source.) Often a single evaluative statement can supply the current that joins the individual paragraphs: 'this poem treats death so powerfully because it does so unsentimentally'; 'the poem brings together an impression of spoken fluency with elaborate formal artistry'; 'the force of the poem is in its fluid movement between different perspectives'. Aim for a judgement that gives latitude for development.

The main differences between a commentary and an argumentative essay are the range of materials you are required to consider and – consequently – the scope of the argument that you are expected to develop. To some extent, the task is just to extend your argument across a larger range of examples, but to do that may well entail making that argument more ambitious and wide-ranging. It is likely that an argumentative essay will be prompted by a question. Obviously, you will need to respond to what the question asks, but the best essays have the confidence to define their field of interest on their own terms: essay questions usually aren't written with 'expected' answers in mind. Imagine, for instance, you were faced with the instruction:

> Discuss the contention that poetry is a medium better suited to the exploration of feeling than the presentation of intellectual argument.

There are numerous ways in which you might respond. You may simply want to agree or disagree with the contention, perhaps considering a poem based upon the exploration of feeling and a poem based upon the presentation of argument alongside one another to support your case. But then 'disagreement' might take different forms: you might want to argue that poetry can handle both emotion and intellect equally well; you might want to argue that a clean distinction between feeling and intelligence is false. Other responses might put pressure on key words: if you want to write an essay about feeling in poetry, you could examine the significance of 'exploration' – how do its implications differ from another verb you might have expected, such as 'expression'? Likewise with 'presentation' – do poems really 'present' arguments or do they 'develop' them as they go? Yet another path through the question might isolate the issue of what is distinctive about poetry as a 'medium', perhaps comparing some poems with passages of prose, or drama. These are just a few of the ways in which the question could be handled or interpreted. Without deviating from its terms entirely, you can treat the question as a springboard for the argument you want to pursue.

And in this light, we might come to see any apparent murkiness in the question of what makes a successful literary essay not as vagueness but flexibility. The best essays will have the confidence to see the pliability of the marking criteria as an opportunity, not a cause for panic. They will treat the absence of any 'expected' answer as the chance to define their own aims. The flexibility is literature's great strength as a subject; it is one of the main ways in which it proves your intelligence and prepares you for life. It asks you to set your own notion of what you want to achieve. Of course, what you are trying to achieve has to be ambitious, and imaginative, and related to the task at hand: but establish a confident sense of what you are up to, and your marker will see you taking the essay by the scruff of the neck and will reward you.

What Sort of Plan Should You Make?

Having established some ideas and a sense of what you want to do with them, you can start to plan your essay, giving thought to the best order in which to deliver your points. It is important that you develop a sense of how your thoughts are going to develop *in order* – a spider diagram, while a useful way of overseeing the range of your ideas, will not help you to articulate your ideas coherently. Still, don't waste too much time on this: what you need is a rough outline of the sequence in which you are going to work through your material, perhaps organised as a list of bullet points describing the central idea in each paragraph. It's easy to spend hours devising an elaborate plan which will suffocate your argument rather than give it the breathing space to develop as it goes. There is truth in the old motto that you won't get anything done by planning.

How Should You Begin?

How should you begin? Broadly speaking there are three things the opening of an essay should do: (1) fix your reader's attention; (2) establish succinctly the terms and scope of the essay, signalling the ground it is going to cover and the direction it is going to take; (3) enable you to get swiftly into the main body of the essay.

There are innumerable ways of achieving these objectives, and the best way to learn them is to read essays by other writers and observe how they kick things off. You will find that writers often grab your attention by beginning with something concrete that raises the question they want to address: an anecdote, an illustrative quotation, a sharp critical observation. In this way they can strike immediately to the heart of a subject and open out the questions they are going to pursue from there. In a commentary essay you might even begin with the beginning of the poem under discussion, before stepping back to show how it establishes the larger issues you are going to show to be at stake. If you have been given a question that includes a quotation from a poem or a critic, get to grips with it immediately – show how it raises an issue central to the topic that you want to address.

An introduction needs to introduce, succinctly, the subject matter under consideration. This does not mean supplying your reader with screeds of directionless information about your poets or poems, but rather setting out the facts pertinent to your argument. In a commentary essay, you might offer some details about the poet's life or about the poem's composition or reception – so long as they help to inform and orientate your approach. In a more argumentative essay, you are likely to have some freedom over the poems and poets that you are looking at, and you will need to justify your choice. To construct a coherent argument, there needs to be coherence and logic to the materials you are bringing together in support of it. It might be that you want to build an argument about poems or poets from a particular period; it might be that you want to look at writers using the same form; it might be that you want to unify your poets by genre or subject matter. It might even be that you want to cover a deliberately eclectic range of writers, to illustrate a diversity of achievement. Whatever the case, it will pay to explain your choice of poems, authors, or passages as you introduce them: tell your reader why you have chosen them and what story they will allow you to tell.

Somewhere at the heart of your introduction will have to be a distillation, perhaps in a single sentence, of the position you are going to test out or the case you are going to make. Give this statement prominence: it might occur at the end of your opening paragraph as a culmination of your opening reflections; or you could even begin your essay with it, as a way of laying your cards on the table. But you need to show, too, the context that frames what you want to say. This does not mean giving a full rundown of a work's critical history, but rather isolating the fundamental aspects of the existing debates out of which your own position emerges. How is your argument going to situate itself in relation to the key disagreements or the most productive lines of enquiry? What are the gaps that you hope to address? Some of these matters may of course be indicated by the question you are answering. It may even be that you want to follow on from the question you have been given by raising further questions, rather than by stating your argument from the off – such an approach has the benefit of setting up your conclusion. In all cases, it pays to be brisk. Don't become ensnared in distinctions irrelevant to what you want to discuss. Don't let a question railroad you into issues peripheral to your main area of focus. Engage with it on your own terms and use it as a springboard for the line of argument you want to pursue.

Even if you write a draft of your introduction first, return to it last: the essay you write is likely to turn out differently from the essay that you think you are going to write, and you need to ensure that the argument that you are introducing is the one you have actually made.

Informing and Arguing

An introduction states and situates an essay's argument. What is involved in carrying that argument out?

We have returned once or twice already to Samuel Johnson's definition of literary criticism as a process of 'improving opinion into knowledge'. 'Knowledge' is not 'fact': literary criticism doesn't often deal in incontrovertible proof like the sciences. But 'knowledge' is also different from 'opinion': literary criticism is not a field in which anything goes and everyone's position has equal validity. Arguments have to be formed and supported. 'Knowledge' is substantiated opinion.

An essay turns 'opinion' into 'knowledge' by building an argument upon the analysis of evidence. An argument looks to persuade, not to insist. It engages the reader as a thoughtful listener who could be imagined as responding to, or questioning, its claims. The way to substantiate an argument is through the careful presentation and consideration of evidence – that is to say, whenever you are writing about a poem, you will need to introduce and analyse appropriate quotations to support your points. The body of the essay should present all the evidence necessary for your arguments to be understood. Of course, you can't cover everything. Much of the art of writing an essay lies in how well you select and handle your quotations. Managing quotations well entails three main things:

- **Contextualisation:** give a sense of the place the lines which you are quoting occupy in the poem at large. Many essays falter because they neglect the responsibility to *inform*; they assume the reader will be familiar with all the ins and outs of the material under discussion, rather than doing them the courtesy of refreshing their memory. If you are quoting some lines from the middle of a poem, describe what has led up to them; show how details fit within the whole.
- **Engagement:** thorough introduction and presentation of the evidence is only the first step. An essay needs to build beyond description into analysis (investigation of the poem's effects and how they are created) and evaluation (judgement of the particular way in which the poem succeeds; response to its emotional, intellectual, and imaginative impact). Make sure you pay close attention to the lines you have quoted: what do they show us, and how do they show us it? Isolate words, phrases, techniques and show how they shape the aspects of the poem's vision and significance that you want to talk about.
- **Flexibility:** don't worry if some of the evidence you quote challenges or complicates your initial standpoint. Some development of your argument as it goes is to be welcomed; it shows that your argument is dynamic, evolving as it engages with the evidence. A good essay takes

shape organically: it builds arguments from the ground up rather than imposing a pre-established position in spite of the evidence.

The way to act practically on these issues is to think about the content and composition of individual paragraphs. Paragraphs are not just ways of interposing regular pauses for breath. They are units of argument. As you start to organise your annotations into the points that are going to form the basis of your argument, consider how you can use paragraphs to enable you to introduce, support, and explore these points. Think of your paragraphs as having a three-part structure:

1. **A headline section** where you introduce and unpack the main idea or point of focus: aim to begin with a single succinct 'topic sentence' which states the theme of the paragraph.
2. **The evidence you are using to support your point** or to bring it into focus, introduced and contextualised to give a sense of the place of this particular detail within the poem as a whole.
3. **Analysis and exploration of that evidence:** what are the formal and verbal qualities of the passage you have quoted? How do they contribute to the poem's vision and how do they feed into your argument at large?

Once you have established this basic rhythm, you'll discover all sorts of variations you can play on it. The advantage of a structure like this is that it means you are forced to think at the start of each paragraph about how the point you want to make relates to and advances your main line of argument, and that it forces you to anchor that point in a piece of concrete evidence. Essays are liable to go awry when they lose sight of their main path or enter the realm of gesture and speculation rather than evidence-based argument.

You may also wish to support and refine your argument by engaging with other critics. Probably the most frequent question markers are asked is 'how many critics do I need to include?' It is an odd question, which imagines, wrongly, that examiners have a secret set of criteria which they guard from students. What matters is not how many critics you stuff into an essay, but how you stuff them in. Evidently, in an extended piece, you will need to situate your argument within a broad and representative awareness of the critical field. As we have observed, this can be the job of the introduction; it might well involve summary, rather than direct quotation, of arguments. Your aim is to show a command of the range of positions that define the debate into which you are entering. In the body of the essay, you may well want to quote a critic directly, in order to address a particular aspect of their argument. As when quoting from a poem, don't just throw in critical quotations without context; give a sense of how the particular phrase you are quoting is representative of a critic's position at large. The key is to be active in your engagement with the quotation. Don't introduce someone else's argument only in order to make a point for you. Use critics to define and direct your own argument. You might want to bounce off a quotation to advance an alternative perspective. Perhaps you want to bring a remark into contact with some lines from the poet under discussion, in order to show how it illuminates them. Remember that critics aren't some alien breed with an insight into the poetry that is unavailable to you: by writing an essay, you too are becoming a critic and adding your voice to an existing debate.

The Body of the Essay

How should you arrange the individual paragraphs that make up the body of your essay? One rule of thumb applicable across both kinds of essay is to keep your argument moving: make sure each paragraph introduces a new point or idea that grows out of the previous one and into the next one.

In a close-reading essay, the challenge is to find a shape that organises your observation of local details into a coherent whole. Broadly, there are two ways of doing this. You can allow your reading to take its shape from the poem itself – working through chronologically and devoting a paragraph to each stanza, or quatrain, or sentence, for example. The advantage of this approach is that it allows you to keep close to the details of the poem; the risk is that the larger direction and emphasis of your argument becomes swamped by all the individual moments you are responding to. Alternatively, you can address different areas of the poem in turn – first establishing its central arguments and preoccupations, for instance, then returning to look back over the poem and investigate how these are shaped by its use of rhyme, metre, imagery, diction, etc. Here you are able to work through a clearer argumentative scheme but risk blurring the order in which you work through the poem. Neither approach is inherently preferable – it is up to you to decide which one allows you to convey your reading and your argument most clearly and persuasively.

You also need to be selective, working out which aspects of the poem you have most to say about. A successful commentary involves managing to 'tell the story' of the poem (in terms of its form, not just its content) while realising that you cannot say everything. The most eloquent essays will vary their pace and approach, lingering over the lines or moments they take to be the most suggestive or significant while still conveying an assured sense of their position within the development of the thought, feeling, and sense of the passage as a whole.

You have more freedom in deciding how to arrange an argumentative essay. But the fundamentals of your task remain the same: you need to show an intelligent understanding of the poems you have chosen, and you need to convey a sense of their structure, development, and impact. It might even be helpful to think of the essay as a series of close readings which you then step back from and knit together into a larger argument. Alternatively, you might like to run different poems side by side, comparing aspects such as the way they begin, or their handling of a particular form, or the way they use imagery. Comparison can be an effective method of bringing out the distinctiveness of the poems you are considering, but it requires care to establish good grounds for comparison (such as a shared aim, genre, or technique) and not to run accounts of multiple poems into a confusing jumble.

As in a commentary essay, you need to sustain a coherent logic of development in your movement from one paragraph to the next. It pays to focus on individual poems in a chronological, line-by-line or stanza-by-stanza order rather than jumping about all over the place. As you move between poems and poets, or between different stages of your argument, keep in touch with the terms of the question. Here is your chance to step back, vary the pace and focus, and keep up a conversation with your reader about how your argument is evolving: draw contrasts and similarities between the writers or works you are considering, showing how they illuminate the key issues you are addressing; show how the evidence you are considering helps to develop your answer in new or unexpected directions. It is tempting to glue an essay together in moments of transition by asserting the similarities between poems or poets. Yet it is often the precise differences within broad areas of similarity that are most interesting. Don't flatten out reality for the sake of your argument. Bring out the distinctiveness of each writer.

How Should You End?

Concluding an essay is challenging. Again, the question to keep in mind is what you are trying to achieve: you need to find a way of gathering together the various threads of your argument without simply repeating yourself or drifting off into unsupported generalisation. Reading other essays and asking how a writer has managed to do this is the shortest way to acquiring a sense of the possibilities.

You will need to revisit the position you took or question you asked at the start of the essay and think about how far your attention to the poem or poems has confirmed, challenged, or extended that position or answered that question. But you want to remain engaged and specific: usually in an essay you are working to a strict word count – there is little point just recapitulating what you have already said in more general terms. Suggest further lines of enquiry; introduce some contextual or biographical information which helps you pan out and see the poem's impact from a wider angle; find a line or image which distils everything you've been arguing up to this point; bring the essay to a close in tandem with discussion of the ending of one of the poems you are discussing. However you choose to close, it pays to be imaginative about your essay at this stage – there are few more disheartening sights for a marker than that of the phrase 'In conclusion . . . ' rearing its tedious head at the start of a closing paragraph: try to leave your reader with a sense of your individual voice.

How Should You Review Your Work?

One sure way to improve your writing is to leave yourself time to review and edit your work before you submit it. Essays are often hampered by mistakes which are easy to make but also easy to eliminate if you give yourself the distance to read your work as though through another's eyes. If you can bear it, it can be helpful to read an essay aloud to yourself.

As you read back over your work, attend to the following issues:

1. **Clarity of argument:** can you summarise what your essay says in a single sentence? Obviously such a sentence is likely to be a simplification of your argument, but if you can't summarise your case succinctly then it is unlikely that your reader will easily grasp it either – and remember, you are writing to make your ideas and understanding understood.
2. **Clarity and coherence of structure:** does the argument evolve logically from paragraph to paragraph? A useful technique to deploy in this respect is to turn your essay into a list of bullet points. Take a blank sheet of paper and work through your essay, summing up the central point or topic of each paragraph in a single sentence. If you can't summarise the central point of the paragraph, then it needs more

work: either the argument needs refining, or some sentences need ejecting, or the paragraph needs breaking into two. Once you have a 'map' of the essay, you should have achieved a bird's eye view of how your argument develops: ask yourself whether there are any gaps, wrong turns, or inconsistencies: do you need to add in another paragraph? Cut a paragraph? Re-arrange the order?

3. **Clarity of prose:** have you made your points as concisely and as precisely as possible? Writing is very difficult: there will always be small ways in which your expression could be improved. One easy route is through cutting. Be harsh with yourself: ask if every paragraph, every sentence, and every word earns its keep. Adding full stops helps to curtail meandering sentences. It pressures you to say what you mean and not hide behind a mass of words. Beyond making cuts, the surest way to improvement is through practice, both by writing and by reading other writers and emulating the way they manage things. Some common and easily addressed pitfalls include:
   - Redundant or confusing adverbs and adjectives – cut them! Strip away words to get to the substance of your point. 'Walcott's poem is tragic' has more force and clarity than 'Certainly, Walcott's poem is almost tragic'.
   - Sentences lacking a clear connection between subject and main verb: keep a spinal cord of 'subject – verb – object' running through each sentence.
   - Disagreement between main and subordinate clauses. 'Born in 1917, Brooks's poems depict urban life' makes no sense, because the subject of the sentence is 'Brooks's poems', not Brooks herself. 'Born in 1917, Brooks wrote poems which depict urban life' is better.
   - Overlong sentences: a sentence should develop a single unit of thought. Look for places where you might put in extra full stops.
   - Speculation in place of argument: phrases such as 'it seems that . . . ', 'it could be argued that . . . ', 'perhaps such-and-such wanted to say that . . . ' sound vague and uncertain unless you are trying to pinpoint moments of vagueness and uncertainty.
   - Repeated words or phrases. Everyone will have their own bad habits: 'arguably' (if something is arguable, argue it); 'almost' (almost always redundant); 'relatable' ('relate-to-able?' – consider the implications of the word: do we only admire literature that we can connect with our own experiences?); 'incredibly' (seldom meant literally); 'clear' (which usually makes things less clear); 'important'

(why is it important?); 'bias' as an adjective ('I am bias' . . .); 'this' without specifying what 'this' is that you are drawing attention to; words such as 'moreover', 'furthermore', 'in addition' as ways of beginning paragraphs (they generally imply insufficient thought has gone into how one idea leads into the next); saying that a poem 'references' something (find a more precise verb to indicate how the poem calls whatever it is in to play); saying that one thing 'links to' another without saying who is doing the linking or describing the nature of the link; the habit of describing all contrasts as 'stark'.

- Passive rather than active constructions. 'The theme of love can clearly be seen in the third stanza' makes it sound as though the idea has just appeared from nowhere (and who is doing the 'seeing'?); 'Byron turns his mind to the pains of love in the third stanza', attributes agency and makes you think about an author's artistic decisions.
- Uses of the word 'I': students often feel that, for some mysterious reason, the word 'I' is forbidden. It is not. The reason the word is often flagged up in essays is that when used to express an argument, it makes that argument seem at once flimsier and, oddly, less personal. Compare the sentences 'I think that the poem makes fun of social conventions' and 'The poem makes fun of social conventions'. The second is more confident, but also more forceful: the words 'I think' are redundant – your reader knows that this is what you think, otherwise you would not be writing it (and, in any case, the business of an essay is not just to say what you 'think' but to substantiate those thoughts). Such self-consciousness can be effective – say, when you want to concede that the point you are making is more tendentious than others – but in most cases, it pays to get rid. At other times, particularly when you are discussing the direction of an essay, 'I' can make your writing purposeful and efficient. 'I shall begin by discussing Spenser, and then move on to Milton' is more direct and economical than 'First, Spenser will be discussed before a discussion of Milton will be undertaken'.
- Quotations which are not properly integrated into sentences: including a quotation is not an excuse to abandon correct grammar and syntax.
- Statements of the obvious: 'Rossetti uses the word "love" to indicate deep affection'.
- Pretentious language: 'lexical' or 'semantic field' when you mean 'language', 'muse' when you mean 'think'. Choose the plainer word.

4. **Persuasiveness:** are all of your points backed up by evidence? Is your evidence presented in a way that gives as full and as coherent a picture as possible of the work under discussion? Have you 'squeezed all the juice' out of the lines you have quoted? Are there further words, or images, or techniques that you could say something about? A good question to ask yourself is: 'what impression would I get of the poem I am discussing if I weren't already familiar with it or didn't have a copy of it to hand?' If the answer to that question is 'an inaccurate, confused, limited, or even a dull one', then it'll pay to revisit your work and address the issue.

Above all, keep in mind that you are not writing into a void. There is a human being on the other end of your words. As a reader, one wants to come away from an essay thinking 'yes, this person has got a real grasp on this poem/these poems/this poet' – or even, 'yes, I hadn't noticed that this poem/these poems/this poet was so good in this way before'. Aim to convey reasoned enthusiasm for the work in question.

Epilogue: What Should You Read?

One of the reasons we gave for reading poetry at the start of this book came from Keats: it is 'a friend to man'. What friends should you keep, and how do you pick them? We all get on with different people and crave different company in different moods. The answer to the question 'what should I read?' will change from person to person and from occasion to occasion. Sometimes we want a chatty, light-hearted companion; sometimes we might want a voice that responds movingly to feelings of isolation; sometimes a reminder of the beauties of nature does the trick. It pays to become familiar with as wide a range of poems and poets as possible. All the same, there are people who, by common agreement, are more worth spending time with than others. Everyone wants to avoid the tedious oaf who tells the same two anecdotes over and over in the same colourless language; we all want to find the person whose conversation mixes elegance and honesty, and who shows us something new about the world with every meeting. How do we find them?

Start by getting hold of a good anthology. The suggestions in the Further Reading on page 238 offer broad samples of poetry in English. Use the poets you already know to orientate you. Perhaps you've been reading some poems by Coleridge: look up other poets who wrote around his time – Smith, Wordsworth, Shelley, Hemans. Make comparisons. Build a sense of the similarities and differences in their style, concerns, and outlook. Likewise, you might follow the fortunes of a particular form, or genre. If you've been studying contemporary sonnets, say, then look for earlier poems written in the same form to see how poets' sense of what the sonnet can do, and what can be done with the sonnet, has developed over time. If you've been studying Chaucer, seek out other narrative poems for comparison, from anonymous ballads to the mock epics of the late seventeenth and early eighteenth centuries.

Alternatively, use the anthology to generate a sample of reading that will enable you to cover new ground and encounter surprises. Starting on page one and moving through is a bad idea; progress will become laborious without the onward pull of narrative suspense. Instead, try dipping in every fifty pages, hopping across the evolving history of poetry. Be promiscuous. Open yourself to the variety of ways in which poets have seen the world and show you what they've seen.

Be patient. Don't expect to absorb a whole tradition of poetry in one burst. It is far better to read one or two poems deeply than to skim across ten without taking them in. If you find a poet who provokes a strong response in you – pleasure or displeasure – then ignore the others and stay with them. Get hold of an edition of their work. Read them and re-read them; get to know their way of presenting the world; attune yourself to their voice.

Make reading personal. Work out who you like and why you like them. See if you can persuade others round to your tastes. In exchange, listen to others. You are not the first person to ask the question 'what shall I read?' Let yourself benefit from the experience of those who have asked it before you. Doing so might force you to go against the grain of what you think are your own preferences. Part of the point of reading is to come to terms with the achievements which are commonly regarded to define and embody the values of a culture. Perhaps you can see no appeal in the poetry of Alexander Pope. But it is at least worth reflecting that for three centuries varied and intelligent readers *have* found something to value in Pope's work and that your supposed dislike of him leaves you in a minority.

Read to enter dialogue with others. In becoming familiar with the body of poetry written in English – what is sometimes called the *canon* – we discover a tradition of astonishing depth and variety in which the readers of the past have found companionship, inspiration, consolation, joy. We encounter the expression of a whole culture's ideals and understanding of the world. Sometimes this tradition is criticised as the work of a set of dead white European men. The adjectives demand contemplation. The idea that we shouldn't read someone on the grounds that they are dead is to miss the fundamental power of poetry, which allows us to transcend our contemporary perspective: 'you do not want a steady diet of contemporary literature', as Lydia Davis says: 'You already belong to your time.'[1] But the same argument works in the opposite direction in relation to ethnicity, place, and gender. It is natural for readers to be drawn to the works and traditions which shape the culture to which they belong, whether their home is Sri Lanka, Scotland, or St Lucia – to read is to find community. At the same time, we understand our local culture more fully by realising its multiplicity and by setting it alongside others. Anyone with an appetite for reading will be grateful for the work that has been done to rediscover previously occluded lines of women's writing or to open our ears to voices from a range of geographical and ethnic backgrounds – particularly when it gives proper prominence to the imaginative richness of these writers' work. Listening to these recovered voices need not be to repudiate established writers, though we may find that an expanded tradition harmonises in a new way. English poetry's great strength is its inclusiveness. A tradition is not a static monument, but an evolving consensus, and we may find that we want to change it, as much as we allow it to change us. As readers we play a small part not just in gathering our inheritance from the past but in shaping it for the future, and in reading to encounter what is strange rather than familiar to us we ensure we pass on something of renewed focus and variety.

Most of all, read to deepen and expand your awareness of life. Reading poems won't make you a better person, but it might make you more aware of the ways in which you can live a valuable life and give you a richer sense of why life is worth valuing. To read poetry is to embrace the fact that there are – and have been – people with more ample and nuanced visions of the world than our own: people with quicker wit, more lively imaginations, a more magisterial command of language. Enjoy their company.

Note

1. Lydia Davis, *Essays: One* (New York: Farrar, Straus and Giroux, 2019), 238.

Glossary of Common Forms and Genres

Ballad: a narrative poem, usually in *abcb* quatrains; originally a product of oral culture, though literary appropriations are common.

Ballad stanza: quatrain rhymed *abab* or *abcb*, often with alternating tetrameter and trimeter lines.

Blank verse: unrhymed lines of iambic pentameter.

Dramatic monologue: a poem in the voice of a character other than the poet, usually with an implied audience and narrative.

Elegy: a poem of mourning, usually following a process of development from the expression of grief to consolation.

Epic: an ambitious narrative genre, recounting the adventures of a hero in a way that tells the story of a culture's foundations; often serves as a compendium of other genres.

Heroic couplets: iambic pentameter rhymed *aa bb*.

Haiku (or hokku): a three-line Japanese lyric form consisting of lines of five, seven, and then five syllables.

Ode: an elevated mode of lyric, often involving apostrophe to an object, entity, or muse, upon which the poet meditates; characterised by ornate metrical and rhyming structures.

Ottava rima: an eight-line stanza of iambic pentameter rhymed *abababcc*.

Panegyric: poetry of praise for an individual or institution.

Pastoral: a mode which constructs simplified, idealised visions of rural society as a means of contrasting and exploring the complexities of civilised life.

Rhyme royal: seven-line stanza in iambic pentameter rhymed *ababbcc*; overlaps a cross-rhymed quatrain with a closing pair of rhymed couplets.

Romance: a poem which takes part in an imaginative realm – often of the past; tends to play longing for escape against an awareness of the need to return to reality.

Satire: writing devoted to the exposure and denunciation of vice and folly through irony, wit, and humour.

Sonnet: a poem of fourteen lines: can be rhymed in any number of ways, but two common variations are the Shakespearean (three quatrains and a closing couplet, rhymed *abab cdcd efef gg*) and Petrarchan (an octave followed by a sestet, rhymed abbaabba cdecde) patterns. There is often a *volta* or 'turn' in the argument between the octave and sestet, or before the closing couplet.

Spenserian stanza: a nine-line stanza of iambic pentameter rhymed *ababbcbcc*, with an elongated, six-foot final line (an alexandrine).

Stanza: a discrete unit of verse, often arranged according to a recurring pattern of rhyme and metre.

Terza rima: tercets with an interlocking *aba bcb* rhyme scheme.

Verse paragraph: a unit within a poem in a continuous form such as couplets or blank verse, marked off by a blank line or an indentation at the start of a line.

Villanelle: a nineteen-line poem in five tercets (rhymed *aba*) and a quatrain (rhymed *abaa*), with the first and third lines recurring alternately at the end of each stanza and in the closing two lines.

Further Reading

Many books and essays have been helpful in writing this book. I have listed here a short selection of items that will help develop your pleasure in poetry.

Anthologies

Essential Poems from the Staying Alive Trilogy, ed. Neil Astley (Tarset, Northumberland: Bloodaxe Books, 2012) – a compilation from three lively anthologies, *Staying Alive*, *Being Alive*, and *Being Human*.

The Norton Anthology of Poetry, 6th ed., ed Margaret Ferguson, Tim Kendall, and Mary Jo Salter (New York: Norton, 2018).

The Oxford Book of English Verse, ed. Christopher Ricks (Oxford: Oxford University Press, 1999).

Poems and Critics: An Anthology of Poetry and Criticism, ed. Christopher Ricks (London: Fontana/Collins, 1972) – short anthology of poems with companion critical discussions; invaluable introduction which sets out an understanding of literary criticism as 'the giving of reasons for thinking and feeling as one does about a work of literature'.

The Rattle Bag, ed. Seamus Heaney and Ted Hughes (London: Faber and Faber, 1982).

Handbooks

Derek Attridge, *Poetic Rhythm: An Introduction* (Cambridge University Press, 1995).

Stephanie Burt, *Don't Read Poetry: A Book about How to Read Poems* (New York, NY: Basic Books, 2019).

Terry Eagleton, *How to Read Literature* (New Haven, CT: Yale University Press, 2013) – brilliant guide to closely reading poems, plays, and novels, and a starting point, too, for raising questions about a poem's historical and social contexts; useful companion to the same author's *How to Read a Poem* (London: Wiley, 2006).

Stephen Fry, *The Ode Less Travelled: Unlocking the Poet Within* (London: Arrow, 2005) – lively guide from the perspective of someone trying to write poetry.

Alistair Fowler, *How to Write* (Oxford: Oxford University Press, 2007) – step-by-step guide to writing.

Philip Hobsbaum, *Metre, Rhythm, and Verse Form* (London: Routledge, 1996).

John Hollander, *Rhyme's Reason: A Guide to English Verse*, 4th ed. (New Haven: Yale University Press, 2014) – jaw-dropping illustration of the effects of different verse forms.

John Lennard, *The Poetry Handbook: A Guide to Reading Poetry for Pleasure and Practical Criticism*, 2nd ed. (Oxford: Oxford University Press, 2005).

James Longenbach, *The Art of the Poetic Line* (Minneapolis, MN: Graywolf Press, 2007) – sharp guide to the significance of lineation.

Mary Oliver, *A Poetry Handbook* (New York, NY: Harvest-Harcourt, 1994).

The Princeton Encyclopaedia of Poetry and Poetics, 4th ed., ed. Ronald Greene, *et al.* (Princeton, NJ: Princeton University Press, 2012) – invaluable encyclopaedia of poetic terminology.

James Reeves, *The Critical Sense: Practical Criticism of Prose and Poetry* (London: Heinemann, 1956).

Timothy Steele, *All the Fun's in How You Say a Thing: An Exploration of Metre and Rhythm* (Athens: Ohio University Press, 1999) – alongside Attridge, the best introduction to poetic metre.

Rhian Williams, *The Poetry Toolkit: The Essential Guide to Studying Poetry* (London: Bloomsbury, 2009).

Criticism and Histories

Lascelles Abercrombie, *The Idea of Great Poetry* (London: Martin Secker, 1925) – dated but suggestive tour of the question of poetic 'greatness'.

John Carey, *A Little History of Poetry* (New Haven, CT: Yale University Press, 2020).

William Empson, *Seven Types of Ambiguity* (London: Chatto and Windus, 1930) – classic study of multiple meanings in poetic language.

Laurence Lerner, *The Truest Poetry: An Essay on the Question: What is Literature?* (London: Hamilton, 1960).

Ronan McDonald, *The Death of the Critic* (London: Bloomsbury, 2007) – history of the role and concept of the literary critic.

Bernard O'Donoghue, *Poetry: A Very Short Introduction* (Oxford: Oxford University Press, 2019) – succinct analysis of the question of what poetry is.

Michael O'Neill (ed.), *The Cambridge History of English Poetry* (Cambridge: Cambridge University Press, 2010).

Claude Rawson, (ed.), *The Cambridge Companion to English Poets* (Cambridge: Cambridge University Press, 2011) – essays on major English poets.

Christopher Ricks, *The Force of Poetry* (Oxford: Oxford University Press, 1976) – exemplary readings of a number of poets.

Michael Schmidt, *Lives of the Poets* (London: Weidenfeld & Nicolson, 1998) – dazzling, readable history of poets in English; great place to start reading about any poet.

Alex Wong, 'Duties of Care in the Study of Literature', *The Fortnightly Review*, 21 July 2015, https://fortnightlyreview.co.uk/2015/07/duties-care-study-literature/ – stimulating intervention in debates around the expansion of the literary canon.

Online Resources

For Better for Verse: https://prosody.lib.virginia.edu/ – interactive website with exercises to practise hearing poetic metre.

The Guardian 'Poem of the Week': https://www.theguardian.com/books/series/poemoftheweek – long-running series written by Carole Rumens offering an introductory reading of a different poem each week.

The Poetry Archive: https://poetryarchive.org/ – recordings of poets reading their poems.

The Poetry Foundation: https://www.poetryfoundation.org/ – online website of the publisher of *Poetry* magazine, contains poems, essays, and introductions to innumerable poets.

Copyright Permissions

I am grateful for the permission to reproduce the material from the following works:

Ai, "The Kid". Copyright © 1979 by Ai, from VICE: NEW AND SELECTED POEMS by Ai. Used by permission of W. W. Norton & Company, Inc.

Samuel Beckett, extract from 'what is the word' from COLLECTED POEMS OF SAMUEL BECKETT, ed. Seán Lawlor and John Pilling (London: Faber and Faber, 2013). Reproduced by permission of Faber and Faber.

Anne Carson, 'Lines' from DECREATION: POETRY, ESSAYS, OPERA by Anne Carson, copyright © 2005 by Anne Carson. Used by permission of Alfred A. Knopf, an imprint of the Knopf Doubleday Publishing Group, a division of Penguin Random House LLC. All rights reserved.

Amy Clampitt, 'The Cormorant in its Element' from THE COLLECTED POEMS OF AMY CLAMPITT by Amy Clampitt, copyright © 1997 by the Estate of Amy Clampitt. Used by permission of Alfred A. Knopf, an imprint of the Knopf Doubleday Publishing Group, a division of Penguin Random House LLC. All rights reserved.

Wendy Cope, extract from 'An Attempt at Unrhymed Verse', TWO CURES FOR LOVE: SELECTED POEMS, 1979–2006 (London: Faber and Faber, 2008). Reproduced by permission of Faber and Faber and printed by permission of United Agents (www.unitedagents.co.uk) on behalf of Wendy Cope (© Wendy Cope, 2009).

Dick Davis, 'I see no love in anyone'. Extract of the poem 'I see no love in anyone' by Hafez is from *FACES OF LOVE: HAFEZ AND THE POETS OF SHIRAZ*, translated by Dick Davis, © 2012 Mage Publishers, www.mage.com

Emily Dickinson, 'They shut me up in Prose', THE POEMS OF EMILY DICKINSON: READING EDITION, edited by Ralph W. Franklin, Cambridge, MA: The Belknap Press of Harvard University Press, Copyright © 1998, 1999 by the President and Fellows of Harvard College. Copyright © 1951, 1955 by the President and Fellows of Harvard College. Copyright © renewed 1979, 1983 by the President and Fellows of Harvard College. Copyright © 1914, 1918, 1919, 1924, 1929, 1930, 1932, 1935, 1937, 1942 by Martha Dickinson Bianchi. Copyright © 1952, 1957, 1958, 1963, 1965 by Mary L. Hampson.

U. A. Fanthorpe, 'BC:AD' from CHRISTMAS POEMS (Enitharmon Press, 2002). Reproduced by kind permission of R. V. Bailey.

Ivor Gurney, 'After War' from COMPLETE POEMS (Carcanet Press, 2004). Reproduced by kind permission of Carcanet Press.

Ted Hughes, extract from *Gaudete* from COLLECTED POEMS, ed. Paul Keegan (London: Faber and Faber, 2003). Reproduced by permission of Faber and Faber.

Kathleen Jamie, 'The Shrew' from THE BONNIEST COMPANY (Picador, 2015). Copyright © Kathleen Jamie 2015. Reproduced through permission of the licensor through PLS Clear.

Donald Justice, 'Mrs Snow' from COLLECTED POEMS by Donald Justice, copyright © 2004 by Donald Justice. Used by permission of Alfred A. Knopf, an imprint of the Knopf Doubleday Publishing Group, a division of Penguin Random House LLC. All rights reserved.

Arun Kolatkar, 'Irani Restaurant Bombay' from COLLECTED POEMS IN ENGLISH (Bloodaxe, 2010). Reproduced by kind permission of Bloodaxe Books.

Philip Larkin, extract from 'Toads' from THE COMPLETE POEMS, ed. Archie Burnett (London: Faber and Faber, 2012). Reproduced by permission of Faber and Faber.

Denise Levertov, 'Caedmon' by Denise Levertov, from BREATHING THE WATER, copyright ©1987 by Denise Levertov. Reprinted by permission of New Directions Publishing Corp.

Arvind Krishna Mehrotra, 'The cock crows' from THE ABSENT TRAVELLER: PRAKRIT LOVE POETRY FROM THE GATHASAPTASATI OF SATAVAHANA HALA (Penguin, 2008). Reproduced by kind permission of Arvind Krishna Mehrotra.

Charles Olson, 'Merce of Egypt' from THE COLLECTED POEMS OF CHARLES OLSON: EXCLUDING THE MAXIMUS

POEMS, ed. George F. Butterick (University of California Press, 1987).

Alice Oswald, extract from DART (London: Faber and Faber, 2002). Reproduced by permission of Faber and Faber.

Srinivas Rayaprol, 'A Letter for Mother', 'Life Has Been', 'On Approaching Fifty', 'This Poem' from ANGULAR DESIRE: SELECTED POEMS AND PROSE (Carcanet Press, 2019). Reproduced by kind permission of Aparna Rayaprol.

Stephen Spender, 'An Elementary School Classroom in a Slum' from NEW COLLECTED POEMS (Faber and Faber, 1984). Reproduced with Permission of Curtis Brown Group Ltd., London on behalf of The Estate of Stephen Spender Copyright © Stephen Spender, 1933.

Rosemary Tonks, 'Farewell to Kurdistan' from BEDOUIN OF THE LONDON EVENING: COLLECTED POEMS AND SELECTED PROSE (Bloodaxe, 2016). Reproduced by kind permission of Bloodaxe Books.

Exhaustive and exhausting pains have been taken to trace, contact, and receive a response from copyright holders. If you think a permission has been overlooked, please get in touch.

Index